Cosmo-nationalism

Cosmopolitanism did not merely sink to the ground, pale and exhausted; and the new national idea did not then spring up in its place, unimpeded and victorious. Cosmopolitanism and nationalism stood side by side in a close, living relationship for a long time.

                Friedrich Meinecke, *Cosmopolitanism and the National State*

Philosophical vocabulary has taken different turns even in the most closely related languages, with the result that many distinctions made in Greek or Latin or German are all but impossible to make in English. In the case of poetry, such barriers are, at once, a contingent disadvantage and a symptom of integrity. But so far as philosophy goes, problems of untranslatability strike at the heart of the whole philosophical enterprise. As early as the *Cratylus* and *Parmenides*, we are made to feel the tension between aspirations to universality, to a critical fulcrum independent of temporal, geographic conditions and the relativistic particularities of a given idiom. How is the particular to express the universal?

                                          George Steiner, *After Babel*

The idea of national philosophy carries in it a strange contradiction. In one sense, we are very accustomed to hearing of German, French, Italian or Anglo-Saxon philosophies; their division seems so inscribed in philosophical institutions that this idea seems to be completely self-evident. Authors and philosophical texts would be by differentiating degrees identified, amongst other criteria, by their adhesion to a 'national group.' Without doubt, the difficulty would be then to know the nature of this group (cultural, political or other?), and the principles by which one might become a member of it – the inscription of philosophy in a determined language, the nationality of the philosopher, dependence on a tradition. But, as problematic as each of these terms is (culture, nation, tradition, nationality), the actual existence of national philosophies would not be called into question.

            Marc Crépon, 'L'Idée de "philosophie nationale"' (my translation)

# Cosmo-nationalism
*American, French and German Philosophy*

Oisín Keohane

EDINBURGH
University Press

Edinburgh University Press is one of the leading university presses in the UK. We publish academic books and journals in our selected subject areas across the humanities and social sciences, combining cutting-edge scholarship with high editorial and production values to produce academic works of lasting importance. For more information visit our website: edinburghuniversitypress.com

© Oisín Keohane, 2018

Edinburgh University Press Ltd
The Tun – Holyrood Road
12(2f) Jackson's Entry
Edinburgh EH8 8PJ

Typeset in Monotype Ehrhardt by
Servis Filmsetting Ltd, Stockport, Cheshire

A CIP record for this book is available from the British Library

ISBN 978 1 4744 3115 6 (hardback)
ISBN 978 1 4744 3117 0 (webready PDF)
ISBN 978 1 4744 3118 7 (epub)

The right of Oisín Keohane to be identified as the author of this work has been asserted in accordance with the Copyright, Designs and Patents Act 1988, and the Copyright and Related Rights Regulations 2003 (SI No. 2498).

# Contents

*Acknowledgements* vi

1  Introduction  1
2  The Making of Brothers: Kant the Nationalist, the Internationalist and the Cosmopolitan  24
3  The Presentation of National Philosophies: Kant on the French and German National Character  55
4  The Metaphysics of Nationalism: Fichte and the German Language as a National Philosophical Idiom  92
5  Philosophical Rights-of-Way: Tocqueville and the American Philosophical Method  116
6  The Transcendental Declaration of Independence: Emerson and American Philosophy  155

*Bibliography*  193
*Index*  207

# Acknowledgements

This book is based on doctoral research undertaken at the European Institute, LSE, a place which shaped me in more ways than one. I would like to thank, first and foremost, my doctoral supervisors, Prof. Simon Glendinning and Dr Jennifer Jackson-Preece. Prof. Glendinning often had a better sense of my idiom, and what I wanted to say in my idiom, than I did. Dr Jackson-Preece, in turn, ensured that my idiom was always intelligible to others.

I would also like to express my gratitude to the staff at the UC Irvine Critical Theory Archive, and Professor Peggy Kamuf and Professor Geoffrey Bennington, who were most accommodating when I viewed the Jacques Derrida Papers. My trip to this archive as well as my doctoral work were funded by the Arts and Humanities Research Council (AHRC) and by the European Institute. Without their financial support, this book would not have been possible. I would also like to acknowledge the backing of the following institutions, which enabled me to complete the manuscript: the Institute for Advanced Studies in the Humanities at the University of Edinburgh, the National Research Foundation of South Africa and the Department of Philosophy at the University of Johannesburg, the Humanities Research Centre at the National Australian University, and, above all, the Andrew W. Mellon Foundation and the Jackman Humanities Institute at the University of Toronto. I would also like to thank more generally the following for their support and many profitable conversations over the years, which have guided this work in one form or the other: Prof. John Breuilly, Prof. Alex Broadbent, Dr Amy Devlin, Prof. Robert Gibbs, Dr Áine Mahon, Prof. Ruth Marshall and Prof. Jonathan White. I also owe a debt of gratitude to my copyeditor, Eliza Wright, whose keen eye was invaluable, and the artist Yang Yongliang, whose image adorns the front cover of this book.

On a more personal note, I wish to thank my family, and in particular, my grandparents, Michael and Florrie Keohane, who believed in me from the start, and who introduced me to another world, one I could believe in, and participate in with the joy they shared from day to day. I would not be on the path I am today without them. Betty and Donal Geary also deserve my heartfelt thanks for the warmth and kindness that they have shown in welcoming me into their family.

Finally, the greatest thanks go to Elizabeth Geary Keohane. One of the best definitions of marriage I have ever come across derives from John Milton, who said that the chief and noblest end of marriage is 'a meet and happy conversation'.[1] I have known Elizabeth for the last decade and a half of my life, but I confess that my happiest conversations in life have already been with her. To know that our conversation is not yet ended, and that we have so many conversations ahead of us about which I know not what, but which I know promise more future happiness, gives me more hope in the promise of life, and the worth of living it, than I would have thought possible as a child. I find the same springs of joy expressed sublimely and yet humbly by J. S. Mill: 'What marriage may be in the case of two persons of cultivated faculties, identical in opinions and purposes, between whom there exists that best kind of equality, similarity of powers and capacities with reciprocal superiority in them – so that each can enjoy the luxury of looking up to the other, and can have alternately the pleasure of leading and of being led in the path of development – I will not attempt to describe. To those who can conceive it, there is no need; to those who cannot, it would appear the dream of an enthusiast.'[2]

Some of the material in this book has been previously published in different forms. I would therefore like to acknowledge the editors and publishers of the following texts: 'Fichte and the German Idiom: The Metaphysics of the *Addresses to the German Nation*', in vol. 19, issue 2 of *Nations and Nationalism* (2013), pp. 317–36; 'Out of Earshot of the School: Tocqueville and the "American Philosophical Method"', book chapter in *Stanley Cavell, Literature and Film: The Idea of America*, edited by Áine Kelly and Andrew Taylor (2013), Routledge, London and New York, pp. 132–57; 'Tongue-tied Democracy: The Bind of National Language in Tocqueville and Derrida', in vol. 4, issue 2 of *Derrida Today* (2011), pp. 233–56.

---

[1] Milton 2016: 68.
[2] Mill 1989: 211.

For Florrie

CHAPTER I

# Introduction

## ON THE PROBLEM OF ASSIGNING A NATIONALITY TO PHILOSOPHY

Nationalism has been one of the most significant social and political phenomena of the last two centuries, and it is very likely to remain a feature of our world for some time to come. Yet, except as a form of irrational and 'unphilosophical' prejudice, it has long been ignored as a topic in political philosophy. This is not accidental; philosophy has always, insofar as it understood itself, pictured itself to be the project of universality, and has wished to present itself as something that takes place outside or beyond the national as such; something that is, therefore, ultimately detachable from language, culture and history. Whilst the 'birth' of philosophy may thus be traced to Athens or other Greek *poleis*, if not reduced to them – one can recall the enigmatic figure of the Stranger or the figure from Egypt in Plato's dialogues – and whilst the Greek heritage may remain a privileged site or locus for philosophy, something for it constantly to overcome and to think otherwise, its Greco-European origins were never intended to limit its scope, its worldwide ambition, its universal validity. Accordingly, when Plato and Aristotle discussed the Greek concept of *ousia*, for example, they did not think its scope would be necessarily limited due to the fact it was a Greek word – they did not think it was a property belonging solely to the Greeks or to the Greek language. In short, Plato and Aristotle did not think they were producing 'Greek philosophy' or even 'Greek Theory' when they discussed and produced their philosophies, and the ideas contained in Aristotle's *Politics* were not limited to being applied to what Aristotle called 'the Hellenic race [*genos*]' (Aristotle 1996: 1327b1 30–1).

Philosophy from its inception has thus always acknowledged that while it may have specific cultural and historical origins, for example, in Greece, it has, from the start, sought to transcend those original limitations so as to maintain its claim to be a project of universality. The universal projected in this way is therefore not conceived of as a given, but rather is announced as a task. In other words, the idea of the universal project, one which is not bound by linguistic, territorial, ethnic or cultural limitations, has been seen as a *process* of universalisation, rather than something guaranteed to philosophy by its very self-definition. The idea of philosophy may thus be said to have always had the central ambition to deterritorialise itself – to export itself across borders.

But if philosophy is always traversing the boundaries and limits that may enclose it at any given moment, if it is always displacing its own limits, it may be said to cross not only territorial borders, and so national borders, but also the borders of the *idiom*, that which borders on the self because it signifies what is properly *one's own*. For as Jacques Derrida reminds us, the idiom is not solely a linguistic matter, even if the linguistic idiom is not one determination of idiomaticity among others, because the idiom (*idion*) is nothing less than 'the proper [*le propre*]', 'it is about propriety/property/ownership [*propriété*]', the 'singular feature, in principle inimitable and inexpropriable' (Derrida 1992a: 4; translation modified). The idiom is consequently about belonging and belongings; it is the sphere of what is most 'mine' – what belongs to one's own people, one's own family, one's own home and property. Philosophy therefore should, properly speaking, have nothing to do with the idiom, let alone the national idiom.

As a result, the national register of philosophy is seen as a secondary accident, an addition, something that may be sociologically or historically useful for grouping certain thinkers together, but which has no philosophical bearing on the works produced by these thinkers. We may thus find in a philosophical encyclopaedia, headings such as 'German philosophy' or 'American philosophy', but no examination of what the adjective 'German' or 'American' might mean under such circumstances. This reflects the fact that these national inscriptions in philosophy are taken to be only an incidental feature of the subject, something which comes to it from the outside and only by chance. It is thus no accident that philosophy concludes that any national dimension it may possess is always something it should and finally can discard, transcend or overcome.

To consider the problem at hand, one may consider the difference between talking about 'French literature' and what we might call 'French mathematics'. If someone were to define 'French literature' straightforwardly as literature written in the French language, one might think of asking them, for example, of how they would account for those literatures of France written in a language other than French, and so the presence and history of so-called *patois*. Or, alternatively, of how they would account for literature in French written outside of France, and so the idea of *la Francophonie*. While 'French literature' is thus a contested term, one continuously fought over, it is still widely used. But what would it mean to speak of 'French mathematics'? What would it mean to speak of mathematics or a *mathesis universalis* in national terms, to say that mathematical objects such as numbers and points had a national basis or were nationally specific?[1] The problems one encounters in the designation 'French mathematics' are in some ways akin to the designation 'French philosophy'. For the idea of 'national philosophies' – philosophies demarcated in national terms – appears to contradict some of the most basic tenets and deep-seated presuppositions of philosophical discourse, namely, that as a cosmopolitical project, it has no linguistic or national borders. Indeed, its problems are thought to be philosophical precisely because they are deemed to have universal relevance, a relevance that transcends any or every linguistic or geopolitical boundary: philosophy is the thesis of universal translatability.

Yet, if philosophy is in-its-vocation universal, it is in-its-actuality always embodied in a particular language, or set of languages, in a particular time and in a particular place. This problem has become more acute and visible since the demise of Latin and the rise of so-called national languages. In this book I will explore how certain philosophers at the end of the eighteenth and beginning of the nineteenth century – specifically, Immanuel Kant, J. G. Fichte, Alexis de Tocqueville and R. W. Emerson – addressed the issue of how philosophy by its very constitution strives for the universal, even when it speaks within national categories to announce its universal project. This book hence explores how far philosophy can account for its national inscriptions and yet still think of itself as universal in scope. My aim is to find a way of coming to terms, conceptually and politically, with the very idea that philosophy can be inflected and differentiated in terms of nationality – for example, 'German philosophy' – without having simply to sacrifice its commitment to being a universal mode of reason free from such national or regional inscriptions.

What the foregoing brings to light is that there is a notion of universality inherent in the discipline of philosophy that makes the topic of the national in philosophy, as Derrida notes, a scandalous subject for the discipline. Yet, as he also observes, 'we know that the "philosophical world", assuming it still has unity, is not only divided into "schools" and "doctrines" but also [. . .] divided according to linguistico-national borders that are more difficult to cross than political borders' (Derrida 2004a: 215). Indeed, we might note that since the beginning of the twentieth century so-called international philosophical congresses – like the World Congress of Philosophy that has been organised every five years since 1948 by the International Federation of Philosophical Societies – have taken place with increasing frequency across the 'philosophical world'. Derrida in fact draws attention to how national differences in philosophy become more explicit when transmissions between national formations deepen. He writes that it 'is at the very moment at which there is an intensification of what takes the form of exchanges, meetings, [and] so-called philosophical communication', when 'influences, grafts, deformations, hybridisations' occur, 'that national demands show up more clearly, or even become exasperated and tense up into nationalism' (Derrida 1992a: 6).

Concomitantly, we might also add that there has also been a proliferation in the appearance of encyclopaedic entries on what is called 'French philosophy' or 'German philosophy' in the twentieth century, following on from their introduction at the end of the eighteenth century, that is, the moment when Latin ceased to be the language of philosophy and of instruction, even if major philosophical works were still being translated into Latin, for example, Immanuel Kant's *Critique of Pure Reason* (though as we shall see in Chapter 3, this is more complicated since the first *Critique* itself systematically uses Latin to *establish* Latin–German 'equivalents' in philosophy). Although the distance that lies between these 'schools', 'doctrines' or 'traditions' cannot be reduced to the effects of nationality and language, they both nonetheless remain part of the problem. We must thus ask ourselves, it seems today more than ever, what we can do to understand present philosophical configurations and displacements – how we might repair or relate national philosophical differences, rather than simply repeat or ignore them, or indeed, repeat them by ignoring them.

In my view, one of the most important ways we might do this is to find a way of acknowledging the two intertwined strands of the national and the philosophical. One can think about this relationship in three main ways. First, in terms of the philosophy of nationalism; second, in terms of philosophers and nationalism; and third, in terms of philosophical nationalities. The first is the most traditional, and consists of asking classical philosophical questions like 'What is x?', so for example, asking the ontological question: 'What is a nation?' This is an area that nearly all scholars of nationalism pursue, even if they do not always pursue it under the name of the philosophy of nationalism. The second consists of asking historical questions about the role of philosophers in the rise of nationalism. This strand most famously originated in the work of Elie Kedourie, who argued that philosophers like J. G. Fichte played a pivotal role in the ascent of nationalism. Lastly, one can consider the issue of philosophical nationalities. This heading leaves the way in which one is to read the national and the philosophical intentionally open; it thus combines two questions, the question of the national character of philosophy and that of the philosophical character of the national. This last strand, in other words, examines how philosophers have thought of the national whilst at the same time assigning a nationality to philosophy, since the thinkers I will examine in this book did both. My proposal will be that they have done it through understanding the nation as a schematic affiliation, something bridging the empirical and non-empirical. The nation as a schematic affiliation thus becomes not only an object of philosophy, but a vehicle for philosophy.

However, as we will see, this has not meant that these thinkers freed themselves from the possibility of the worst when it comes to nationalism, rather, the idea of the nation as a schematic affiliation produced a certain strain of nationalism that I will call cosmo-nationalism. I will define this strain of nationalism as one that in fact utilises, rather than opposes, ideas in cosmopolitanism to advance the aims of one particular nation. For instance, cosmo-nationalism often turns to the cosmopolitical idea of 'humanity' to advance the claim that one particular nation best embodies or represents all of humanity. Cosmo-nationalist thinkers thus claim that one particular nation is privileged not because it is nationally superior, be it in genetic or cultural terms, but because this nation is exemplary of cosmopolitical values. The superiority of the nation in this case lies in the fact it is supposedly more cosmopolitan than its neighbours. Accordingly, another way of thinking about cosmo-nationalism is that it names a system of ideas and ideals that uses the apparatus of the nation, and, indeed, one particular nation, as a vehicle to accomplish a given set of cosmopolitical aims. It could thus be understood to be a hybridisation of cosmopolitanism and nationalism and so a mutation of both. First, however, I want briefly to explore how the theme of the national is taken up outside of philosophy: in the field of inquiry in the social sciences now simply called 'nationalism studies'.

## THE NATIONAL AS UNDERSTOOD BY NATIONALISM STUDIES AND BY PHILOSOPHY

As Umut Özkirimli notes in his *Theories of Nationalism*, the topic of nationalism became a subject of academic investigation in its own right specifically in the twentieth century, and one can examine the historiography of nationalism studies in several different ways. He himself argues that the theoretical debate on nationalism should be divided into three stages, namely, 1918–45, when nationalism first became a subject of academic inquiry; 1945 to the late 1980s, when the debate became more dominated by sociologists and political scientists; and from the 1980s to the present, when scholars attempted to transcend the 'classical' debate. One passing matter that Özkirimli interestingly observes is the changing emphasis on the orientation of nationalism studies, from its beginnings prior to World War I, which were largely ethical and philosophical, to its more contemporary sociologically orientated frame of reference, especially since the 1960s.

It can even be argued that since its formation as a discipline or an area of interdisciplinary studies in the 1980s, nationalism studies, or at least some of its leading theorists, have tended to dismiss the philosophical – or more broadly ideational – aspect of nationalism as epiphenomenal, or at best, assign this philosophical aspect of nationalism only a secondary and derivative role. This is most evident in Ernest Gellner's theory as to how nationalism developed, which stresses the social conditions of both modernity and industrialisation. Gellner's account was explicitly developed so as to counter Elie Kedourie's thesis that nationalism arose due to a series of 'philosophical' factors, including the misapplication of Kant's theory of the autonomy of self to the political arena of national self-determination, the impact of the French Revolution on young German intellectuals, and the efforts of Fichte (Kedourie [1960] 1993).

As John Breuilly notes in his introduction to the second edition of Gellner's *Nations and Nationalism*, while Gellner agreed with Kedourie that nationalism preceded the existence of nations, and that nations were effects rather than causes of nationalism, Gellner

> could not agree [with Kedourie] that this was due to the power of nationalism *as an idea*, or of an intelligentsia as the bearer of this idea. The *idea* of nationalism was product, not producer, of modernity. Its success was not due to its intellectual power but to its function with a modern social order. (Breuilly 2006: xxi)

As Gellner himself puts it, 'the ideological or doctrinal history of nationalism is largely irrelevant to the understanding of it' (Gellner [1983] 2006: 125). Or as he writes in *Encounters with Nationalism*, 'Nationalism as an elaborated intellectual *theory* is neither widely endorsed, nor of high quality nor of any historical importance' (Gellner 1994: 65).

Anthony D. Smith similarly argues against Kedourie's position on the ground that it gives too much weight to 'ideas' alone, that it is elite-centric and falls prey to what Smith calls 'intellectual determinism' (Smith [1971] 1983: 39). Finally, Benedict Anderson in his *Imagined Communities* goes even further and states that one of the paradoxes of nationalism is 'The "political" power of nationalisms vs. their philosophical poverty and even incoherence. In other words, unlike most other isms, nationalism has never produced its own grand thinkers: no Hobbeses, Tocquevilles, Marxes, or Webers' (Anderson [1983] 2006: 5). Anderson thus posits that not only is there no philosophical dimension to nationalism, but that its 'power' partly stems from its *lack* of philosophical power, even its philosophical incoherence.[2]

Jacques Derrida, in his first seminar on philosophical nationalities and nationalism (which, tellingly, was the first ever seminar he held under the aegis of the *École des hautes études en sciences sociales* – EHESS – an institution that names itself as a specifically 'social sciences institution') in fact invokes the monopoly of authority that certain social scientists claim when analysing the national.³ Derrida thus states that one of his aims is to problematise not only the claims that philosophy would traditionally make with regard to other disciplines, for example, that it is the so-called queen of sciences since it provides the grounds of 'general' or 'fundamental' ontology in contrast to 'regional' ontologies, but also 'a certain authority of the same type that a given social science might claim over the treatment of this problem [surrounding the national], and as to its competence to deal with it' (Derrida 1992a: 8). Derrida thus suggests that if the problem of philosophical nationalities is not entirely definable and determinable on the basis of the social sciences, it will not be the aim of his project to simply replicate the old familiar gesture of philosophy dismissing the empirical fields of study outright as incapable of addressing the issue at hand – as Martin Heidegger did in his lectures from 1934 when he dismissed the ability of 'census-takers, cartographers, or civil administrators' to define 'the essence of a *Volk*' or 'Germany' (Bambach 2005: 125).

However, one of the few commentators on Derrida's very first seminar session on nationalism, Richard Beardsworth, comes very close to replicating Heidegger's position, when he states in *Derrida and the Political* that one of the main consequences of Derrida's claims about the philosophical dimensions of the national are that

> since a nation is a philosopheme, an idea rather than a fact, it can never be definitely accounted for on the basis of the kind of evidence available to the human sciences: it is not the possible object of an ethnography, a discourse of racial characteristics, a linguistic or social analysis. No such discourse can examine the nation without presupposing in advance a definition of the nation. (Beardsworth 1996: 62)

The problem with this kind of gesture is not only that it treats the 'social sciences' as an undifferentiated block, which is admittedly something Derrida is guilty of too in this first seminar session, but that it ignores the fact that Derrida states in his opening sentence that if his purpose is not to proceed

> to the historical, social, linguistic analysis of what would be called a philosophical nation or nationality [. . .] Such an analysis (in terms of the social or human sciences) is of course not excluded from the seminar, and *will even be necessary in it*. (Derrida 1992a: 3; my emphasis)

It is not my ambition in this book to critique directly the idea of the national 'idea' in thinkers like Gellner, or in Beardsworth in his exposition of Derrida, and show why it is radically inadequate to any rigorous idea of the 'idea'. In part, this is because the 'idea' idea itself has never been homogenous in the history of philosophy – one thinks, for example, at the very least, of the differences between Plato, Aristotle, Kant and Marx on the idea of the 'idea' – and that it has never been simply equated to the 'non-material'. Indeed, somewhat ironically given that the Greek word *eidos* means 'form' as well as 'idea', the idea of the 'idea' has always had uncertain boundaries and contours. The particular difficulty of circumscribing the 'idea' of the national is highlighted by the fact that Derrida does not reduce the national-philosophical thematic to the involvement of philosophers, and what they say (their 'ideas'), in the history of nationalism (an issue discussed earlier under the heading of 'philosophers and nationalism'). As Derrida argues, the national assertion that involves a philosophical structure

> does not necessarily take the form or the representation of a system stated by professional philosophers in philosophical institutions; it can show up as spontaneous philosophy, an implicit philosophy but one that is very constitutive of a non-empirical relationship with the world and a sort of potentially universal discourse, 'embodied', 'represented', 'localised' (all problematic words) by a particular nation. (Derrida 1992a: 10)

In other words, even before philosophers become involved with the 'idea' of the national, the national already has a philosophical structure.

Rather than thinking of the nation solely as an 'idea' rather than a 'fact', I will therefore suggest that a more rigorous and insightful way to think about the nation, one that Derrida in fact mentions in passing, is through the notion of the schema, a schema that is analogous to the Kantian *Schema* – that is, the mediating element, the 'third thing' that participates in both empirical (sensory, material) and non-empirical (conceptual, ideal) elements at once through the faculty of imagination. That it is the nation as a schematic affiliation that explains the philosophical character of the national and the national character of the philosophy. The central claim of my work is that national philosophies co-emerge with various forms of cosmo-nationalism, and that national philosophies have a philosophical structure – a schema – that mediates the particular (e.g. 'What is German?') and the universal ('What is Man?'). I hence show that nationalism frequently involves a non-empirical construal about what man is, and specifically about what is most proper to mankind. This non-empirical construal is essential to a national assertion that a particular people is best placed or most fit to or duty bound to represent humanity. The claim that philosophy is implicated within nationalism is thus not advanced solely as a historical claim within the history of ideas, but as a methodological point regarding the non-empirical structure of the national.

The problems associated with the particular and the universal are, of course, an integral part of philosophy from its inception, as is evident in the schematic discussion of *khôra* as a 'third genus' (*triton genos*) in Plato's

*Timaeus*. However, it will be argued that it is really only with the eighteenth century and Immanuel Kant – examined in Chapters 2 and 3 – that the distinctive formation of philosophical nationalism becomes unavoidable. Indeed, it is the development of this formation in Kant, and emerging debates around the nation, that encourages figures such as J. G. Fichte – examined in Chapter 4 – to explicitly characterise their work as the embodiment of a 'national philosophy', as the active nationalisation of philosophy, a nationalisation, moreover, paradoxically allied with and not contrasted with the cosmopolitical. Another figure who will be seen to develop this cosmo-national schematism will be Alexis de Tocqueville – examined in Chapter 5 – when he claims that the USA has a national philosophical method that is both democratic and French, or rather, which is democratic because it is French in origin. Tocqueville's logic of generality – for example, his claims about general ideas and the role of generalisation – will be seen to play an analogous role to the function of schematism in combining the empirical with the non-empirical when the question of 'Man' is at stake. Finally, as a closing response to the idea of philosophical nationalities, Ralph Waldo Emerson – examined in Chapter 6 – will be seen to explore the notion of philosophical nationalities in a more distinctively hospitable way; that is to say, a way that is open to the foreign as such, even if one particular nation is once again problematically identified as the 'home' of 'Man'.

As should be clear from this summary, this book argues against the common tendency to view nationalism as a strongly particularist worldview, one which is incompatible always and everywhere with cosmopolitanism as an equally strongly universalist worldview. Instead, I will argue that there is an ineradicable universalist element to cosmo-nationalism (a conception of 'Man') and an ineradicable particularist element to cosmopolitanism (rooted in the need to speak one 'natural' or 'national' language *above* another – still too particularist – 'natural' or 'national' language). Accordingly, I argue that not all forms of nationalism are opposed to cosmopolitanism, and that the dichotomy between the national and the cosmopolitical tends to be drawn too starkly, and in an oppositional way, in the leading theories of nationalism and cosmopolitanism, for example, by such theorists as Jürgen Habermas or Brian Barry. We have thus lost the early insights of scholars such as Friedrich Meinecke in his *Cosmopolitanism and the National State*, who demonstrated the close relationship that cosmopolitanism and nationalism could have to one another. However, it should also be recalled that Friedrich Meinecke only did this to lionise the national state and that he only examines Prussia and Germany in any depth. My work will go beyond these territorial limits, to show just how far afield cosmo-nationalism can be found. The cosmo-national will thus be defined as a form of the national that is actually complicit with, rather than in tension with, the cosmopolitical. In addition, each of the four thinkers we will consider in this book will be classified as thinkers of the cosmo-national, whether this focus be implicit or explicit in their work.

The reluctance of philosophy to consider the nation contrasts with a definite and continuous interest in the concept of the State. For if the project of philosophy has always been concerned, from the start, with expropriation, delocalisation and deracination, the *politeia* Plato and Aristotle outlined in their political works could be said to belong to the same universal project insofar as it is a 'form' that could be constructed anywhere and by any architect. It was inherently mobile. This early emphasis on the *polis* and the *politeia* that a *polis* may adopt remains true of the entire political philosophical tradition, which has nearly always been a philosophy of the State. From 'Greek Philosophy' to the 'Latin Tradition' to 'Social Contract Theory' to 'Contemporary Political Thought' (say, from Rawls to Habermas), philosophy has nearly always concerned itself with and analysed the State rather than other forms of political community, even if the nation continues to haunt – and, in a certain sense, *be* the haunt of – the politico-transcendental imagination since the eighteenth century.

There is, in other words, an interesting affinity between the State and philosophy; they are, as it were, 'politically cooperative': both are models that can be replicated elsewhere, and so instantiated anywhere. If the Hellenic *genos* were rooted to a birthplace, the 'forms' of government were free to roam. Or again, whereas the *genos* could only expand, the *polis* and its associated *politeia* could be universalised. This highlights that political philosophy has thus traditionally been very equivocal when it comes to the mother and concepts derived from maternity (e.g. mother country, motherland, mother tongue), even occasionally using the words of a mother to express these worries, as in Plato's *Menexenus* – considered in Chapter 2 – when Socrates the 'midwife' recites the speech of Aspasia, rather than beget his own. The *polis* has thus stood at the centre of politics like some sort of capital, providing the very heading of politics, whilst issues about the *khôra*, for instance, have stood in the periphery, like some kind of borderland, undecidedly political, neither political nor apolitical, a third thing.[4]

An exemplary instance of this trend is Charles Taylor's analysis of nationalism in his essay 'Nationalism and Modernity', an essay that engages with scholars of nationalism like Ernest Gellner and that invokes such canonical philosophical names as Immanuel Kant and G. W. F. Hegel, but which never asks how philosophy *itself* may be implicated or always positioned within the discourse of the national – not only historically, but methodologically: in terms of how philosophy may be situated *within* the topic of nationality and nationalism before it comes to examine the national as such (Taylor 1997). Taylor's engagement with the philosophy of nationalism and his simultaneous avoidance of the national aspects of philosophy – bar his occasional references to Herder – is emblematic of the discipline as a whole.

It should be noted from the outset that while my work is aware of the contested nature of terms like 'nation', 'nationality' and 'nationalism', above all, by scholars of nationalism, it will not be applying pre-established definitions, be they modernist, ethnosymbolist, primordialist or constructivist interpretations. Rather, it will be seeking to determine how the texts under examination – ranging from Kant's *Anthropology from a Pragmatic Point of View*, to Fichte's *Addresses to the German Nation*, to Tocqueville's *Democracy in America*, to Emerson's *Essays* – are themselves articulating notions of the 'nation' and 'nationality' by means of philosophical schemata. My work will thus be informed by nationalism studies, unlike Derrida's work, which in fact took place in the same years as some of the leading books on nationalism were published or republished – for example, Benedict Anderson's *Imagined Communities*, Ernest Gellner's *Nations and Nationalism*, Eric Hobsbawm and Terence Ranger's edited *The Invention of Tradition*, and Anthony D. Smith's second edition of *Theories of Nationalism*, all of which were published in 1983, the year that Derrida embarked on his seminars. However, my work will (nevertheless) seek to contest their appropriation of philosophical categories (spirit, *Geist*, *esprit*, etc.) when they have reduced these to empirical typologies. Insofar as my concern is with the nation addressed as a philosophical schema, the emphasis will thus be on the idea of the national as both something partly produced by philosophy, and something that, in turn, produces and transfigures philosophy.

My project will thus be in opposition to the usual direction of scholarship, specifically as formulated in the history of (political) ideas, and often associated with Elie Kedourie and Isaiah Berlin, which seeks to understand the effect of philosophy on nationalism by examining the 'practical' or 'concrete' ramifications of philosophical 'ideas'. While it will be informed by such an approach to philosophical texts, occasionally discussing, for instance, the various translations of certain key terms in Fichte in the last two centuries, for example, the German term *Geschlecht*, and the uses certain individuals have made of texts like Fichte's, it will in the first instance offer close readings of the texts, and in particular, what we may call the *political logic* rather than simply the political philosophy they use to deploy the 'idea' of the national. This book will thus consider at times matters not usually considered by classical political philosophy, for instance, questions around 'schematism' or 'abstraction'. My discussion will thus analyse what roles the nation, nationality and nationalism play in these texts, as well as how the authors reconcile their national affirmations with the universality of philosophy.

Which is not to say that it will confine itself to discussing what is 'internal' to the text, since what is in question in this book is precisely the question of the 'internal' and 'external' limits of philosophy – for example, its relation to, as well as its crossing of, certain national languages, national cultures, and national histories. As Derrida notes, if certain key historical or political events are not always talked about in texts, they are often '"talked" about *through [à travers]*' texts (Derrida 2004a: 15). As we shall see, though some of the texts under examination do not explicitly discuss the concept of the nation, and indeed, sometimes make a deliberate effort not to do so – as in the case of certain, but, significantly, not all of Kant's texts – each and every one of them is *traversed* by the problem of the national. The texts are occupied, we might say, at the most fundamental level by the very forces that not only constitute, but also partition and demark borders; namely, by the national and the philosophical. The texts are thus always involved in the parti(cipa)tion between the national and the philosophical, in the *schema* that lies between both.

## GERMAN IDEALISM, FRENCH CARTESIANISM, AMERICAN TRANSCENDENTALISM AND THE 'PHILOSOPHICAL NATIONALITY AND NATIONALISM' SEMINARS OF JACQUES DERRIDA

The objects of study in this book will be various texts by philosophers from the movements of 'German Idealism', 'American Transcendentalism', and what we might call, following suit, 'French Cartesianism'. The fact that the former two national designations are common to philosophy, are found regularly in philosophical texts, courses and curricula, and yet are not analysed, is telling of how philosophy ignores the national in its own constitution. In this book, however, these movements have been selected precisely in the light of their 'pretensions to philosophical nationality' and their claim to 'recognise national philosophical characteristics', in their own body of work or in others, whether it be to 'praise' these characteristics or to 'discredit' them (Derrida 1992a: 5). My book thus does not cover philosophers who do not present their philosophies specifically as an instance or species of national philosophy, or at the very least a confrontation with it. The existence of national philosophies is of course not restricted to Germany, France and the USA, and hopefully some who are inspired by this work might in the future delve into the other national philosophies that came into being, but Germany, France and the USA will always be historically privileged when giving an account of the rise of national philosophies since their philosophers were among the first to recognise national philosophical characteristics and self-consciously identify as producing distinctly national philosophies. In other words, it is in Germany, France and the USA above all that this question of a national philosophy takes place as a question, begins to articulate itself and produce its own terms and thereby establish itself.

Whilst there is an ongoing dispute within nationalism studies as to when the nation first arose, few scholars of nationalism would dispute that nationalism came into being from the French Revolution onwards, when sovereignty was explicitly transferred from the French king to the French nation. In addition to the already examined matter of schematism, the philosophers focused on in this book (Kant, Fichte, Tocqueville and Emerson) all wrote specifically about the concept of the nation in the aftermath of the French Revolution; indeed, some of them wrote about the French Revolution at length (Kant, Fichte and Tocqueville).

Four further reasons for the selection of these philosophers can be identified. First, they all purported to recognise national philosophical attributes in other nations, as well as sometimes even claiming their own work to be the embodiment of a 'national philosophy' as such. These philosophers, in other words, begin to self-consciously write about their own relationship to the nation, and they do so in philosophical terms, that is, in terms not reducible to empirical particularisms.

Second, they all hold philosophical views on the role of language, and not only the role of language in philosophical discourse generally, but language in its socio-political or cultural dimension. I will foreground this in the case of each thinker, even if one of them is typically thought (erroneously, as we shall see) to disregard it altogether (Kant), and one is typically thought (erroneously, as we shall see) to identify the privileged status that belongs to speaking a certain national language – German – with the empirical capacity to speak that language (Fichte). The issue of language is important not because of a 'linguistic turn' but because, from Kant onwards and partly due to Kant, philosophers abandoned for most of the nineteenth century (at least until Frege) the project of creating a so-called universal characteristic; a purely formal and mathematical language that would be free from the kind of ambiguity and equivocation found in 'natural' and 'national' languages.

A third reason for this choice of philosophers is that they are all thinkers who engaged with the question of cosmopolitanism alongside the question of the national, even if some of these thinkers are more associated with nationalism (Fichte and Emerson), and some more associated with cosmopolitanism (Kant and Tocqueville).

Kant and Fichte were professional philosophers, holding positions in the Prussian State. Tocqueville and Emerson, by contrast, conducted most of their work outside of the academy, becoming what would now be called 'public intellectuals'. Nevertheless, and this is the fourth reason for selecting them, all engage with the question of whether philosophy can be a popular matter, and so were interested in the availability of philosophy outside of the school – what we may think of as the relation of philosophy to 'the people'. Kant addressed the issue of the popularity of philosophy in the preface to his *Metaphysics of Morals*, one of his most important works on political philosophy. Fichte's

*Addresses to the German Nation* were given outside of the university, but addressed the question of national education, and the possibility of teaching metaphysics in school. Tocqueville stated in *Democracy in America* that Americans were Cartesians without having to go to school and learn Descartes. And Emerson was part of what was called the 'lyceum circuit', travelling most of the USA to give lectures at various centres and halls to those wished to advance their 'adult education'.

While these reasons for selection are, I think, strong, it is striking that the authors I have chosen are rarely studied together. Indeed, they are more usually examined in different disciplines. Kant's work is examined in detail most often by professional philosophers, though it can be found to have had an enormous impact on many disciplines outside of philosophy. Tocqueville's work is usually only examined in detail by social scientists, and in particular, political scientists and sociologists, and is ignored by professional philosophers. Emerson's work is usually only examined in detail by literary critics and Americanists, and its philosophical import not so much ignored, like Tocqueville's, as actively denied by professional philosophers, despite a series of readings by Stanley Cavell. Fichte's work, moreover, has an even more unusual relationship with the academy insofar as his different works remain completely separated between disciplines: his different versions of *Wissenschaftslehre*, for instance, are usually studied only by professional philosophers, whilst his *Addresses to the German Nation* is usually only examined closely by social scientists, and in particular, scholars of nationalism. This no doubt reflects the belief of philosophers of all kinds that the national, as such, is not strictly philosophical, and thus does not need to be examined. The selected thinkers do not only get treated in different disciplines, they are also normally treated as being central figures in different political traditions. Kant, for instance, is normally read as the arch-federal-cosmopolitan; Fichte as the arch-ethnic-nationalist; Tocqueville as the arch-democratic-liberalist; and Emerson as the arch-literary-nationalist. That the juxtaposition of these figures can belong to a coherent and compelling discussion of 'philosophical nationality' is, of course, the task of my work as a whole.

In terms of approach and the means of analysis, this book builds on the work of Jacques Derrida, who is one of the very few major thinkers to have addressed how philosophy can be intertwined with, complicit with, or in tension with forms of nationalism. It is for this reason that his corpus provides my primary theoretical framework. Furthermore, while Derrida's work on subjects like phonocentrism, animality and deconstruction has elicited much critical attention, the attention paid to his work on nationalism has been minimal. Nevertheless, philosophical nationality was not a merely passing interest for Derrida, and made up one of the largest seminar series he ever conducted. The series in question goes under the name of 'Nationalité et nationalisme philosophiques' (Philosophical Nationality and Nationalism) and was held between 1984 and 1988 under the auspices of the EHESS (Derrida 1984–8). Indeed, some of this material has been published under various names, including the so-called *Geschlecht* series, *Of Spirit*, 'Khôra' and 'Kant, the Jew, the German'. These seminars on nationalism will lead, in turn, to the series on 'Politics of Friendship' (1988–91), and then to the longest of the seminar cycles, which is entitled 'Questions of Responsibility' (1991–2003). This last series examines issues such as hospitality and sovereignty, and so carries on many of the themes that are treated in the nationalism seminars.

This book draws most of all on the first four seminar sessions of his 1984–5 seminars: 'Le fantôme de l'autre: nationalité et nationalisme philosophiques' (Philosophical Nationality and Nationalism: The Phantom of the Other). This is because Kant and Fichte, as well as Emerson (indirectly through Harold Bloom), briefly appear in these seminars, and because a whole seminar session is devoted to Tocqueville – a figure Derrida has hardly spoken about in public (one of the few mentions of Tocqueville is in *Rogues*). The other sessions in the first half of the 1984–5 course discuss Adorno, Arendt and Adonis, whilst the second half mostly examines Heidegger. None of this other material will be examined here (it can be noted though that most, if not all, of this material on Heidegger is published in Derrida's 'Geschlecht II: Heidegger's Hand', and that these sessions on Heidegger are discussed by David Farrell Krell in his *Phantoms of the Other: Four Generations of Derrida's Geschlecht*). I will, however, make occasional recourse to Derrida's later seminars on nationalism; namely, the 1985–6 seminars 'Littérature et philosophie comparées: mythos, logos, topos'; his 1986–7 seminars 'Théologie – Politique' (which is the source material for Derrida's 'The Eyes of Language: The Abyss and the Volcano'); and his 1987–8 seminars 'Kant, le Juif, l'Allemand'.[5] The only other major work to date that discusses these seminars as a whole is Dana Hollander's *Exemplarity and Chosenness*, though her focus is more on the religious and Jewish dimensions of the idea of the 'chosen people'.[6]

It should also be noted though that this interest in the philosophical character of the national and the national character of philosophy is evident from the very beginning of Derrida's work, above all in relation to the experience of language a philosopher is supposed to have in order to be a philosopher. As Derrida puts it, the fact that

> philosophy is written and written in an idiom, was for a long time disavowed by the philosopher, whether because he claimed to transcend his idiom in view of a sort of universal and transparent language, or whether because – and this amounts to the same thing – he considers the natural

language in which he speaks to be an empirical accident and not an experience tied to the exercise of thought. (Derrida 1995b: 374)

This highlights that the problem of untranslatability and the irreducibility of the idiomatic strikes at the heart of the whole philosophical enterprise. That philosophy is the very thesis of translatability – the belief that one can separate word and concept from one another, or ('cultural') use and ('universal') meaning. As Derrida reminds us, the notion of translation as a philosopheme is not classically thought of as 'an active, productive, transformative *"hermeneia"* [a word that means both translation *and* interpretation]' but instead as 'the transport of a univocal meaning, or in any case a controlled plurivocality, into another linguistic element' (Derrida 1988: 140). Derrida was from the start a thinker of the possibility and impossibility of translation, and was interested in the language politics of philosophical discourse from his earliest works; it is thus no surprise that the word 'nationalism' appears there too, for example, in a footnote to 'Violence and Metaphysics', which first published in 1967 (Derrida 1978: 409), and in the 'bottom band' of 'Living On: Borderlands', an essay first published in 1979, when he states that

> what this institution [namely, the university] cannot bear, is for anyone to tamper with [*toucher à*; also 'touch', 'change', 'concern oneself with'] language, meaning *both* the *national* language *and*, paradoxically, an ideal of translatability that neutralises this national language. Nationalism and universalism – indissociables. (Derrida 2011: 122; original emphasis)

Thus, as well as his unpublished seminars which explicitly deal with nationalism in the 1980s, my work will also be able to draw on Derrida's published works too, his numerous books and essays, many of which already hint at or are themselves traversed by the problem of philosophical nationalities and nationalism.

This book's way of proceeding is also indebted to Derrida insofar as it conducts what might be called a genealogical style of deconstruction when it comes to the question of cosmo-nationalism, but it does so alongside an examination of certain formal structures or aporias. It thus considers questions both from a historical perspective (when did cosmo-nationalism arise?, How did it arise?, Which thinkers and forces in society allowed it to arise?) and from a formal perspective (how do cosmo-nationalism and philosophy interact with one another?, How can philosophy be said to have a nationality if it strives for universality?).

These questions also raise the difficult matter of Derrida's relationship to politics. Geoffrey Bennington in 'Derrida and Politics' usefully highlights the complications that arise when one thinks of Derrida's work in relation to what one calls, in our tradition, 'political philosophy'. Examining how Aristotle discusses metaphysics, and alternatively, politics, as providing the ultimate ends of philosophy, Bennington writes of 'how the philosophical concept of politics [in the tradition] is both subordinate to metaphysics and superior to it' (Bennington 2010: 23). Bennington hence notes that there is a 'fundamental ambiguity' in

> the concept of politics itself, which, perhaps more clearly than any other (with the possible exception of 'law') betrays a radical instability in the metaphysical concept of concept itself – and one plausible way of reading Derrida's work as a whole is that it shows up an irreducible conceptual politics even in the most theoretical or speculative domains of philosophy. (Bennington 2000: 24)

Bennington's notion of 'conceptual politics' is helpful for explaining one of the reasons why I have focused on the notion of the schema, which at first might not seem as politically relevant to nationalism as certain other notions (such as sovereignty). The schema we might say plays a particularly significant role in the 'conceptual politics' of cosmo-nationalism because it works as a bridge between the concept (our concept of the concept) and the political (our concept of politics). The work done in this book can thus be understood as making visible the conceptual politics which underwrites the nation as a schematic affiliation.

The same might be said of the 'idiom', the concept I opened the book with. The emphasis on the idiom also explains why there are passages in this book where I provide the original French or German alongside the translation. I also at points compare a number of translations of the same text, such as Fichte's *Addresses to the German Nation* or Tocqueville's *Democracy in America*. It might thus be useful to elucidate Derrida's position when it comes to idiomaticity.

In one of Derrida's seminar sessions devoted to philosophical nationalism, in a session that considers Heidegger and that is dated 11 March 1985, Derrida analyses Heidegger's concern with how language is viewed in the modern age, which for Heidegger is in fact equivalent to the question of how language is 'used up and abused', because of the way it has become 'an indispensable but masterless, arbitrarily applicable means of communication, as indifferent as a means of public transportation, such as a streetcar, which everyone gets on and off' (Heidegger 2000: 53). In distinction to this machine-like relation to language, Heidegger ominously mentions those organisations that aim 'for the purification of language [*Reinigung der Sprache*] and for defense against its progressive mutilation [*Sprachverhunzung*]', 'institutions', he states, that 'deserve respect' even if they exemplify the fact that no-one knows, least of all linguistic technocrats, 'what language is all about' (ibid. 54).

Derrida explains how Heidegger's concern in this passage is about the need to save language, and in particular, the wish 'to save language from contamination by foreign languages [*pour sauver la langue des contaminations par les langue étrangères*]'.[7] Moreover, Derrida observes that this wish to safeguard language from the foreign is not restricted to 1930s Germany, and that it is not so alien even 'here, now [*ici, maintenant*]' in the France of the 1980s.[8] Derrida thus alludes to recent events, as he frequently does in his seminars; in this case, the creation by President Mitterrand of the *Commissariat général de la langue française* and the *Comité consultatif de la langue française*, two governmental bodies set up so as to defend and illustrate the French language, at a time when, as the French government no doubt understood, English was becoming increasingly dominant in and outside of France (thus the division of the agencies, one dealing with the threat of anglicisms and so-called Franglais, and the other with what I call 'Anglobalisation', via the notion of *la Francophonie*). One can thus consider Derrida's use of foreign words. To take an example which is not an example among others, consider the use of the English word 'analysis' in *Politics of Friendship* at the very moment Derrida is discussing the bond, the bond of language and the bond of union. Derrida is commentating on the proper name Lysis and the dialogue by Plato entitled *Lysis*, and states:

> Maieutic as an effect of *analysis* [in English in the original], the Lysis quotes within itself its homonym [*son homonyme*], thereby tying itself [*se lie*] to the common name (lysis), which designates, as if by chance, unbinding [*déliaison*], detachment [*détachement*], emancipation [*l'affranchissement*], untangling [*dénouement*], the tie [*lien*] undone or dissolved by *analysis*. (Derrida 2005c: 78)

Derrida thus quotes, as if by chance, the foreign word 'analysis' at the very moment he is discussing the bond of the body politic. Moreover, he does not merely describe this breakdown, this act of lysis which occurs in the proper name Lysis; he enacts the act of lysis in his own writing, incorporating foreign words like 'analysis' to describe this lysis in French. His prose consequently depicts the breaking down or dissolution of French (national) cells, specifically, those hostile to foreign bodies. What is so striking in Derrida's writing, we might state, is therefore that it not only breaks its tie with the French language while continuing to inhabit it, but that it does so by incorporating the very foreign word ('analysis') that names the breaking of the tie. Accordingly, the idiom is divided in, and of itself.

Indeed, this gesture is exemplified by Derrida's constant use of the English expression 'double bind' throughout his works, including in *Politics of Friendship*. The first time it appears in that text is in parentheses after the expression *double constraint* when he is discussing the expression "'if there is one [*s'il y en a*]'" (ibid. 38). This doubling of languages, however, is elided in the English translation, which simply eliminates the expression 'double constraint' altogether and goes straight to the 'double bind' (ibid. 39). As George Collins renders it: 'By specifying recurrently: "if there is one" ... a double bind occurs in interposition.' The translation thus eliminates the double bind, the very *inter*position between French and English which exists in the so-called French original: 'd'une double contrainte (*double bind*)' (Derrida 1994a: 59). One may find fault with Collins's translation; it is, nevertheless, revealing, and hard to remedy, for what we discover is that translation finds itself in a double bind. As Derrida has repeatedly asked, how does one translate something written in more than one language? This doubling of languages in *Politics of Friendship*, which analyses the bind *of* language, and so the bind language produces, is all the more critical since every subsequent time the expression 'double bind' is used in the text, it appears outside of parentheses, in the main body of the text, and thus 'in' the French, or rather, in a certain angle to the French. Derrida thus 'uses' and not merely 'mentions' the English expression (to use a distinction in 'analytic philosophy' he often uses but also repeatedly questions). Moreover, crucially, at one point he even uses the expression 'double constraint' *alongside* the expression 'double bind' to demonstrate the relation of one *with* the other, the constraint of the double bind, that is, the very relationship of being-with the other (Derrida 2005c: 174). This suggests that the experience of language, the double bind of idiomaticity, is what most deeply informs Derrida's thoughts on being-with, a being-with made possible by the non-self-identical nature of the idiom. As he writes in 'Fidélité à plus d'un':

> The idiom is never proper or the proper identity of oneself [*à soi du propre*], it is already different from itself, it is only of difference. It inscribes a deviation [*écart*] in itself, in the self-same. This deviation conditions its irreducible economy in a language [*langue*] that it at the same time announces, without waiting, because of the deviation, the work of translatability. Already inside only one language [*langue*]. It is the idiom itself which one would then say was known as the social bond [*liaison*] or the social unbinding [*déliaison*]. (Derrida 1998a: 224; my translation)

The importance of the idiom is thus that it can unbind as well as bind, that it is the experience of belonging *and* non-belonging, that is has two fidelities, two-as-one. The moment of unbinding is thus as crucial as the moment of binding, neither is possible without the idiom. Moreover, in using the English word 'analysis', Derrida uses the resources of Greek not to create a liaison between 'his' language and Greek, as Heidegger so often did, but so as to open it to the singular other, to simultaneously 'de-Frenchify' *and* enfranchise his idiom.

His writing thus embodies a certain form of hospitality by remaining open to the work of foreign bodies. As a result, his writing, rather than showing a looseness of concepts, demonstrates how foreign words can loosen the tongue – the tongue that is his and not his.

Accordingly, his writing resolves at once to cultivate *and* deracinate the French language. So as not to be bound solely to 'his' language, to be its captive, he welcomes the analysis of the other, the one only the other can provide. What Derrida imparts in his practice of writing is thus that the idiom is never given *to* myself or purely invented *by* myself. Which is to say, Derrida overturns 'his' idiom – estranges it in the presence of such homely words as 'dwelling'. The kind of dwelling envisaged by Heidegger, for instance, when he banked on the resources of the German word *Anwesen* to re-establish a link between 'dwelling' and 'coming-to-presence', following on from the Greek word *ousia*, whose 'pre-philosophical proper meaning', Heidegger writes, was the household or homestead, that which is synonymous with 'property, possession, means, wealth' (Heidegger 1988: 108).

A final word on the subject matter of this book. Since Kant, Fichte, Tocqueville and Emerson are the subject of examination for this book, its emphasis and orientation is on Germany and America, using France via Tocqueville alongside Cartesianism as a bridge between the two. The fact that the book starts with Germany ostensibly reproduces the well-known and often criticised privilege that Kedourie gave to Germany when understanding the rise of nationalism. Derrida himself notes that he thinks there is a 'specific modernity' to this 'national-philosophism' and that Germany in the nineteenth as well as twentieth century 'is not a sequence amongst others'. On the contrary, Derrida thinks 'it marks an incomparable event that played an irreplaceable role in the constitution of the national-philosophical thematic'.[9] Derrida at this point in the session invokes the phenomenological technique of eidetic variation – the technique of asking what features or properties an entity must have in order to be the kind of entity it is. The invocation of this technique suggests the problems at hand when defining the 'essence' of philosophical nationalism, not only because eidetic variation takes place in the imagination according to Husserl, and is therefore not reliant solely on factual events, but because the 'essence' derived from this technique should be by definition indifferent to the conditions of space and time – it requires us to step outside of historical inquiry. But the matter of philosophical nationalism and nationalities is precisely about the question of time and history, and the relationship philosophical discourse has to its own time, its passage through space(s) and language(s). It is thus no surprise that Derrida's early work presented itself as a critique of Husserl's dismissal of history – even if Derrida accepted in part Husserl's rejection of historicism – a dismissal he thought remained unchanged in Husserl's work right up to the end, contrary to appearances. But it should also be born in mind that if Derrida rejected the view of *philosophia perennis*, the notion of an eternal philosophy independent of time or culture, he did not, like Michel Foucault, believe that the philosophical could be completely enclosed in a factual and determined historical structure. As he writes in 'Cogito and the History of Madness', the 'historicity proper to philosophy is located and constituted in the transition [. . .] between that which exceeds the totality and the closed totality, in the difference between history and historicity' (Derrida 1978: 74).

The historical sequence of philosophical nationalism, and its association with 'this difficult thing' called Germany, consequently has the unusual position of traversing the usual distinctions between history, understood as the examination of the particular or the singular, and philosophy, understood as the examination of the universal. It is, we might say, another instantiation of the 'third thing'. Indeed, Derrida, in 'Interpretations at War: Kant, the Jew, the German', states that this 'national exemplarity does not belong only to the German nation'. This structure of exemplarity can, in other words, be found in other nations. Derrida thus does not maintain, as Kedourie does, that there is really only *one* version of nationalism, or that German nationalism was the mainspring of all nationalisms, but *neither* does he propose to treat all nationalisms as the same or of equal importance in terms of understanding nationalism. He thus constantly retreats (from) 'Germany', never ceasing to be occupied by it, treating it as a singularity, but one that is exemplary in its exemplarity. As Derrida writes, 'What would one say to the statement that this exemplarity does not belong to it [Germany] except in an exemplary manner?' (Derrida 2008: 292).

On the other hand, while Germany has a certain emphasis in Derrida's writings, it is not always Germany alone. In both the essay on Kant mentioned above and in the seminars on nationality and nationalism, Derrida never ceased to discuss what he calls the 'Americano-Germanic thing'[10] or the 'Germano-American axis'.[11] As Derrida states in his very first seminar session on philosophical nationalities and nationalism:

> the United States of America has played a quite odd and revealing role in this question of philosophical nationalisms since the beginning of the nineteenth century. Today, it is the market or the *Kampfplatz*, as you wish, [this German word, which appeared famously in both of Kant's prefaces to his first *Critique* when describing *metaphysics* as a conflict, reminds us that this conflict for Derrida is not reducible to geopolitical or even linguistic issues, even if these areas remain central], which is the most open to the greatest intensity of exchanges, debates, evaluations of the Philosophical International (it would be easy to show that the USA is the major place, the obligatory passage for all philosophical circulation

[. . .] What is happening [or comes to pass: *se passe*] today in the USA, what passes and does not pass via the USA is a central or unavoidable symptom for what is of interest to us. (Derrida 1992a: 18–19)

Indeed, the first paper Derrida delivered that combined the motifs of internationalism, nationalism, democracy and what he calls 'national philosophies', namely, the 'Ends of Man', was delivered in 1968 in the USA at a conference sponsored by the French government and the International Cultural Co-operation Committee of the American Philosophical Association (McQuillan 2009: 71). Nationalism thus has no borders for Derrida and no community is immune from it. This book will thus itself negotiate a passage to America via Germany and France, starting off chronologically with Kant, and then moving on sequentially to Fichte, Tocqueville and Emerson.

## NOTES

1. It might be noted though that mathematics has, if infrequently compared with literature, been differentiated by means of its nationality. A notorious case of this is Ludwig Bieberbach and his notion of *Deutsche Mathematik* rooted in a notion of intuition (*Anschaulichkeit*) that he claimed was absent in 'Jewish' mathematics.
2. With regard to scholars of nationalism, one notable exception to the dearth of studies on the national character of philosophy is Michael Billig's chapter 'Philosophy as a Flag for the Pax Americana' in his *Banal Nationalism*, which considers the figure of Richard Rorty. As Billig notes, 'At first sight, the great traditions of philosophy seem to have no place in banal nationalism', which Billig characterises as everyday as opposed to extreme nationalism, but he argues, through analysing the various uses Rorty makes of the first person plural – for example, the 'we' of a philosophical school, or the 'we' of a whole political culture, or a universal 'we' – that 'Rorty's philosophical texts can be seen as flags for the nationalism of the Pax Americana in the new global order' (Billig 1995: 154, 161). Billig even uses the phrase 'philosophical nationalism' at one point to characterise Rorty's position (ibid.: 172). If Billig's attempts to analyse the national character of philosophy are laudable, he does not extend his analysis elsewhere, and he does not address the philosophical character of the national as such.
3. Derrida highlights the importance of the institutional setting of his seminar in an instructive aside contained in parentheses. He asks whether his move from the ENS to the EHESS means 'that *de jure* or *ipso facto* the discourse I shall be producing or the teaching I shall be giving here will fall under the social sciences, social sciences talking about philosophy or "philosophical institutions" (since this is the title of the post I chose to occupy?) [. . .] What has to happen for a social sciences institution to receive into itself – *de jure* – someone or some discourse statutorily defined by an essential relation to the philosophical? There's a question I leave hanging for the moment but which I did not want to evade in this opening session' (Derrida 1992a: 9). It might be added that Derrida's remarks complicate, if not exactly refute Simon Critchley's claims that unlike the 'Frankfurt School', which adopts a position on the 'necessary interdependence of philosophical and sociological reflection', Derrida's work is '*too exclusively philosophical*

[. . .] it is [therefore] possible to argue that his theoretical categories lack sufficient sociological mediation insofar as they are derived too directly from an engagement with tradition conceived in exclusively metaphysical or logocentric terms' (Critchley 2006: 101; original emphasis).
4. See Derrida's essay 'Khôra' in *On the Name* (1995). It might be noted that, in one of the original versions or drafts of 'Khôra', Derrida entitled his essay 'Politiques de la Khôra' and in fact highlights its 'politico-territorial' dimensions first, as opposed to the published version of 'Khôra', which highlights its 'metaphysical' dimensions first (Derrida 1984–8, Box 61, Folder 1; see note 5 below). Derrida's revision of this title from its unpublished to published version might thus lead us to ask the Aristotelian question: what is first, philosophy, politics or metaphysics? It might even lead us to interrogate the *genus* of the disjunction, especially since the logic of the disjunction (division, dissolution, disbanding, *dialuō*, dialysis, analysis, lysis, separation, unbinding, rupture, untying, secession, *écart*, etc.) plays as important a role in politics as it does in metaphysics, even if disjunction has always remained in the shadow of conjunction (joint, alliance, covenant, bond, bind, *Bund*, web, tie, fabric, weaving, *sumplokē*, succession, etc.), like some kind of political secret.
5. These seminars can be consulted at the UC Irvine Critical Theory Archive in the USA (and photocopies of them can also be found in the IMEC archive in Caen, France). Derrida's seminars have begun to be published, but since the team involved in publishing them is mostly working backwards, that is, from the very last seminars, it will take some years, likely a decade or more to reach the seminars on nationalism. It should also be emphasised that the scale of Derrida's work in this area alone is monumental, and will require several volumes to publish. My book thus touches only on a fraction of the archive material. The first year alone comprises of thirteen seminar sessions, and as indicated above, there are four years of material devoted specifically to this topic (though later seminars also relate to it, for example, the 1988–9 seminar 'Politiques de l'amitié'). Derrida often cites these seminars in his published work on philosophical nationalism, counting – as he notes in the foreword to *Politics of Friendship* – on their future publication to make sense of the premises and horizon of his work in this area. References to the Jacques Derrida Papers (hereafter Derrida 1984–8) will be made in this book by noting the box number, the folder number, the seminar number, and, where possible, the page number. The translations are mine unless otherwise noted.
6. Also noteworthy is a special issue (issue 1.2) of *Bamidbar: Journal for Jewish thought and Philosophy* (2011), ed. Willi Goetschel, which examines the place of Spinoza in Derrida's nationalism seminars.
7. Derrida (1984–8), Box 18, Folder 15, p. 9.
8. Ibid. p. 9.
9. Derrida (1984–8), Box 18, Folder 2, Seminar 2, p. 3.
10. Ibid. p. 5.
11. Derrida (1984–8), Box 18, Folder 2, Seminar 4, p. 1.

CHAPTER 2

# The Making of Brothers: Kant the Nationalist, the Internationalist and the Cosmopolitan

> The land [*Land*] itself is a fraternisation [*Verbrüderung*] out of a common [*gemeinschaftlichen*] father.
> Immanuel Kant, 'Reflections on Philosophy of Law',
> Reflection no. 7686 (from 1770s) [19:490]

It has become commonplace to take Immanuel Kant as the exemplary thinker of cosmopolitanism. Indeed, Kant as the thinker of the 'State', of the 'interstate' and of the 'cosmopolitical' is a familiar figure. But what about Kant as the thinker of the 'people', of 'fraternity' and of the 'nation' – does such a Kant exist? Could we recognise the 'national' as something that is essentially and thoroughly embedded in Kant's work, something that demands further analysis in the same way his notion of the State does? Is the only legitimate question in the Kantian political dossier the question of the State – be it in the singular or in the plural? The aim of the following two chapters is to identify and reconstitute another strand of philosophical thinking in Kant, one about nationalities as they relate to philosophy, one which has been eclipsed and overlooked in his work, even if this eclipse, as we will see, had already been prefigured by Kant himself.

The place of Kant in Derrida's seminars on philosophical nationalities and nationalism is ostensibly peripheral. While there are brief excursions and examinations of Kant throughout the seminars, they are always pursued in relation to another thinker and another problem at hand. The most sustained examination of Kant's own writings in these seminars comes very early, in the second session of the first year, when Derrida offers a reading of Theodor Adorno's 1965 contribution to a radio broadcast entitled 'On the Question: What is German?' (*Auf die Frage: Was ist Deutsch?*) and in particular, Adorno's belief that Kantian thought is the best place of resistance to nationalism. Derrida observes that Adorno in this piece relies on an interpretation of Kant that places practical reason and autonomy at the centre of Kant's thought, rather than an emphasis on finitude and temporality in the imagination, as we find in Martin Heidegger's 1929 *Kant and the Problem of Metaphysics*. Derrida thus complicates any straightforward notion of the German inheritance of Kant, a difficulty he expands upon when he recalls the Davos debate – if a 'debate' is what it truly was, Derrida mindfully notes – between Heidegger and Ernst Cassirer that led to Heidegger's text. By noting the multiple and conflicting appropriations of Kant, within a single language, as well as between languages, Derrida thus underscores all the political and institutional questions that are involved in the use of such titles as 'neo-Kantianism', the 'Marburg school' and what he calls the 'Judeo-German Psyche' (Derrida 2008: 291). The pertinence of these national and international appropriations comes to light in recalling that the Davos 'debate' was itself not only a part of larger so-called international university course sponsored by the governments of Switzerland, France and Germany, but something that was brought about so as to achieve a 'reconciliation' between French-speaking and German-speaking philosophers (Friedman 2000: 9).

With such different readings of Kant available – marked by school, by tradition, by language, amongst other factors – Derrida notes that one could no doubt draw different conclusions about the Kantian interpretation of nationhood and language (*langue*). He proceeds, in turn, to examine a small number of passages from Kant's *Anthropology from a Pragmatic Point of View* (1798), with the aim of complicating the faith Adorno places in Kant as a 'star witness of the German tradition', one who can undo 'the unreflected supremacy of the national' because Kant's 'thought is centred upon the concept of autonomy' (Adorno 2005: 206). But Derrida warns that though he has discussed Kant, one would have to return to the work of Kant and examine a wider range of texts, and indeed, at much greater length, to understand all the difficulties that are involved in Adorno's faith in Kant as a thinker who resists nationalism. Derrida does indeed return to Kant, but in a very different way, in the last year of those seminars, namely, in 1987–8. In fact, the proper name 'Kant' can even be said to haunt these *séances* and underline their very possibility, as when Derrida titles this last year of seminars on nationalism: 'Kant, le Juif, l'Allemand: nationalité et nationalisme philosophiques'. For this group of seminars – which were partly published under the bilingual title of 'Interpretations at War: Kant, le Juif, l'Allemand' – does not so much consider the work of Kant, as the 'insistent recurrence of the *reference* to Kant, even to a certain Judaism in Kant, on the part of those who, from Wagner and Nietzsche to Adorno sought to respond to the question "*Was ist Deutsch?*"' (Derrida 2002a: 261; my emphasis).

We are thus left in the philosophical nationality seminars with only fleeting reflections on or of Kant in the writings of other thinkers. The import of this strategy is no doubt tied up with the logic of the *psyché*, the two-sided mirror that Derrida invokes when he considers the aforementioned 'Judeo-German Psyche', as well as what is at stake if the concept of interpretation, and all that involves, is itself the scene of misunderstanding; if wars take place not only between different (national) interpretations, but between different (national) interpretations of what constitutes a legitimate interpretation. Derrida's work thus raises the question of where to position Kant and his philosophical legacy in the history and development of philosophical nationalities. The following two chapters of my book will thus examine Kant, and in particular, how his work is both a *symptom* of these newly established national-philosophical formations (e.g. 'French philosophy', 'German philosophy', etc.) as well as an *acceleration* of them. It is indeed often noted that the notion of 'German philosophy' is itself tied to Kant – that the title 'German philosophy' came into being because of Kant, even though he was not the first significant philosopher to write in the German language (one thinks, for instance, of Herder). An illustration of such identification can be found in Terry Pinkard, who states in his *German Philosophy, 1760–1860: The Legacy of Idealism*, that

> starting in 1781 [the year that the first edition of Kant's *Critique of Pure Reason* appeared], 'German' philosophy came for a while to dominate European philosophy and to change the shape of not only how Europeans but practically the whole world conceived of itself [. . .] From its inception, it was controversial, always hard to understand, and almost always described as *German* [. . .] Yet the fact that there was no 'Germany' at the time indicates how little can be explained by appealing to its being 'German', as if being 'German' might independently explain the development of 'German' philosophy during the period. If nothing else, what counted as 'German' was itself up for grabs and was being developed and argued about by writers, politicians, publicists, and, of course, philosophers, during this period. (Pinkard 2002: 2; original emphasis)

If Pinkard notes the significance of the repeatedly attached 'German' predicate to philosophy in this period and ever since, he does not pursue Kant's own thinking about what was 'German', let alone Kant's relationship to the newly emerging national inscriptions of philosophy. This is particularly significant since these new means of demarcating philosophy – that is, by nationality – often pose, as described in the Introduction, the most difficult of problems to the most trenchant and long-standing traditions of the subject.

If Kant does not settle the question of philosophical nationalities, he is not one figure among others in the history of their development. For Kant's work will be posited as central to understanding the rise and formation of philosophical nationalities, philosophies differentiated by means of nationality *and* nations differentiated by means of philosophy. Yet, as we will see, what the following chapters show is that Kant's writings on philosophical national characteristics and the newly established idea of the nation are ambiguous insofar as the very philosophical nationalities they claim to recognise are also *marginalised*. They are included in such a way, we might say, as to be effaced. This suggests, in turn, that the eclipse of these issues in the Kantian archive – and so contemporary philosophy insofar as it is inescapably constituted by this archive – was already prepared by Kant himself. But if this is so, this project will also claim that the means and instruments by which to uncover these other readings of Kant are also partly already present in the Kantian archive. As Derrida notes with regard to the Kantian heritage in his essay 'Privilege':

> The Kantian heritage is not only the Kantian heritage, a thing identical to itself. Like every heritage, it exceeds itself to provide (or lay claim to) the analysis of this heritage, and, better, the instruments of analysis for every heritage. This 'supplementary' structure must be taken into account. A heritage always surreptitiously bequeaths to us the means of interpreting it. It superimposes itself *a priori* on the interpretation we produce of it, that is to say, always, to a certain extent, and up to a line that is difficult to determine, that we repeat of it. (Derrida 2002c: 49)

Recognising that the Kantian heritage is divided, not identical to itself, allows us to see how this heritage both expresses *and* represses the pressing issue of philosophical nationalities, precisely because this heritage has not remained indifferent to how it is read. Kant's 'political writings' – but even this belongs to what remains to be thought – are presented, and moreover, present themselves as a 'reading' of the State. In other words, the texts open up the question of philosophical nationalities always under the shadow of the State. They would enjoin us to say, or rather, to say-without-saying it, that 'German philosophy' rightly sees that philosophy ought to engage with questions of the State – *contra* Herder. Yet, if the texts' defences ensure that they are read in a certain manner, there remain, undoubtedly, other traces, including, we might say, traces of the national. This raises the question of how we are to read Kant, to continue reading him in a way that does not simply follow the route of interpretation that the texts themselves legitimise and lay out for us in advance. The kind of interpretation, for example, that privileges the State as a philosophical site; the site which facilitates, or better yet, sponsors philosophy, and which philosophy proper in turn should think about and legitimise.

For if Kant famously never produced a 'Fourth Critique' on politics, if his explicit political philosophy did not appear in another *Critique*, but only in articles and essays mostly for the *Berlinische Monatsschrift* from the mid-1780s onwards, it should also be recalled that these essays themselves privilege the field of the statal, meaning that when the nation appears, it appears in the margins. We thus need to pay attention not only to which texts are eclipsed in the Kantian archive, but also to what issues are eclipsed within those texts – how certain themes and problems are relegated to being secondary, derivative and accidental. Derrida, following this line of thought, asks:

> must one not at least begin by bringing to light those effects of authority that are already, strictly 'within [*à l'intérieur*]' (if one can put it this way, for this language is still Kantian) his oeuvre, by studying its hierarchizing, canonizing, marginalizing, and disqualifying procedures, the 'internal' structure of the text, the exclusion (that is, the externalizing [*la mise en extériorité*]) of the Opuscules [that is, what are thought to be *minor* works], Parerga [that is, what are thought to be *incidental* pieces], or Remarks? (Derrida 2002c: 50)

Derrida's question raises the possibility of reading Kant in a way which does not simply abandon the Kantian heritage, nor which simply reproduces the very privileges that this same heritage has in turn prepared. The logic of the problem before us can be defined as follows: in order to gather the conceptual tools needed to articulate the limits that this heritage has imposed upon us, we need to draw on the very *same* heritage that we seek to bring into question. With regard to the question of philosophical nationalities, something that has not traditionally been a legitimate research topic in philosophy, be it in so-called analytic *or* Continental philosophy, we might turn to the divided nature of the Kantian heritage.

For on the one hand, Kant provides us with a reading of national characteristics that suggests that national characteristics are never completely exhausted by a given set of empirical predicates. On the other hand, he never directly engages with the classical questions of language and philosophy, let alone the usage of so-called natural language *in* philosophical discourse; the usage of natural language *as* philosophical language; other than when he claims, as we will see, that there is at least one language, namely, French, which is implicitly an obstacle to the pursuit of reason free from the sensibility of the nation. This is despite the fact he claims that philosophy by necessity *cannot* present itself as a mathematical demonstration, that it is essentially *discursive* and must use words and not mathematical signs (as Leibniz, who wrote mostly in Latin and French, had dreamt when he advocated a *characteristica universalis* – a universal language, one independent of any 'natural' language). But this emphasis on the discursive nature of philosophy coupled with Kant's denunciation of the French language at least signals that the topic of the idiomatic can become unexpectedly important for the Kantian 'critical project', even if it understands the idiomatic – that is to say, the French idiom – as only a negative condition, something which endangers rather than enables the universal vocation of philosophy.

But if Kant's writings prepare the way for an explicit positing of the national dimension of philosophy, I wish to claim that his work also remains deeply problematic, especially with regard to its supposed ability, as Adorno claims, to resist forms of nationalism, xenophobia and national belligerence. Kant's work will thus not be simply situated against nationalism, but shown in its various equivocations to be, at certain points, as possibly *complicit* as resistive to forms of nationalism. The two following chapters elaborate the aforementioned tension between the universal and the particular by tracing some of the ways the project of reason as outlined by Kant is *implicated* in the question of national differences in philosophy – the manner in which such differences do not befall the project of reason as merely secondary or derivative accidents.

Accordingly, this chapter demonstrates that philosophical commentators who link Kant solely to cosmopolitanism – for example, Georg Cavallar – ignore the complexity and unresolved tension between the nation and cosmopolitanism in Kant's work, and thus pass over the strategic exclusion and inclusion of the nation in his political outlook. It does this by examining a set of analogies between citizenship and kinship – as well as State and motherhood – that are never completely eradicated by Kant, even when he warns that the *juridical* sense of people, a State, should not be confused with the *empirical* sense of people.

In addition, it shows that the difficulties Kant faces over this tension between the national and the cosmopolitical are relevant not only to what is called his 'political' philosophy, but also to his vision of philosophy as such – to the universal philosophical discourse premised on reason. That the faculty of reason may itself be involved here is to acknowledge the manner in which Kant deploys a *political* conception of reason, one divided in terms of strict legitimate *jurisdiction*. As Onora O'Neill astutely states in her *Constructions of Reason*:

> The close connections between the short political essays and the central critical writings suggest not only that the essays are part of Kant's systematic philosophy, and not marginal or occasional pieces, but also perhaps that the entire critical enterprise has a certain political character. If this is the case, it is no accident that the guiding metaphors of the *Critique of Pure Reason* are political metaphors. If the discussion of reason itself is to proceed in terms of *conflicts* whose *battlefields* and *strife* are scenes of *defeat* and *victory* that will give way to lasting peace only when we have established through *legislation* such courts, *tribunals* and

*judges* as can weigh the issues and give *verdict*, then it is not very surprising that Kant links his discussion of politics very closely to larger issues about the powers and limits of human reason. (O'Neill 1989: 29; original emphasis)

It should also be noted that within nationalism studies the importance of Kant is disputed. According to Elie Kedourie, who explains nationalism in terms of a revolution in 'European philosophy', nationalism started inadvertently with Kant and the political consequences drawn from his ethical and epistemological theories by a class of intellectuals (Kedourie [1960] 1993). My own work, in contrast to Kedourie's, will uncover the conceptual apparatus Kant himself provides for understanding national characteristics, or rather, those belonging to France, England and Germany, since, as we will see, these examples are privileged for Kant and cannot be reduced to empirical typologies in the same way Spain, Italy, Poland, Russia and what he calls 'European Turkey' can. My interpretation thus reveals why an understanding of these privileged national characteristics cannot be – in Kant's own terms – exclusively an empirical task. This enables me to begin uncovering how philosophical nationalities, even when they are formulated in the most troubling manner, can exist without vitiating the universality that philosophy from its foundation promises. The claim that Kant is implicated within nationalism will thus be advanced not, like Kedourie's, as a historical claim within the history of ideas, but as a methodological point regarding the partly non-empirical structure he provides for understanding English, French and German national characteristics. This will develop one of the major claims of this project, that although it is not entirely philosophical, nationalism can only be fully understood by taking into account its philosophical dimensions. In contrast to Kedourie, Ernest Gellner thinks that an emphasis on Kant as a source of nationalism is misplaced at best and incoherent at worst irrespective of whether one believes in what Gellner deems to be a 'doctrinal' and intellectually led account of nationalism, or a 'materialistic' and socially determined account (like, presumably, his own, which emphasises the process of industrialisation, mass literacy and modernity). This is because, for Gellner, 'it is hard to think of a writer whose ideas provide less comfort for the nationalist [. . .] Kant is the very last person whose vision could be credited with having contributed to nationalism' (Gellner [1983] 2006: 126). Kant is 'the very model for that allegedly bloodless, cosmopolitan, emaciated ethic of the Enlightenment' (ibid. 126).

Indeed, Isaiah Berlin, in his essay 'Kant as an Unfamiliar Source of Nationalism', states that

> at first sight nothing would seem more disparate than the idea of nationality and the sane, rational, liberal internationalism of the great

Königsberg philosopher. Of all the influential thinkers of his day, Kant seems the most remote from the rise of nationalism. (Berlin 1996: 232)

However, if Berlin proceeds in the essay to undermine the prevalent view that Kant was a thinker of great remove from nationalism, he does so by analysing ideas, like Kedourie, in what he takes to be Kant's 'ethical writings', particularly the ideas of self-determination and 'the choosing self', rather than those texts which explicitly mention or invoke the '*Volk*' alongside the Latin term '*natio*' or the German term '*Nation*', terms Berlin, in fact, ignores. This chapter will thus analyse what has been long neglected – the Latin and German political terms of Kant. As we shall see, the equivocations in Kant's various texts around the notion of the '*Volk*' and the '*Nation*' suggest that he is in various ways closer to nationalism than previously thought and, in some ways, more distant.

## KANT AND THE TOWER OF BABEL

The account of reason which Kant develops in his *Critique of Pure Reason* is deemed to be, in 'The Doctrine of Method', an unfinished edifice or building. As Kant notes, it is an edifice which is necessarily unfinished and which must be built in spite of

> the babel of tongues [*Sprachverwirrung*], which inevitably gives rise to disputes among the workers in regard to the plan to be followed, and which must end up by scattering them all over the world, leaving each to erect a separate building for himself, according to his own design. (Kant 1933: A707, B735)

The appropriateness of Kant's allusion to the tower of Babel is evident when we recall that this is the story *par excellence* about the project of universality, the programme, projection and promise of universal reason. The original story from the Book of Genesis, chapter 11, declares that the great Semitic family – that is, the tribe of Shem – will build themselves a city and a tower whose height reaches the heavens, so that they can 'make a name for themselves' and not 'be scattered all over the face of all the earth' (Genesis 11: 8). It is worth noting that Kant does not mention, in his retelling of the story, that part referring to the making of a 'name', the making of a unique genealogy, a genesis that would be singular and whole. There is no record of the 'Shem' in the *Critique of Pure Reason*, no record of the name 'Shem', no record of the name that means 'name' in Hebrew. The absence of this name in Kant's retelling is of course in accord with the original idea of philosophy, that it must not be limited to a *genos*, to a people, to a lineage, that it must, in a word, be universalisable – we must be able to dissociate philosophy in the last instance from the singularity of a proper name, and above all, from that of 'Babel', to what precedes and comes first in the very name Ba-bel ('father', *Ba* and 'God', *Bel*, according to Voltaire).

But if Kant's exclusion of 'Babel' as a proper noun, as a place name, as the foundation of a unique genealogy is already telling, his sole focus on the centrifugal motif, the dispersion of people across the world, is just as revealing. In particular, it shows that he sees the picture of people building according to their own regional and local habitat, solely as a threat, something that can only bring about the collapse of the edifice of philosophy, rather than something that can help sustain it. For although Kant recognises that there have been historically specific *ways* of philosophising, he will not accept that there could be, in different times and places, distinct and yet equally adequate philosophies. If there is only one form of reason, there can only be one true rational philosophical system. The problem of whether there could be more than one philosophy, of whether there was a multiplicity intrinsic or possible within philosophy, was not foreign to Kant, as he writes in the preface to his *Metaphysics of Morals*:

> Not only have there been different *ways* of philosophising and going back to the first principles of reason in order to base a system, more or less successfully, upon them, but there had been many experiments of this kind, each of which made its contribution to present-day philosophy. Yet since, considered objectively, there can only be one human reason, *there cannot be many philosophies*; in other words, there can only be one true system of philosophy from principles, in however many different and even conflicting ways one has philosophised about one and the same proposition. (Kant 1996a: 4 [6:207]; my emphasis)

In other words, even if for Kant reason is something that is not given to itself, or grasped by itself, once and for all, and from the start, it is not vulnerable to the same conditioning that empirical processes must suffer. Reason cannot seemingly be subject to differences of nationality, language and geopolitical boundaries. There can only be one edifice and one plan for one true philosophy. The fear thus lurking behind these worries of fragmentation, expressed so succinctly by Kant, is that philosophy will perish under a babel of tongues, that it will no longer be able to gather itself into a single unifying edifice, even one so humble, or down-to-earth, as a 'dwelling-house [*Wohnhaus*]' (Kant 1933: A707, B735).

Philosophy must be sheltered for Kant and it must be housed in a single building. Moreover, this domicile must be in order, or better yet, it must reflect the order of things. Like the Greek *arkheoin*, the dwelling-house of philosophy is thus a symbol of the home *and* of the law. The architectural imagery at play, one so often found in the project of reason, underscores a further sense of the word 'Babel', one cited by Jacques Derrida in his essay 'Des Tours de Babel' when he mentions Voltaire's 1764 entry on the subject in his *Philosophical Dictionary*, namely, that the word 'Babel' also functions as a *common* noun, meaning 'confusion', the kind that descends on architects when they find themselves interrupted amid construction, as well as the kind that undoes the bind, the *fusion* of a 'people'. That the narrative of Babel is not tangential to Kant's discussion of reason in 'The Doctrine of Method' is brought further to light when we recall that the original story is itself concerned with the very project of universality that reason gives to itself. As Derrida puts it in his aforementioned essay:

> the Semites want to bring the world to reason *and* this reason can signify simultaneously a colonial violence (since they would thus universalise their idiom [not language as such, and certainly not a *characteristica universalis*, but their 'lip', their idiom, and not the idiomatic as such, but the *Semitic idiom*, one in principle inimitable *not only* because it belongs to the idiomatic, *but also* because it is a sacred language]) *and* a peaceful transparency of the human community [insofar as their community aspires to be, quite 'literally', above divisions of family and tribe by making one 'name']. Inversely, when God imposes and opposes his name [by giving his name to the city of Babel and by bringing confusion into that city by means of his name, so that henceforth 'Babel' would *mean* confusion and be susceptible to the *effect* of a certain confusion], he ruptures the rational transparency but interrupts also the colonial violence or the linguistic imperialism [. . .] he delivers a universal reason (it will no longer be subject to the rule of a particular nation [*nation* is Derrida's word, following the Louis Segond translation of the Bible he cites earlier in the essay]), but he simultaneously limits its very universality: forbidden transparency, impossible univocity. (Derrida 2002a: 111; my emphasis)

For Kant, we must not reach as high as the Semites, but neither must we abandon the vocation of making philosophy, by means of reason, a single coherent construct or edifice. We will return to this scene of language and idiom as it is presented in Kant more thoroughly in Chapter 3. What needs to be emphasised first is that the babelian motif of 'making a name', postulating a genealogy by means of the 'name', in fact reappears when Kant analyses the notion of a people, a *Volk*, in his aforementioned 1797 text *Metaphysics of Morals*:

> As natives of a country [*Landeseingeborene*], those who constitute a nation [the actual word used in the German text is *Volk*, but as we will soon see,

the translator is not so much erroneously identifying the two words, as anticipating Kant's association of a *Volk* with the German term *Nation* only a year later, in another text. However, as will also become apparent, Kant already marks the community of birth in *this* text by means of Latin] can be looked upon to be descendants [more literally, by means of analogy: *nach der Analogie der Erzeugung*] of the same *ancestors* [*parental* ancestors: *Elternstamm*] (*congeniti*) even though they are not. Yet in an intellectual sense and from the perspectives of rights [*in intellektueller und rechtlicher Bedeutung*], since they are born of the same mother [*von einer gemeinschaftlichen Mutter*] (the republic) they constitute as it were one family (*gens, natio*) whose members (citizens of a state) are of equally high birth [*ebenbürtig*] and do not mix with those who may live near them in a state of nature. (Kant 1996a: 114 [6:343]; original emphasis)

Pauline Kleingeld – one of the few commentators on Kant who has addressed the topic of nationalism and patriotism as it appears within Kant's work – notes in her essay 'Kant's Cosmopolitan Patriotism' that Kant uses the analogy between the nation and family in several places. Another, for instance, is in 'On the Common Saying', where Kant differentiates a paternalist (*Väterliche*) government with a patriotic (*Väterländische*) government, stating that the latter 'way of thinking [*Denkungsart*]', which he upholds against the former, 'regards the commonwealth [*das gemeine Wesen*] as the maternal womb [*mütterlichen Schoß*]' (Kant 1991: 71). However, for Kleingeld, the crucial question is not whether he uses it or not, but 'in *what* regard the family and the nation are analogous' (Kleingeld 2003: 313; my emphasis). She states that defenders of what she calls 'nationalist patriotism' take the family and the country as analogous insofar as both 'are claimed to imply *special duties* on the part of their members towards co-members' (ibid. 314; original emphasis). But she claims that for Kant, on the contrary, the analogy is supposed to merely lie in 'the fact that all members are *of the same rank*' (ibid. 314; original emphasis). She highlights this by noting that Kant refers to *ebenbürtigkeit*, with its connotations of equality and shared family origins, and thus concludes that 'membership in a republic should be understood as analogous with the shared *birthright* that comes from a shared ancestry. Just as all children in a family are of the same social class, all citizens in a republic are equal' (ibid. 314; my emphasis).

## PLATO'S *MENEXENUS* AND THE ATHENIAN *POLIS*

But we might also ask if Kleingeld is aware of the immense history of this particular analogy. For within the Athenian tradition of the *polis*, and this is not just any tradition for Kant, can be found the mother, the transformation of the republic into a mother, a provider and nurturer to her children – the citizens of a *polis*. An example of this – even if the text does not subscribe to the analogy – can be found in Plato's *Menexenus*, when Socrates recites a funeral oration he attributes to Aspasia for the war-dead of the city of Athens. It is what we might call, following Benedict Anderson and Nicole Loraux, a recitation of 'ghostly *national* imaginings' (Anderson [1983] 2006: 9).[1] In this recitation Socrates not only praises the city of Athens by calling her a mother, but also secures by means of this claim, proof that the equality of rights in Athens *descends* from a prior equality of birth. The claim in *Menexenus* is as follows:

> 'The reason we have this polity is our equality in birth. The other cities have been put together from people of diverse origin and unequal condition, so that their polities are also unequal – tyrannies and oligarchies. Some of their inhabitants look on others as slaves, while the latter look on the former as masters. We and our fellow-citizens, *all brothers sprung from one mother*, do not think it right to be each other's slaves or masters. Equality of birth in the natural order makes us seek equality of rights in the legal.' (Plato 1997: 238E–239A; my emphasis)

Civic equality, or *isonomy*, is thus founded on an equality of birth, or *isogony*. One is led to an equality of rights in law (*nomos*) because there is a *prior* order assigned by birth, by nature (*physis*). Kant's definition of the republic as a mother when seen from the perspective of *Recht* thus repeats and yet reconfigures the order of precedence found in *Menexenus* between natural and juridical law. For Kant, it is not any kind of 'proper' or 'noble' birth that makes us seek equality of rights in the legal order, but the perspective of right (*Recht*) itself. Yet, this *isonomy* is not without a familiar and familial example – we are to treat fellow citizens *as if* they possessed the same equal high birth (*ebenbürtig*). The fraternity that governs and links the citizens of a State together will not be *founded* on the 'proper birth', but it will use the language of kinship, the order of the familial, to articulate the civic relationship.

We might thus suspect that certain problems around this configuration have not been diminished, for even if in Kant the equality of rights in the legal order is something that is established *separately* to any equality of birth in the natural order, it is nevertheless something that for him should *model* itself on this equality of birth found in nature. The example of equality that *isonomy* will follow, the one it will seek to imitate, is none other than the one which originally governed it in the Athenian *polis* – the equality of *isogony*. The rupture with the law of natural birth is thus not absolute. For the equality of citizens in a republic should not be established by repressing or denying family, kinship, or blood as such, but by treating all citizens of a republic *as if* they were brothers, they must 'constitute *as it were* one family (*gens, natio*)'

(Kant 1996a: 114 [6:343]; my emphasis). They must, in other words, act *as if* they were familial figures united by a common birth and a common ancestor.

The price Kant pays for this is not simple. On the one hand, it allows him to escape the Athenian definition of a *polis* as made up of an indivisible unit rooted in the soil of a specific homeland. On the other hand, it makes it finally impossible for him to fully escape the politics of fraternity, a configuration of politics which invokes, at whatever distance, blood, birth and nature – be it autochthonal or not. To understand first of all how Kant widens the Athenian definition of the citizen, we may return to *Menexenus*:

> 'The nobility of these men's origin [in Athens] is rooted in that of their ancestors. The latter were not immigrants and did not, by arriving from elsewhere, make these descendants of theirs live as aliens in the land, but made them children of the soil. Really dwelling and having their being in their ancestral home, nourished not, as other peoples are, by a stepmother, but by a mother, the land in which they lived.' (Plato 1997: 237C)

The invocation of the mythic origins of Athens, the autochthonous emergence of its people from its soil, posits an original and indivisible unity for the *polis*. It opposes the Athenians, the legitimate city-sons of the city, to those it identifies as 'immigrants' and 'foreigners'. In fact, as Loraux points out in her *Born of the Earth*, the word *epêlus*, often translated in the above passage as 'immigrant', more accurately means an 'arrival' or a '(late) arrival' (Loraux 2000: 162). The figure of the outsider, the stranger, is someone who arrives; it is the one who is a latecomer, who is belated. The semantic shift of 'immigrant' to '(late) arrival' registers the temporal as well as spatial dimensions at stake: the belief that the non-autochthones could never have claimed the land in the way the autochthones did, precisely because they arrived at a particular temporal juncture – their movement took place within a temporal dimension that was not only not needed by those born from the soil of Athens, but which did not take place in time at all. If this secured the mythic origins of the city, the only thing that the citizens of Athens had to do to ensure that this autochthony of the first ancestor continued, that it was inheritable, was to stay in the same place, to reside on the soil of their ancestors.

In contrast to this, Kant writes that 'climate and soil' cannot furnish the key to explain the national character of a *Volk*, 'for migrations [*Wanderungen*] of entire peoples have proven that they do not change their character as a result of their new place of residence [*Wohnsitze*]' (Kant 2007: 408 [7:313]). The implication is thus that Athenians could be Athenians outside of Athens, that territory, or permanent occupation of soil, does not define a people. They may still require a proper place, a place which is their own, to be entitled to call themselves a people, but it need not be the place of their origin. While the *propius* – that which is one's own, that which is pure and that which belongs to property – thus dominates, it does not determine the place of a people. This is of course linked, if not reducible, to Kant's effort in such texts as *Perpetual Peace* and the *Metaphysics of Morals* to broaden the notion of right (*Recht*) from one grounded exclusively in the domestic sphere, and so the rights a citizen has in the State to which he belongs, to one that includes all individuals who share the same ground, that is, the same terrestrial globe, and so the rights an individual has on foreign soil – what Kant famously inaugurated under the name of the cosmopolitical order and the right to hospitality.

The gender-specific determiner ('he') used in the previous sentence is no accident. It is emblematic of the fact that Kant wishes to both dissociate *and* associate, at some level, kinship with citizenship, and so, gender with citizenship. For as Nicole Loraux has argued in *The Children of Athena*, there was no female citizen in the ancient city of Athens – there was only the world of the *andres*, the male citizen-soldiers of the city (Loraux 1993). This is in keeping with the equality of rights, for the *andres* are of equal standing in the city, not only because they are of Athens, its progeny, but because they are its sons. Recall that the analogy between country and mother in *Menexenus* held that Athenians are '*brothers* sprung from one mother'. Athenian politics, then, is not only a language of kinship; it is a language of the brother, of the uterine brother.

We might think Kant escapes such a fate when he avoids the myth of autochthony, but to think he has escaped the difficulty of dissociating citizenship, kinship and fraternity in this manner would be to forget the important distinction Kant makes between the 'active' and the 'passive' citizen in his *Metaphysics of Morals*. He proclaims there that active citizens are those who are not only part of the commonwealth or republic, but members of it; in contrast, passive citizens are those who 'lack civil personality' and whose 'existence is, as it were, only [a matter of] inherence [*seine Existenz ist gleichsam nur Inhärenz*]' (Kant 1996a: 92 [6:314]). Crucially, the passive citizen includes not only the figure of the minor and the dependant in general, but the woman. This is in fact in accord with the semantic family of the Latin word *gens*, one of the words Kant associates with the word *Volk*, for its semantic field (from *gen-*) includes not only genus, generic, genre and generation, but also gender.

## KANT'S DEFINITION OF THE NATION

But the word *gens* has further import, for if one of its earliest uses in Ancient Rome, as noted by C. J. Smith in his *Roman Clan*, was to refer to a 'people', it developed in due course a separate sense, namely, the name of a 'familial group', one alleging kinship and shared ancestry. Indeed, Smith claims that 'the earliest references to the *gens* in the sense of a familial group are found in Cicero' (Smith 2006: 13). The *gens* that names the people thus also names by the time of Cicero – a thinker who is pivotal for Kant, as we will see in the next section – the patrimonial clan, the one united by a common name, by a common *nomen*. The equivocation at stake here is further complicated by the fact that there is 'a parallel to be drawn between the search for familial ancestry and the process of identifying the founders of nations, or searching for the *origines gentium*' (ibid. 14).

The *gens* of the nation and the people is thus already haunted, even before the founding story they themselves tell, by the alleged kinship of the family. The spectral dimension, which was previously claimed by Anderson as an element of the national imagination, underscores the fact that this kinship of the *gens* posits relations not only in the human realm, but in legendary genealogies and mythical ancestors – the lost body of the founding king or the mythic hero who once founded a nation.[2] As Smith notes, in relation to the *gens*, this is no more evident than in the political discourses pertaining to the institution of the Roman funeral. If the same holds true for Athens, it is not least because of such mythic Athenian kings and founding heroes as Cecrops and Erichthonius, but because the repetition of the myth of autochthony is to be found in nothing less than the '*epitaphioi logoi* (funeral orations), in which the official orators collectively ascribe to all Athenians an autochthonous emergence from the soil of the city' (Loraux 1993: 7).

If one will always confuse the *gens* with the *familia*, it is because of the burial of the dead, those ghostly national imaginings and funeral orations which appear everywhere from the *Menexenus* to the 'Gettysburg Address' of Abraham Lincoln. Everything that takes place between *khôra* – a Greek word which can be variously translated as 'locality', 'spacing', 'country', 'village', 'birthplace', 'territory of the city' and 'civic soil' – and the cemetery. As Derrida declares, 'the founder of a spirit [*esprit*] of a people, one could show, always has the figure of the *revenant-survivant*, a ghost-survivor' (Derrida 1994c: 182). The French word *revenant*, meaning at once that which returns or comes back, and the ghost or spectre, emphasises that the appeal to a national affirmation always presupposes the return, at least the expected return, of a sort of spectral entity, an entity that embodies or incarnates the spirit, the spirit of a people. As we will see in Chapter 2, the word *esprit* is not just any French word for Kant.

The importance of this Greco-Roman history from *Menexenus* to Cicero is manifold for Kant, but one of the most important elements is that it founds a rational philosophical universal history. As detailed in his 1784 *Idea for a Universal History with a Cosmopolitan Aim*, this would be a telling of 'history [*Geschichte*]' according to a 'hidden plan of nature', rather than an aggregate of human actions without plan (Kant 2007: 116 [8:27]). Moreover, this history would provide us with a view towards the 'perfect civil union of the human species [*die vollkommene bürgerliche Vereinigung in der Menschengattung*]' (ibid. 118 [8:29]). But this teleological project can only be achieved for Kant by following the exemplary example of a *single* people, namely, the Greeks. For in the ninth proposition of this text, Kant claims that it is *only* Greek history that preserves or at least authenticates 'every other older or contemporaneous history' (ibid. 118 [8:29]).

This includes, he observes in a footnote, the 'Jewish nation [people: *Volk*]' (ibid. 118n. [8:29]). The Jewish people will only have a history insofar as they interact with the Greek people, and this came about for Kant only through the translation of the Hebrew Bible into Koine Greek at the time of Ptolemy II, in other words, with the Septuagint. Jewish memory, their historical legacy, in the end, can count for Kant only with the assistance of the Greeks. They had to be Hellenised; they had to pass through Greek thought in order to enter history (*Geschichte*). The vast and complex question of Kant and Judaism, what Kant wrote on the Jews, be it as a religion or what he sometimes also called a people, as well as his relationship to German Jews, and so his relationship to Mendelssohn – all of which is a continual theme in Derrida's aforementioned 'Kant, le Juif, l'Allemand' seminars – will not be pursued here. But let us briefly note that Kant's effacement of the name 'Shem' can be compared and associated with another name Kant insistently does not invoke, namely, Johann Gottfried Herder. That this absence of Herder is no accident, that it has its own significance, is revealed when we recall that Herder's model of the nation was none other than Hebraic. For Herder, Ancient Israel is the oldest institution of nationhood, a 'most excellent example [of the *Volk*]' (Herder, cited by Barnard 2003: 20). This was not only, crucially, because of their common heritage and their shared language and folklore memory, but because – in a gesture that is paradoxically Kantian – of their *juridical* system. This was expressed for Herder in the self-reflective image of Jewish law in Moses, that the legislation of Moses was not 'only moral and philosophical, but also national' (ibid. 21). Even though Herder emphasises the importance of law, the juridical system as at once universal *and* national, nothing could be further from Kant's distrust of the Jewish people and his belief that they erode rather than sustain the *civic* nature of the body politic. It is not the continuation and expansion of the Hebraic model of nationhood that Kant seeks, whatever that may be determined to be, but the expansion of the Greek model of the *polis*. Kant's silence on such issues as the Jewish 'election' is thus no accident.

That the continuation of the Greek was indeed the very task that philosophy was charged with for Kant, is evident from his claim that the Greek inheritance is supposed to be an *unbroken* chain that links all peoples of Europe – and so eventually for Kant, the world – together. As he states, 'only a *learned public* that has endured uninterruptedly from its beginnings up to our time can accredit ancient history' (Kant 2007: 118n. [8:29]; original emphasis). The site of Ancient Greece will name and will always name, in its foundations, in its roots, not only the beginnings of the history of philosophy, but the philosophy of history. As Kant notes, the Roman people (*des römische Volk*) 'only matters so much because it "swallowed" up the Greek *polis*, because it continued on a conception of politics which was both *rooted* in Greece *and* which was already in destination and orientation universal' (ibid. 119). Greece, like the 'rational belief' examined in Kant's essay 'What Is Orientation in Thinking?', functions as something akin to a 'signpost' and a 'compass' (Kant 1991: 245).

The logic at stake is one where the *polis* is devoted to *deracinating* itself because it was tied to a conception of humanity, of universalisation, which was founded uniquely in Greece. The total political unification of humanity will thus have begun in Greece, but this movement or teleology will always have been from its foundation marked by something that exceeds Greece. It will continue to spread and overcome all geopolitical division, all borders and frontiers, by relying on this 'compass' to point the way ahead, providing the example of a destination still to be reached, that is, the complete *future* unification of mankind. That this task is one performed by a discourse that calls itself philosophy should not surprise us when we recall Derrida's essay 'Tympan', where he states that philosophical discourse is the same

> discourse that has always insisted upon assuring itself mastery over the limit (*peras, limes, Grenze*) [the Greek, Roman and German examples of the 'limit' and the 'border' are of course not examples among others, especially in the political realm and in relation to those tongues that have always remained privileged in philosophical discourse – even as this discourse also claims mastery over these linguistic limits]. It [that is, philosophical discourse] has recognized, conceived, posited, declined the limit according to all possible modes; and therefore by the same token, in order better to dispose of the limit, has transgressed it. *Its own limit* had not to remain foreign to it. (Derrida 1982: x; original emphasis)

The importance of Rome is reaffirmed, however, in this teleology outlined by Kant, when he names that part of the *Volk* which is in a civil condition a *civitas*, thus using the Latin word for Roman citizenship to describe the civil condition when taken as a whole, that is, when taken as a totality. As Kant states:

> This condition of the individuals within a people in relation to one another is called a *civil* condition [*bürgerlicher Zustand*] (*status civilis*), and the whole of individuals in a rightful condition, in relation to its own members is called a *State* (*Civitas*). Because of its form, by which all are

united through their common interest in being in a rightful condition [*im rechtlichen Zustande*], a State is called a *commonwealth* [*das gemeine Wesen*] (*res publica latius sic dicta*) [. . .] Because the union of the members is (presumed to be) one they inherited [*angeerbter*], a State is also called a nation [in fact, contrary to what the translator indicates, Kant uses a circumlocution to *avoid* using the German term nation precisely at this moment; Kant instead says, a stock of people or an ancestral people, *Stammvolk* – the word nation not only does not translate *Stammvolk*, it reintroduces into the programme the very thing to be avoided by Kant] (*gens*). (Kant 1996a: 89 [6:311]; original emphasis)

If Kant invokes the Roman *civitas* at the moment he is describing the civic condition of a people, of a *Volk*, he also associates these concepts with the *gens*, above all, when he links the *civitas* and the *Volk* to a form of inheritance. The importance of the *gens* is thus not peripheral; it comes from the fact that the union of members that constitute a given State is not taken to be ahistorical, even if the social contract that binds them – as an Idea (*Idee*) of reason – is. This implicit reference to the social contract is brought out a few sections later, when Kant declares 'the act by which a people [*Volk*] forms itself into a State is the original contract. Properly speaking, the original contract is only the *idea* of this act' (ibid. 92–3 [6:315]; my emphasis). So not only need there not be an actual, documented and archived social contract for Kant in order to justify a State, but he foresees through the figure of the *gens* that a State will be inherited. Moreover, unlike Rousseau, he does not make the social contract into a necessary condition, one needed for the establishment of a people *as* a people; rather, he only makes it a necessary condition for that *part* of a people who wish to form a State. The people may thus be entitled to call themselves a people *before* that part of them comes to establish a State, before they enter into civil condition with one another. The people as a whole, the *Volk*, thus precede for Kant the foundation of the social contract.

If the question of kinship in Kant's elaboration of the *Volk* remains then, it is because of the legal fiction of the *gens*: to recognise others as fellow citizens of a State is not enough; one needs to treat them *as if* they were fellow brothers, ones united by descent, through the male line, from common ancestors and a common name. Indeed, we might need to treat our fellow citizens in this way so as to universalise the fraternity that may already exist in a given State – especially if this State is a historical entity, an inheritable entity, as Kant also claims it to be. If empirical determinations of fraternity thus appear as a potential obstacle to civic equality, Kant does not disown or abandon the concept of fraternity, but instead, transforms it into an ideal object so as to embrace a whole State, and by means of this, a federation of States. What we discover in Kant is thus the ideality of fraternity. The State will treat her citizens, from the perspective of right (*Recht*), as if they were brothers, and mankind, in turn, will treat each other from the perspective of virtue, as if they were brothers of the same family.

The cosmopolitical and the inter-State as articulated by Kant thus depend on 'brotherhood', but it is not the brotherhood of an empirical group that it is reliant on; rather, it is the brotherhood of 'Man'. For the same fraternal figure appears in the second half of the *Metaphysics of Morals* – that part dealing with virtue rather than right (*Recht*) – when Kant describes the 'friend of man' (*Menschenfreund*) who loves the whole human race 'as if all men were brothers under one *father* who wills the happiness of all' (Kant 1996a: 217 [6:473]; original emphasis). As we shall soon see in the next section dealing with Kant and Hume, this 'brotherhood of man' in fact reinforces the nationalistic viewpoint, insofar as it too bears witness to a form of humanism, one that makes an alliance, rather than an opposition, between the national and that which is called 'Man'.

It is not without significance that the word *gens* reappears only a year after the *Metaphysics of Morals*, alongside a notion of humanity and the 'citizen of the world [*Weltbürger*]', when Kant publishes his *Anthropology from a Pragmatic Point of View* (hereafter referred to as *Anthropology*) in 1798 (Kant 2007: 232 [7:120]). For the word *gens* appears in a chapter entitled 'The Character of Peoples' (*Der Charakter des Volks*). It is a chapter, we should note, that Martha Nussbaum makes no mention of at all in her essay 'Kant and Stoic Cosmopolitanism', even though she cites the expression 'world citizen' from the opening pages of the *Anthropology* (Nussbaum 1997: 5). As we shall see, this silence on Kant's chapter is not entirely accidental if one wishes to maintain, as Nussbaum does, that any local or regional affiliation is always secondary in Kant's cosmopolitical outlook. The first passage of Kant's chapter reads:

> By the word *people* [*Volk*] (*populus*) is meant the *number* of human beings united by a region [*versteht man die in einem Landstrich vereinigte Menge Menschen*], in so far as they constitute a *whole*. This number, or even the part of it that recognises itself as united into a civil whole [*bürgerliche Ganze*] through common ancestry [*gemeinschaftliche Abstammung*], is called a *nation* [the German term *Nation* is finally unveiled, the community of birth is thus declared, significantly, *in German* rather than in Latin for the first time in Kant] (*gens*); the part that exempts itself from these laws (the unruly crowd within this people) is called a rabble [*Pöbel*] (*vulgus*), whose illegal association is *the mob* [*Rottieren*] (*agere per turbas*); this conduct that excludes them from the quality of a citizen [*Staatsbürger*]. (Kant 2007: 407 [7:311]; original emphasis)

What the passage first of all emphasises is that it concerns itself with a '*Volk*' (the *word*, as Kant emphasises, for 'people') and not of *Volk* as such: one will not so easily eradicate the mark of the word '*Volk*' that blocks our access to the thing itself – the *Volk*. We will thus be dealing with *rival* definitions of the word '*Volk*'. This is exemplified when we contrast Kant's definition of the word '*Volk*' with the definition of '*peuple*' found in Diderot and D'Alembert's *Encyclopédie*. (This contrast is all the more important because Kant's judgement on the French, and particularly on the French language, will be seen to be crucial in the next chapter. It should also be noted that Kant declares in the *Observations on the Beautiful and the Sublime* that he takes his cue of what French national characteristics are partly from D'Alembert, as well as from Montesquieu.) The French article, written by the Calvinist noble Louis de Jaucourt, notes the difficulty of defining the word *peuple* because different ideas are made of it in diverse places and in different times, and it examines some of these changes – for example, it notes the shift of meaning from one that included merchants, men of letters and men of the law, to one that only included workers and agricultural labourers. It also notes the connection between the word *peuple* and the word *nation*, stating that the word *peuple* always forms the most numerous and the most necessary part of the nation. The use of both words in the *Encyclopédie* article on '*le peuple*' highlights the difficulties of defining the word 'people' separately from the concept of a 'nation', even at this time. Indeed, that there is a separate article on the word *nation* is itself a significant fact in the *Encyclopédie*. This other article provides a definition of the word *nation* as 'a collective word used to express a considerable quantity of people, which lives in a particular stretch of country [*pays*], enclosed within definite limits, and which obeys a single government' (de Jaucourt, cited by Balibar 1994: 76). As Michel Foucault observes in his *Society Must Be Defended*, this definition of the word *nation*, one of many competing definitions existing in France at the time, provides a Statist definition of the nation, one which 'settles the nation within the frontiers of the State on the one hand, and within the very form of the State on the other' (Foucault 2003: 142).

The different definitions of the nation provided by Kant and the *Encyclopédie* are themselves revealing, as they highlight that Kant's definition of the word *nation*, unlike the one found in the *Encyclopédie*, requires that a multitude recognise itself as a nation, that its members display a *consciousness* of belonging to a nation. As Kant states, the multitude, the *Volk*, is just an aggregate of individuals in a given area; they need to recognise themselves as united into a civil whole (*bürgerliche Ganze*) in order to be a nation. A nation must thus be partly self-defined and self-constituted for Kant. His definition is thus opposed to the one found in the *Encyclopédie*, where a nation may be completely defined in so-called objective characteristics (e.g. by such factors as possessing a united territory, sovereignty over this territory, a shared government, etc.).

However, this consciousness is as troubling as it is essential for Kant. For once again the model of being united is one of kinship; one is to form the civic body by means of common ancestry (*gemeinschaftliche Abstammung*). If this common ancestry is not to be understood in terms of an empirically given condition of kinship, but a legal relation – like the kind outlined in the *Metaphysics of Morals* that tells us to act *as if* we were united by consanguinity – the effect of Kant's argument is still to leave the juridical fiction of common ancestry reliant on a model of ancestry that alleges some sort of fraternity beyond the regulative ideal of the *as if* (*als ob*). The rupture with nature and the law of natural birth is thus rendered even more problematic at the very instance a people recognises itself, or forms itself, as a nation – a civic whole bound by common laws. By allowing the nation to posit itself, by permitting the nation to make itself and in so doing name itself, one seems haunted by the virulence of a genealogy that insists it is more than symbolic, that it is essentially or properly natural, biological and empirically given. The problem stems from the fact that for Kant, we think ourselves as constituting a *Nation* only if we are members of a civic whole (*bürgerliche Ganze*), but we will not become members of this civic body – that is to say, its citizens – unless we think of ourselves as *already* part of a whole in some way. The nation is left dependant on a form of unity pre-established by a pre-political, quasi-natural condition of the *Volk*. Even if the nation later dispenses with this model, it can never be fully dissociated from it. While the nation is thus not a natural entity for Kant, neither is it something totally removed from the law of natural birth.

It might be thought that Kant's effort to distinguish a *Volk*, on the one hand, as an empirical entity, and, on the other hand, as a juridical entity, enables him to escape this dilemma. Indeed, as noted earlier, Kant, in section fifty-three of the *Metaphysics of Morals*, warns that the juridical sense of people, a State, should not be confused with the empirical sense of people, for the juridical sense must be considered as a transformation of the empirical people according to a juridical norm (*rechtlicher Bedeutung*). However, as Étienne Balibar has argued, the notion of an 'empirical people' still appears on this outline as 'the condition of possibility of a juridical people (that is, of the State), and contradictorily, as the obstacle its constitution must always overcome, the element of naturalness that always remains to be reduced' (Balibar 2000: 110). This suggests why Kant is unable in the end to define a notion of the *Volk* which is completely independent of some notion of natural kinship. If a people are to be understood in a juridical sense, they still necessarily require that element of an empirical people that allows them to recognise themselves as *already* united in some way. Yet, the transformation of an empirical people into a juridical people also requires that this element of naturalness – this pre-established unity – be always reduced or overcome. Thus the tension in Kant between the juridical notion of a people, or a '*Volk*', that removes all traces of the quasi-natural condition and, a notion which invokes, at some level, a schema of affiliation.

## KANT ON HUME, CICERO AND *GENESIS*

Another explanation of how a people come to be united can be found in David Hume's 1748 essay 'Of National Characteristics', a text Kant indirectly acknowledges in his own 'The Character of Peoples'. Hume's strategy is to emphasise the imitative nature of men, the way a similitude of manners is engendered through close and regular contact. As he states:

> The propensity to company and society is strong in all rational creatures; and the same disposition, which gives us this propensity, makes us enter deeply into each other's sentiments, and causes like passions and inclinations to run, as it were, by contagion, through the whole club or knot of companions. Where a number of men are united into one political body, the occasions of their intercourse must be so frequent, for defence, commerce, and government, that, together with the same speech or language, they must acquire a resemblance in their manners, and have a common or national character, as well as a personal one, peculiar to each individual. (Hume 1998: 115)

The source of this sociability is thus naturally rational for Hume, but extends beyond matters of rationality to shared 'passions and inclinations'. His use of the noun 'contagion' emphasises the fact that these common practices can spread unknowingly, unwittingly, among a group of companions, without conscious adoption. The shared practice is itself enough to bind them together. But we also discover that Hume takes these shared manners to be the result, not the formation of a political body. He thus presumes, rather than argues for, the existence of a political body by which these imitative practices might occur. There is thus no account of how imitative practices, or a national character, sometimes precede the formation of a political body. Hume, rather, presumes that the political body will have always already been constituted before any sense of national character (even though, curiously, he speaks of Germany, which at the time was not a united into a political body, alongside France and England). Moreover, he believes that the national character of a nation is to be explained primarily by means of its government.

Hume does this by dividing the causes of national character into two sources, one moral, and the other physical. The moral kind includes 'the nature of the government, the revolutions of public affairs, the plenty or penury in which the people live, the situation of the nation with regard to its neighbours', while the physical kind includes 'those qualities of the air and climate' which 'have an influence on their manners' (ibid. 113–14). Hume discounts the physical kind, the kind advocated by Montesquieu in his 1748 *Spirit of the Laws* (*De l'esprit des lois*) – that Hume had helped to partly publish in translation in Edinburgh in 1750 and which helped to establish the concept of a national character by means of positing an *esprit général* – but he did believe that moral causes

> must be evident to the most superficial observer; since a nation is nothing but a collection of individuals, and the manners of individuals are frequently determined by these causes. As poverty and hard labour debase the minds of the common people, and render them unfit for any science and ingenious profession; so where any government becomes very oppressive to all its subjects, it must have a proportional effect on their temper and genius, and must banish all the liberal arts from among them. (Hume 1998: 114)

Hume thus takes moral causes to be most evident in the power of the government to shape its people according to its own strengths or weaknesses. Kant explicitly rejects such a position in the *Anthropology*. This is because 'To claim that the kind of character a people will have depends entirely on its form of government is an ungrounded assertion that explains nothing; for from where does the government itself get its particular character?' (Kant 2007: 408 [7:312]). Kant thus remains unsatisfied by Hume's account; national character will not remain dependent on the form of government that rules a people.

But there is another crucial argument that takes place between Kant and Hume. It concerns the character of the English nation, or rather, whether the English have a definable national character. For Hume, the English government is unique in being

> a *mixture* of monarchy, aristocracy and democracy. The people in authority are composed of gentry and merchants. All sects of religion are to be found among them. And the great liberty and independency, which every man enjoys, allows him to display the manners peculiar to him. Hence the ENGLISH, of any people in the universe, have the least of a national character; unless this very singularity may pass as such. (Hume 1998: 119; my italics; original capitals)

The English have thus no definable national character and, at the same time, their national character is precisely given by the fact that they alone of all nationalities have no definable national character. The English thus become for Hume the standard by which all national deviation can be measured and they become this standard because of their mixed government and religious convictions. No one form of government dominates England and all sects of religion are to be found there; for Hume, everyone is thus free to acquire their own characteristics unfettered by national influences or prejudices. Kant undermines this claim (though earlier, in the so-called Mrongovius set of anthropology lectures, he had agreed with Hume) and objects not just because he gives little credence to the idea that government shapes national character, but because

> Hume thinks that if each individual in a nation [*Nation*] is intent on assuming his own particular character (as it with the English), the nation itself has no character. It seems to me he is mistaken; for affection of a character is precisely the general character of the people to which he himself belongs, and it is contempt for all foreigners [anything foreign or that comes from outside: *Verachtung aller Auswärtigen*], particularly because the English believe that they alone can boast of a respectable constitution that combines civil freedom [*Freiheit*] internally with power against outsiders [the power against anything foreign and external: *mit Macht gegen Außen*]. (Kant 2007: 407 [7:311])

Kant's argument rests on two claims, which are interrelated: one about the structure of the national character in England, the other about the balance of civic freedom present there. The logic of the first claim entails that the content of a national character should not be thought of as something that is imitative in outcome, but only imitative in terms of procedure. Englishmen need not possess the same national characteristics to belong to the same nation; they need only share the same commitment to acquiring characteristics. Kant thus carefully avoids positing the national character as a homogenous disposition; he instead allows a disposition towards internal differentiation and individualism to be itself the defining trait of the English national character. The English do not escape having a national character for Kant. The mixed government that Hume speaks of may thus for Kant be already influenced and constituted by the individualism associated with the English national character. But this individualism is not unproblematic for Kant, especially when the civic freedom that is supposed to underwrite this priority of the individual is questioned.

For Kant's second claim questions the unique optimum balance that England purports to have with regard to its political and civic freedom. What is at stake here, though Kant does not explicitly name it, is the praise of England not just by Hume, but by Montesquieu, as well as by later *philosophes*, for example, the kind found in Voltaire's 1734 *Philosophical Letters: Letters Concerning the English Nation*, when Voltaire praises the events associated with 1688, that is to say, the establishment of *habeas corpus*, representative government and religious toleration. The reason there can be such a space for individuals in England to acquire their own characteristics – that is, characteristics free from national influence – is because England preserves the freedom of the individual. Liberty in England is first and foremost the liberty of the individual. Kant questions this optimum civic freedom; moreover, not just by analysing how the nation acts towards its own citizens in its domestic sphere, but crucially, in relation to what is deemed to be foreign. Though the question of the foreign would not be reducible to the question of the foreigner – *Auswärtigen* stresses *anything* foreign rather than *anyone* foreign – the figure of the foreigner plays a crucial role in Kant's argument against the English, especially when one recalls his third so-called 'Definite Article' in his *Perpetual Peace*. For in this text the matter of the foreigner, the stranger, the outsider, is taken up, especially in terms of hospitality, the right a foreigner – as opposed to an invited guest – has to reside, following the model of visitation (*Besuchsrecht*) that *Perpetual Peace* establishes.

The salience of this is brought out when Kant writes later in the *Anthropology* that

> For his compatriots the Englishman establishes great, benevolent institutions, unheard of among all other peoples. – However, the foreigner who has driven to England's soil by fate and has fallen on hard times can die on the dunghill because he is not an Englishman, that is, not a human being. (Kant 2007: 410 [7:314–15])

The problem Kant will identify in the national character of England portrayed by Hume is thus the same one Karl Marx will later identify and denounce with regard to the German national character portrayed by Karl Grün: that it presents itself not as a particular representative of mankind, of one among many, but of man as such, the essence of 'Man', the privileged representative of humanity. What we thus discover in Hume's portrayal of the English, according to Kant, is an implicit conception of humanism, which links the national, or rather, one privileged form of nationality, with humanity, with what is most proper to man, with the universal essence of 'Man'. The significance of this critique by Kant is signalled by the importance Kant gave to the question 'What is Man?' Indeed, in his *Lectures on Logic*, Kant stated that

> the field of philosophy in its cosmopolitan sense can be brought down to the following questions: What can I know? What ought I to do? What may I hope? What is Man? *Metaphysics* answers the first question, *morals* the second, *religion* the third, and *anthropology* the fourth. Fundamentally, however, we could reconcile all of this as anthropology, because the first three questions relate to the last one. (Kant 2004: 538; original emphasis)

When Derrida considers the same passages on Hume by Kant in his aforementioned second philosophical nationalities and nationalism session from

1984, he comments that this reveals that even a Humean empirical account of nationality offers the possibility that the 'national' and the 'universal' need not be mutually exclusive, that they may even be allied with one another in certain instances, that this is in the end 'the empiricist version of the same universalism'.[3] The rhetorical move whereby a nationality can come to stand in for humanity in general is indeed for Derrida the very paradox of exemplarity – that which ensures the universal (e.g. 'Man') becomes inscribed 'in the proper body [corps propre] of a singularity, of an idiom or a culture, whether this singularity be individual, social, national, State, federal, confederal, or not' (Derrida 1992b: 72).

What the paradox of exemplarity would thus show is that the site of conflict lies not between competing claims of singularity and universality – or singular and universal communities – but between competing testimonial claims to universality, which compete not only in terms of who is the most universal, but in terms of competing visions of universality. The conflict, in other words, is generated because there is more than one form of universality and because each is inscribed in the proper body of a singularity. What is at stake are thus different conceptions of the universal, rather than a situation whereby singularities are simply opposed to the universal and where we strive to determine which claim of universality is genuinely abstracted from all singularities.

When Derrida discusses this exemplarity in his philosophical nationalities seminars, he does so utilising the Kantian notion of the *schema*, what Kant calls the 'third thing' or the 'mediating representation' that would reconcile sensibility with understanding, and so the sensible with the intelligible, elaborated in the *Critique of Pure Reason* in the famous chapter 'The Schematism of the Pure Concepts of Understanding' (Kant 1933: A138, B177). It is this crucial Kantian mediation between the singular and the universal, achieved by the 'transcendental imagination', that enables universality to be inscribed in the proper body of a singularity. It is also important to recall, when discussing Derrida's use of the term 'exemplarity', that Kant in his 1790 *Critique of Judgement* states that 'if the concepts are empirical the intuitions are called *examples*, if they are pure concepts of understanding the intuitions go by the name of *schemata*' (Kant 1952: 221 [351:20]; original emphasis).

We will return to the issue of schematism in relation to the power of the 'transcendental imagination' and language in the next chapter, but for now, let us note that Derrida in a seminar entitled 'Signatures of Revenge', compares Spinoza with Kant in this regard, because for 'Spinoza there is no mediating schema at least visibly, in a thematic and philosophically assumed way, between the internal and the external, the singular and the universal, the temporal and the spiritual etc [. . .] There is therefore no philosophical nationalism.'[4] In other words, although the problems associated with the particular and the universal are an integral part of philosophy from its inception, it is nonetheless only with and after such figures as Kant that 'philosophical nationalism' can be explicitly posited.

Indeed, for Kant, the love of the fatherland was to accompany, rather than be the opposite of, cosmopolitanism. For the fatherland, the *Vaterland*, was for him the very figure that made citizenship possible – it is what gives one the right to citizenship. As he details in his *Metaphysics of Morals*:

> A country [*das Land*] (*territorium*) whose inhabitants [*Einsassen*] are citizens of it simply by its constitution, without their having to perform any special act to establish the right (and so are citizens by birth [*mithin durch die Geburt*]), is called a native land [*Vaterland*]. (Kant 1996a: 110 [6:338])

Once again though, this civic orientation is not quite what it seems. The importance of the birthright is once again crucial; it is the privileged model of citizenship; in fact, it is the *only* model given. One is a citizen because of one's birth, because the *Land* is that of one's father – as is further evident in a passage omitted from the published version of *Metaphysics of Morals*:

> Patriotism, the love of the fatherland [*Vaterlandsliebe*], also belongs here [in the category of general love of others], as does cosmopolitanism: in both, the determination to love others rests upon common descent, though the former is local, and is properly love of the fatherland when it is directed towards a united national community [united society of peoples: *vereinigte Volksgesellschaft*] that we regard as the rootstock [*Stamm*], and ourselves as members [*Glied:*] thereof; otherwise it is directed to our common world ancestry [*allgemeine Weltabstammung*]. (Kant 1998: 405 [27:673])

The *Vaterland*, the State to which one belongs by birth, was thus to have an essential role in the Kantian cosmopolitical outlook. This is so even if certain forms of patriotism – understood in the eighteenth century as attachment to one's State rather than nation – are without doubt under attack in Kant, as exemplified in his critique of Hume and the civic freedoms purported to exist in England. The omitted passage also shows, unsurprisingly, that Kant simultaneously defended a certain form of patriotism, despite the fact that this civic identification is once again articulated by means of birth and kinship. It is also evident that Kant not only thought that patriotism and cosmopolitanism were compatible, he also thought them to possess a certain affinity of love – when understood as a 'maxim of benevolence', rather than an 'emotion' – when the origins of man were at stake. This position may not seem so foreign to us when we recall that none other than Cicero held the same view, when he opens his *On the Commonwealth* (*De re publica*) with patriotic praise to those heroes who delivered Rome from the terror of Carthage. As Martha Nussbaum admits in a footnote in 'Kant and Stoic Cosmopolitanism', Cicero 'makes many more concessions to local affiliation than other stoic thinkers' (Nussbaum 1997: 7n.23). This is clearly brought out in *On Duties* (*De Officiis*) – which Nussbaum believes was particularly crucial in forming Kant's cosmopolitical outlook – when Cicero writes that

> There are indeed several degrees of fellowship among men. To move from the one that is unlimited, next there is a closer one of the same race [*gentis*], tribe [*nationis*], tongue, through which men are bound strongly to another. More intimate still is that of the same city, as citizens have many things that are shared with one another: the forum, temples, porticoes and roads, laws and legal rights, law-courts and political elections; and beside these acquaintances and companionship, and those business and commercial transactions that many of them make with many others. A tie narrower still is that of the fellowship between relations: moving from that vast fellowship of the human race we end up with a confined and limited one. (Cicero 1991: 22 [I, 53])

If Cicero claims that all of humanity is linked to a greater or lesser extent and that citizens of a *civitas* have closer relations than those linked by means of *gens* and *natio*, he does not exclude the latter non-civic groups from creating some kind of bonds amongst people. Unlike Kant though, Cicero does not derive his juridical model of the State from a genealogical model – the law for Cicero does not emulate the family model, it does not make citizenship a form of legal kinship or fraternity. This makes Kant's coupling of the *civitas* with a *natio* all the more important, since for Cicero, the *natio* – like the *gens* – is outside of the civic sphere. Indeed, we might recall Kant's earlier essay from 1786 precisely on the subject of the origins of man, namely, his 'Conjectures on the Beginnings of Human History'. For this enigmatic essay – that is in part a parody of Herder – posits in a reading of the Book of Genesis that 'the common descent of all human beings from a single family unit was undoubtedly the best means for attaining [sociability as the principal end of human destiny]' (Kant 1991: 222). The 'common world ancestry [*allgemeine Weltabstammung*]' that Kant posits is thus at one with his belief in the Christian origins of mankind, it allows the love of the fatherland (*Vaterlandsliebe*) to be a form of patriotism that is not the opposite of universalism, but rather, a particularisation of it. What is at stake is thus also a Christianisation of fraternisation: the brother – and it is always a brother for Kant – will be a Christian brother, even when the brother is not Christian.

If the omission of the passage about the love of the fatherland in the *Metaphysics of Morals* suggests that Kant was aware of the difficulty this position caused him, it should not lead us to forget what remained in the final published text: references to kinship that fasten Kant's political outlook in various ways to some notion of fraternisation, one which is explicitly brought out when he links the State to the figure of the mother and when he associates the *civitas* in turn with the community of birth (*congeniti*, *natio* and *gens*). It should also be pointed out that Kant evidently does this not so as to counter the international and cosmopolitical order, but rather, to complement it.

But there is also an associated disagreement between Kant and Hume regarding the composition of a nation or a people. This is because for Hume, a nation is an atomistic entity; it is, as he says, composed of 'nothing but a collection of individuals'. But Kant associates the *Volk* not only with a *nation* and a *gens*, but also with the *populus*, a multitude that is not simply an aggregate, but which conveys a sense of the body politic – a united entity. Indeed, if we draw on Cicero and his previously mentioned *On the Commonwealth* again, we may note he also warns that a *populus* is 'not any group of men assembled in any way, but an assemblage of some size associated with one another through agreement on law and community of interest' (Cicero 1999: 18 [I, 39a]). If Cicero emphasises the legal and juridical aspect of the *populus*, a community founded on law, he does not, however, simply equate it with a *civitas*, leaving the latter term to designate the institutional form of the *populus*. This is evident a few sections later when he declares that 'every state [*civitas*]' is an 'organisation of the people [*est constitutio populi*]' (ibid. 18 [I, 41]).

If Kant, like Cicero, also emphasises the fact that a *populus* is a multitude, the greatest number, this can only underscore the emerging importance of the census and the censor for Kant, and everything that links the 'cens' to the enumeration of people. That counting is indeed not far from Kant's mind is revealed when we recall the aforementioned *Idea for a Universal History with a Cosmopolitan Aim*. For it is in this brief text that he will declare that:

> marriages, the births that come from them and deaths, since the free will of human beings has so great an influence on them, seem to be subject to no rule in accordance with which their number could be determined in advance through calculation; and yet the annual tables of them in large countries prove that they happen as much in accordance with constant laws of nature [as changes in the weather]. (Kant 2007: 108 [8:17])

Kant's concern with the numerical, the multitude that is the *populus*, thus seems connected to his concern with statistics, the very science of which, Ian Hacking (1990) notes, came to prominence with Prussian statecraft in the eighteenth century. It was, Hacking further observes in his *The Taming of Chance*, German thinkers such as Leibniz and various statesmen – Hacking does not name them – who brought to full consciousness the idea that the State is essentially characterised by its statistics. If Hacking correctly emphasises the increasing importance of statistics for Prussia, it is no more evident than in the Prussian decree of January 1733 that forbade the publication of the population list, making it into a State secret. Indeed, the growing importance of the population in terms of State power is reverberated in Rousseau – who is widely recognised to have influenced Kant – twenty-nine years later, in one of the several chapters entitled 'The People' in his 1762 work the *Social Contract*, when he declares that 'a body politic can be measured in two ways, by the extent of its territory and by the number of its people' (Rousseau 1997b: 75). When one speaks of statistics, one will thus be speaking, inevitably, about the functions of the State, about biopolitics, the population as a political problem. A multiplicity of men will thus no longer be addressed, *contra* Hume, to the extent that they are nothing more than their individual selves, but only insofar as they form a mass, a multitude, that is affected by overall processes characteristic of birth, death, and so on.

But should this analysis of a '*Volk*' then not provoke us to ask if the Latin designations *civitas*, *natio*, *gens* and *populus* are even, in the final analysis, compatible? After all, according to Kedourie, the word 'nation' prior to the rise of nationalism in the eighteenth century meant 'a group of men belonging together by similarity of birth, larger than a family, but smaller than a clan or a people. Thus, one spoke of the *Populus Romanus* and not of the *natio romanorum*' (Kedourie [1960] 1993: 5). So whereas before different 'nations' – the most famous of which included the aristocracy and the clergy – had existed in a single body, be it a social body or the real, living, bodily person of the king, Kant ensures in his definition of the nation that it remains tied to a *single* body politic. Not all peoples will have their own State, but all States will treat their citizens as making up a single body politic. That part of the *Volk* that is self-conscious of itself is thus at once a State, a nation, a family and a population. So not only is Kant's usage of analogy with regard to a republic and a mother in itself more important than is often realised, but it reveals that analogical extension is precisely what is in question; that Kant is not only using the word *natio*, but transforming the word when he interprets it to be something cognate with a State, *Volk*, *gens* and *populus*.

NOTES

1. It should be noted, however, that Benedict Anderson uses this phrase to describe the '*modern* culture of nationalism' that he thinks is exemplified with the recent practice of dedicating tombs to Unknown Soldiers (Anderson [1983] 2006: 17; my emphasis). He actually compares this practice with that of the Ancient Greeks, but decides that they present a different case, because the cenotaphs the Greeks established, while having no body within them, were meant for specific, known individuals. He does not discuss Greek

funeral orations. Nicole Loraux, on the other hand, calls the first chapter of her *The Children of Athena*, which examines *Menexenus*, 'Autochthony and the Athenian Imaginary' (Loraux 1993: 3) and uses the phrase 'national imaginary' in what is announced to be the sequel to that book, namely, *Born of the Earth* (Loraux 2000: 14). Unlike Edward E. Cohen (2002) though, she never describes the *polis* as a nation, but only ever uses the adjectival 'national' to describe the Athenian civic imagination. She thus seems to invoke the national only in terms of what would be described as 'national sentiments'.
2. This is one of the subjects of Derrida's 1985–6 'Nomos, Logos, Topos' seminars, which constituted the second year of the 'Philosophical Nationalities and Nationalism' cycle. The seminars in that year, however, are for unknown reasons incomplete at the UC Irvine archive. The ones that are left indicate that these seminars continued the reading of Heidegger from the first year around the theme of *Geschlecht* and also marked the beginning of Derrida's reading of *khôra* in Plato's *Timaeus*, a reading that appeared in English under the title 'Khôra' in *On the Name* (Derrida 1995a).
3. Derrida (1984–8), Box 18, Folder 2, Seminar 2, p. 10.
4. Derrida (1984–8), Box 19 Folder 14, pp. 12–13; trans. Joseph Adamson.

CHAPTER 3

# The Presentation of National Philosophies: Kant on the French and German National Character

> Were the German philosophers really [*wirklich*] – philosophical *Germans*?
> Friedrich Nietzsche, *Gay Science*, section 357

Kant's *Observations on the Beautiful and the Sublime* (hereafter referred to as the *Observations*) has a curious place in the history of his writings, not only in terms of its popularity among the public when it first appeared, but because of the so-called belletristic style it adopts. Ernst Cassirer describes this in his essay 'Kant and Rousseau', when he states that Kant became

> a stylist and a psychological essayist [who] established a new standard for the German philosophical literature of the eighteenth century. His *Observations on the Beautiful and the Sublime* display a precision of observation and lucidity and *facility of presentation* Kant never again attained in any later work. At this time he must have possessed a sensitive ear for Rousseau's distinctive literary style. (Cassirer 1945: 6; my emphasis)

We will see later in this chapter that 'style' and 'presentation' (*Darstellung*) will itself become the scene of a national dispute in philosophy, that 'style' will be one of the ways of differentiating national philosophies for Kant, but let us note for now that if Cassirer highlights Kant's preoccupation with 'style', he does not indicate that it is the kind that has led scholars of Kant to ignore the *Observations* as a 'serious' piece of work. Indeed, we might heed Paul de Man's warning that if this text sometimes reads 'like a collection of eighteenth-century provincial platitudes, [it] is not to be dismissed [so] lightly' (de Man 1996: 123).

The importance of the text for de Man derives partly from the fact that it bears similarities to Kant's last *Critique*, published some twenty-six years later, namely, the *Critique of Judgement* from 1790. For de Man the correspondence is close enough to 'make any clear discrepancy between the two texts remarkable' (ibid. 125). Michel Foucault echoes this proximity between the *Observations* and Kant's later texts in his doctoral thesis, 'Introduction to Kant's Anthropology'. He even declares that however different the *Observations* and the *Anthropology* may be in terms of perspective, they are also 'surprisingly similar, even when it comes down to the expressions and the choice of words [. . . as for example, when Kant describes] the distinctive traits that characterise the different nationalities' (Foucault 2008: 29).

The fact that the former was written decades before the latter, or indeed, before any of the *Critique*s, and thus before what is taken to be Kant's mature and 'critical' philosophy, will therefore not preclude, for my purposes, its relevancy to understanding Kant's continual interest in national characteristics, especially insofar as latter texts only adapt claims from the *Observations*, rather than reject them wholesale. Indeed, as James Tully remarks in his essay 'The Kantian Idea of Europe', though the *Observations* was written much earlier than Kant's other more famous political writings, such as *Perpetual Peace*, those later political writings neither repudiate nor contradict the views of national characteristics held in the *Observations* (Tully 2002: 343). Accordingly, if the previous chapter examined a series of concepts and ideas deployed by Kant and retraced some of their *genealogical* history, the present chapter examines Kant's examples of nations – namely, his analysis of the French and the Germans (and more briefly, the English) in his *Observations* and in his *Anthropology*.

There will also be an emphasis on the imagination (*Einbildungskraft*) and on language in this chapter, if not exactly the language of the imagination (though the genre of romance will be seen to be a crucial example for Kant of how not to present philosophy properly). This will be seen to be related to the Kantian schema briefly mentioned in the Introduction and Chapter 2 when discussing the mediation between the empirical and the non-empirical, the 'third term' that participates in both at once. The notion of the schema is once again important in this chapter because, as Derrida states, the Kantian schema

> is also tied in an essential way to the power of the imagination, of the transcendental imagination (with all the enigma that this power has in Kant), to temporalisation or to temporal spacing (cf. Heidegger's reading of Kant), and in a still more enigmatic or problematic way, to symbolic power and to language [*langage*]. Imagination and language [*langage*], we will see that these are the headings, the traditional ones at least, for a great number of questions concerning this schema of consciousness or national affirmation (election, covenant, promise, mission etc. [what

Derrida had earlier called 'neighbouring, though different, conceptual values']), whether it is a matter of images in the language [*langue*] and in sacred texts (rhetoric, interpretation of figures, hermeneutics, etc.) or of the language [*langue*] itself, in the language [*langue*] defining precisely the singular medium in which a universal or non-empirical message would come to be inscribed. Language – or rather, the language, tongue [*langue*] – is, to remain at this very preliminary and rough level, the singularity of a particular body [*corps singulier*] in which a structurally general and meta-empirical ideal signification is incarnated.[1]

Though Kant is known for having little to say about language, especially in relation to the usage of 'natural' language *as* philosophical language, it will be seen that tongues do indeed, if elliptically, matter for Kant, that the invocation of Babel was not an afterthought in the *Critique of Pure Reason*. That the transcendental imagination has an important place in the first *Critique* as well as the *Critique of Judgement* will underline the importance of *Darstellung* in this chapter – how the national dimension of philosophy is not only tied to the question of how to present philosophy as a universal project in a 'natural' language, but with the literary conditions that make philosophy possible. What Kant would call, as we will see, the discursive nature of philosophy, the fact that, like poetic language, it must take place in a 'natural' language – even though Kant always insists that poetic language is the other of philosophy, if perhaps its own other, and so a form of the other it cannot but help regulate and partly constitute. This chapter will thus build on Jean-Luc Nancy's groundbreaking work *The Discourse of the Syncope*, that examines the issue of philosophical *Darstellung*, of how philosophy exhibits itself, in and through the work of Kant and the question of literature.

## KANT ON THE SUBLIME AND THE PUBLIC

Kant's views on national characteristics in the *Observations* are most evident in the chapter entitled 'On National Characters [*Nationalcharakter*] Insofar as They Rest Upon the Different Feeling of The Beautiful and The Sublime'. That Kant's interest in national characteristics is also coupled with his interest in the sublime should come as no surprise when we remember, as Paul de Man has shown in his *Aesthetic Ideology*, that the 'Analytic of the Sublime' in the much later *Critique of Judgement* deploys, beyond its aesthetic vocabulary, a political lexicon. As he states:

> the kinetics of the sublime are treated at once, and somewhat surprisingly, as a question of *power*: the first word of section 28 [. . .] (on the

dynamics of the sublime) is *Macht*, soon followed by violence (*Gewalt*) [also translatable as 'force' or 'dominion'; often in the work of Kant, as in other German thinkers, it signals the *legitimate* use of force employed by institutions of the State] and by the assertion that violence is the only means by which to overcome the resistance of one force to another. (de Man 1996: 78)

Kant's abrupt talk of the notion of might or power, of *Macht*, when moving from a discussion of number to motion thus introduces a quasi-empirical sense of assault, battle and fright into the order of the sublime even before he declares in the same section that 'war itself, provided it is conducted with order and sacred respect for the rights of civilians, has something sublime about it' (Kant 1952: 113 [263:30]). The result is that the sublime always remains as potentially political as it is epistemological. We might also add that it remains as spectral as it is political – if the political is not always already in its very genesis spectral – when we recall how de Man interprets the borderless (*unbegrenzt*) dimension of the sublime. This dimension appears in Kant when he claims that the sublime knows no limits or borders yet must appear as a determined totality, as something phenomenally presented (*dargestellt*). For de Man, this means nothing less than the sublime has 'in a philosophical sense . . . something of a monster, or, rather, a *ghost* [about it]' (de Man 1996: 74; my emphasis). National characteristics will always remain dependent on the ghost, the ghost of the sublime and the spirit of the people it incarnates or embodies. The sublime, when it is present, will always remain an omen, a portent, a sign of that which is not to be determined by the borders of sensible empiricity, but by a spirit. As we will see in the next section, the subject of the sublime is also central to the question of the nation when Kant comes to analyse the 'enthusiasm' found for as well as in the French Revolution, the former of which Kant famously takes as a sign, one regarding the future of mankind.

The epistemological dimension also has a bearing though on the question of a political inscription within the sublime. For the sublime, unlike the beautiful, also crucially informs us of the teleology of its own faculties, specifically about the relationship between reason and imagination, between cognition and pure affect. This is all the more significant when we recall that Kant proceeds by deduction from the sublime to popular or shared feelings, and thus must necessarily invoke the multitude to establish the sublime. As Derrida aptly states, a 'discourse about nationalism is also a discourse on the sublime' (Derrida 2008: 288). But aesthetics is not the only area where Kant finds a national dimension in philosophy, in which he will claim to recognise national philosophical characteristics. He will write in the *Observations* that, in a footnote on France, with regards to its 'metaphysics, ethics, and religious doctrines [*Lehren der Religion*], one cannot be too careful with the writings of this nation [*Nation*]' (Kant 2007: 54n. [2:246]).

Metaphysics has, in some way, become a national issue, something marked by a national and geopolitical landscape. Kant's caution, even in these early so-called pre-critical years, is evident. He does not speak of 'French metaphysics' or of a kind of 'national ontology'; instead, he writes carefully of the metaphysical books or works 'of this nation [*Nation*]'. Yet, Kant seems to be conceding, national inflections of philosophy do exist, philosophical nationalities have formed, or, are beginning to form. What is at stake, we might say, is the very grounding of philosophy, that its ground has seemingly become territorialised and nationalised. For metaphysics as the study of 'fundamental' or 'general' ontology should not, by definition, be susceptible to 'regional' ontologies, let alone national or territorial differences. Yet, Kant admits that metaphysics has come to be influenced by the national insofar as the metaphysical books of one nation are to be treated cautiously. In his *Lectures on Anthropology*, Kant once again cautions his audience about the French, this time because the French 'love bold judgements and judge themselves to be bold in philosophy; thus their writings only glisten for a while' (Kant 2012: 491 [25:1402]).

Indeed, this national dimension to philosophy becomes explicit decades later in Kant's 1799 essay 'On a Supposed Right to Lie from Philanthropy'. For this essay is not only an essay about lying, but in effect, responds to the perceived national dimension of philosophy, and in particular, the right of someone to identify a philosopher by means of his nationality or the language in which his philosophical discourse takes place. If Kant's essay marks a conflict of philosophical nationalities, it may be said to measure Benjamin Constant's attempt to map philosophy, to measure the extent to which a philosopher, or philosophy as a whole, should be thought of as belonging to a national community. What is at stake here in the Kantian essay is thus the firmest of philosophical traditions, that a philosopher should not represent a nationality, that he should not speak from a national platform, that he should instead be contributing to a 'universal community', one beyond nation, beyond State and beyond the limits of a particular language.

The conflict of philosophical nationalities in this essay is not one among others. It concerns a Franco-German exchange, one named in the very periodical that Kant cites at the beginning of his article: *France in the year 1797. From Letters of German Men in Paris* (*Frankreich im Jahre 1797. Aus den Briefen deutscher Männer in Paris*), the journal that choose to translate Benjamin Constant's 1796 *Des réactions politiques* into German and so carried this text, in minimal time, across borders, national, linguistic and otherwise. Kant begins by noting the name of the periodical and by doing so, locating the argument within something called 'France'. He is responding, we might say, to the reception of his work in a national context. Kant also *names* Benjamin Constant at the beginning of his 'On a Supposed Right to Lie from Philanthropy', an act that plays a more rigorous role in Kant's response to a national identification than at first may be imagined. Kant quotes Constant as follows:

> The moral principle 'it is a duty to tell the truth' would, if taken unconditionally and singly, make any society impossible. We have proof of this in the very direct consequences drawn from this principle by a German philosopher [*un philosophe allemand* in Constant's text] who goes as far as to maintain that it would be a crime to tell a lie to a murderer who had asked us whether a friend of ours whom he is pursuing has taken refuge in our house. (Kant 1996b: 611 [8:425])

Kant's response – bar changing the example Constant gives above of a 'friend' to an 'enemy' strategically later in the text – is to make distinctions in *Latin*, distinctions, for example, between harming and wronging someone, that he thinks Constant has overlooked. Kant, moreover, calls the Swiss-born Constant – who had gained French citizenship only in 1796 – 'The French philosopher [*Der französische Philosoph*]' (ibid. 611 [8:425]). Kant thus *identifies* his fellow philosopher using the same terms he was originally identified with – the nation he now belongs to and the language in which his philosophical discourse takes place. But there is a twist. Kant had already named Benjamin Constant in his opening sentence of his essay. The proper name was given before the nationality of the philosopher was declared, so the identity of the philosopher was not provided solely by means of his nationality. We did not need a gesture, like the kind supplied by Karl Cramer – the editor of the aforementioned *Frankreich im Jahre 1797*, who confirmed in a footnote to his translation of the tract that Constant had meant none other than Kant by *un philosophe allemand* – to verify the identity of *Der französische Philosoph*. Kant, supplying both the proper name and then the nationality of the philosopher, draws attention to the fact his own proper name, the name 'Kant', was not treated with the proper care abroad; it did not receive the kind of hospitality a 'foreign' philosopher should surely deserve. But let us note that other 'names' have been produced, ones still allowing transit. As Kant states:

> If we are going to keep the *names* of the persons as they were specified here, 'the French philosopher' [note the sudden introduction of quotation marks] confused an action by which someone *harms* (*nocet*) [note the essential recourse to Latin, something that marks, as we will see later in the chapter, most of Kant's discourse] another by telling a truth he cannot avoid admitting with an action by which he *wrongs* (*laedit*) another [. . .] The 'German philosopher' [again, the national designation has taken refuge behind quotation marks] will therefore not take as

his principle the proposition (p. 214), [that] 'To tell the truth is a duty but only to someone who *has a right to truth*.' (Kant 1996b: 614 [8:428]; original emphasis)

So Kant proceeds cautiously; he declares a reservation, his distrust of the national designation; he is only mentioning the term 'French philosopher' we might say, and no longer using it. Unless, of course, there were invisible quotation marks, hidden scare marks, around the original terms. Kant is either no longer using the national designations with the confidence he displayed earlier in the essay or he is making visible the distrust he had from beginning. In any case, he comes to place the terms 'French philosopher' and 'German philosopher' in quotation marks, he keeps a distance from terms that necessarily imply a distance – be it linguistic or geographical – in the discourse of philosophy, indicating that the national terms, as they stand, are impure, perhaps ambiguous, certainly not to be trusted. Kant will remain vigilant of their danger to philosophy, a vigilance he no doubt finds lacking in Constant.

We can perhaps understand Kant's reaction by recalling his earlier 1784 essay 'An Answer to the Question: "What Is Enlightenment?"' where he made his famous distinction between the public and the private use of one's reason. For Kant's distinction in this essay captures the sense in which philosophy has seen itself as a universal project, or as he puts it, the way it is always a matter of the public (*öffentliche*) use of one's reason, never the private. For the private use of reason does not correspond for Kant to one's individual as opposed to one's communal ties, but the communal identification of oneself, be it, as in Kant's essay, primarily in terms of citizenship, as opposed to the *universality of the worldwide public*. Speaking as an officer, citizen or clergyman – Kant's examples in the essay – one is always speaking on behalf of some sort of bounded community like a State, as Kant declares, 'what I call the private use of reason is that which one may make of it in a certain *civil* post or office with which he is entrusted' (Kant 1996b: 18 [8:37]; original emphasis). But speaking as a scholar (*Gelehrter*) – and one should note this is less an occupation for Kant than someone using their critical reasoning in a public capacity – one is speaking

> as a member [*Glied*] of a whole commonwealth [*eines ganzen gemeinen Wesens*], even of the society of citizens in the world [cosmopolitical society: *Weltbürgergesellschaft*], and so in his capacity of a scholar who by his writings addresses a public [*Publikum*] in the proper sense of the word, he can certainly argue without thereby harming the affairs assigned to him in part as a passive member [of a given community]. (Kant 1996b: 18 [8:37])

In other words, the philosopher as a scholar – and we have plenty of evidence to believe that the philosopher is the scholar *par excellence* for Kant, in accordance with the *privileged* place of the philosopher as someone who is at once subordinate to *and* free of State power in the university, as outlined in *The Conflict of the Faculties* – addresses nothing less than 'the entire public of the *world of readers*' (ibid. 18 [8:37]; original emphasis). The gesture of the essay was no doubt as generative as it was constative in naming a worldwide (*Welt*) readership, but the importance of it lies, above all, with its identification of the scholar, and so the philosopher, as an individual *removed* from a particular bounded community – which need not be a State (like Prussia), but merely a region, and so something as large as a continent (like Europe) or as small as a city (like Königsberg) – he happens to inhabit or dwell in.

The first thing to note is that this is not merely an empirical issue, though its emphasis on the *place* of philosophy is singularly important, as it begins to take note of how different national philosophical traditions can be engendered through different texts, or perhaps even more importantly, the *same* text through different languages, that is to say, those languages called (or instituted as) 'natural' by philosophy and those languages called (or instituted as) 'national' or 'official' by the State. If Latin ceases to be the universal language of philosophy, if it ceases to be the medium of philosophy, Kant draws attention to the fact that the place of publication will matter; it will no longer be of secondary importance.

We will return to the importance of Latin at the end of the chapter, but for now, let us note that the example of France is a telling one. This is most evident when we recall the relationship of the French language to the emerging modern French State under the monarchy of François I. For it was François I who enacted the royal decree of Villers-Cotterêts in 1539, an edict which ensured that French replaced Latin as the administrative and legal language of France. Moreover, as noted by Derrida, this same king *invited* philosophy to be written in French by commissioning and subsidising certain writers (Derrida 2004a: 9). Indeed, this support by the State for philosophy written in the French language can be seen to be further strengthened with the first translations of Plato into French – by Louis Le Roy, for example – soon after 1530, as this event took place with the backing of the monarchy once again, specifically through the figure of Marguerite de Navarre, the sister of François I, who was a keen advocate of Neoplatonism and the patron of Le Roy.

But if the French language has a particular history and role in the juridical, religious and philosophical discourse in monarchic France from the sixteenth century onwards, it is above all because the monarchy ensured and fortified its power by expanding and imposing French over the provinces and dialects of the country (e.g. Breton, Occitan, Franco-Provençal). The political dimension of the language was further complicated by the fact that French was the only language by the end of seventeenth century seen to be capable of replacing Latin as an international language. That this language politics had already affected the question of where philosophy takes place is evident from an article written by Pierre Bayle in 1685 when he claimed:

> from now on the French language will be the bridge of communication for all the countries of Europe [*la langue française est désormais le point de communication de tous les peuples de l'Europe*]. It is a language which we might truly call transcendental [*et une langue que l'on pourrait appeler transcendentelle*], for the same reason that compels philosophers to give that title to natures which spread far and wide and force themselves into every category [*par la même raison qui oblige les philosophes à donner ce titre aux natures qui se répandent et se promènent dans toutes les catégories*]. (Bayle, cited by Vann 1967: 10)

It is important to note that the article advances the exemplarity of the French language not in the name of France, of the emerging French State, but in the name of Europe; the same Europe which would become a so-called republic of letters for Bayle and other scholars. The French language is thus not simply presented here as a 'national' language, a language among others, but as something responsible for Europe, for the languages of Europe. It claims for French the exemplary privilege of universal translation, the language that would translate all other idioms, and perhaps, in due course, replace them. Moreover, its success ensured not only the unity of the philosophical project, but also the unity of a certain Europe, a continent under threat from the loss of an international church – the Christian-Catholic (universal) authority. Bayle's claims are thus not only significant because they were made in one of the first learned journals of the continent, his own French language review *Nouvelles de la république des lettres*, but because this journal was published in Amsterdam, banned in Paris and condemned in Rome.

Kant's emphasis on the place of philosophical texts, that metaphysics, theology and ethics has in some way become a national issue, something marked by a national and geopolitical landscape, is thus not only sensitive to the issue of which 'natural' and 'national' languages are used within a text, but also to the theologico-political dimension of philosophy in Europe since the Lutheran Reformation. It indicates that philosophy in this condition will be necessarily, if it has not been already so, mediated, supported and regulated by the institutions of the State – primarily those attached to the various educational, religious and legal structures of the State, but also those pertaining to the censorship of the publishing sector and its various media and press, including the establishment of various periodicals, learned journals, pamphlets, dictionaries, encyclopaedias, archives, newspapers, etc. This is all the more pressing when – as Lewis White Beck details in a chapter entitled 'A National History of Philosophy?' in his *Early German Philosophy* – 'Textbooks, histories, lexicons, encyclopaedias, and even periodicals devoted to philosophy, appear in Germany earlier, and in greater numbers, than in other countries' (Beck 1969: 7). The project of universality will thus involve questions of circulation and censorship not only within territories, but also between them, and so everything that pertains to translation, to the passage and so-called reception of texts.[2] The broader scope required to ensure that the project of universality, the project of reason, continues was noted by D'Alembert in his 1763 *Discours préliminaire de l'Encyclopédie*, when he ruefully predicted that by the end of the eighteenth century, a philosopher who wished to fully understand the works of the preceding generation 'would be obliged to acquire a knowledge of seven or eight different languages' (D'Alembert, cited by Kohn 2005: 230).

The issue of a project of universality is important to register because for Kant, national differences are *not* exhausted in detailing the empirical differences of nations. This is evident when he details in the *Anthropology* the 'risky attempts to classify the *varieties* in the natural tendency of entire peoples', and states that this must be pursued 'more empirically for geographers than according to principles of reason [*Vernunftprinzipien*] for philosophers' (Kant 2007: 408 [7:312]; original emphasis). What is so striking in this formulation, so provocative, is the fact that it does not deny that the philosopher has *some* role to play in classifying the varieties of people, even if it is smaller than the empirical role of the geographer. For while it is clear that Kant thought empirical differences constituted the majority of differences between nations, he did reserve at least some space for philosophers *in their capacity* as philosophers to describe national differences, not only with regard to those questions concerning the constitution of a nation, a *gens* and a *populus*, but with regard to such examples of a nationhood as Kant takes England or France to be, since he does not take these examples to be reducible to purely empirical or ethnic types. The reason for this is nothing less than the fact that they are the '*most civilized* peoples on earth' (ibid. 407 [7:311]; original emphasis). That is, if one excludes the German people, as Kant importantly qualifies in a footnote: 'It is understood that in this classification the German people [*deutschen Volk*] is disregarded; for otherwise the praise of the author, who is German [*der ein Deutscher ist*], would be self-praise' (ibid. 407n.).

That a level of self-praise may still be active in Kant's reading of the German people will be underscored later in the chapter, but we may note for now that Kant *identifies himself* as German in spite of the fact he will be speaking not only as a geographer, but as a philosopher. But as we will see, the fact he is German will paradoxically allow Kant to declare his nationality without vitiating his philosophical contribution, for the German figure will be held by Kant to be the most cosmopolitan figure possible, the best cosmopolitan;

in other words, what a philosopher aspires to be insofar as the cosmopolitan embodies the universality of philosophical reason itself. The philosopher should always be, if he is not already, a member of cosmopolitical society (*Weltbürgergesellschaft*).

## KANT AND THE ENTHUSIASM OF THE FRENCH

For Kant, these two (or rather, three) examples of nations cannot be restricted or reduced – unlike Spain, Italy, Poland, Russia and what he calls European Turkey – to purely empirical or ethnic typologies, but must be engaged, if one wishes to truly understand their national character, at the level of culture (*Kultur*), of language (*Sprache*) and of reason (*Vernunft*). It is important to note, however, that while France and England cannot be reduced to ethnic types like other nations, Kant still states that if it were not for the lack of 'documents [*Dokumente*]', one could have worked out the 'innate character of the original people of their ancestry [*der angebornen Charakter des Urvolks ihrer Abstammung*]' (ibid. 408 [7:312]). Yet, despite the use of genealogical language and the invocation of an original people (*Urvolk*), it is the faculty of reason (*Vernunft*) that will become the cause of concern for us later on in the chapter, especially when he considers the French nation. Indeed, this explains, at least in part, why the principles of reason, the *Vernunftprinzipien*, are to be used when analysing the varieties of nations. For no empirical investigation by means of itself can determine, or evaluate, the validity or exercise of reason by a given people.

As before, when Kant was suspicious of French metaphysics, religious doctrines and ethics, Kant warns that France has a '*vivacity* that is not sufficiently kept in check by considered principles [*Grundsätze*]'. He invokes 'clear-sighted reason [*hellsehender Vernunft*]' to his side, and if there is any doubt what is at stake, he adds that its 'infectious *spirit of freedom* [*Freiheitsgeist*] . . . probably also pulls reason [*Vernunft*] itself into play, and in the relations of the people [*des Volks*] to the State [*Staat*], causes an enthusiasm that shakes everything [*erschütternden*] and goes beyond all bounds' (ibid. 409 [7:313–14]). The reference to the French Revolution and Terror is unmistakable, and the fact that the imagery is one of vibration, of ground-shaking tremors, no doubt relates to the vibrancy and tone of the French language for Kant, as well as the vibrancy associated with the sublime; but what is equally important to note, is that Kant seems to be suggesting that a form of *Freiheitsgeist* can not only create a national or popular enthusiasm, but can even distort the reason or mind of a whole people, so much so, that the grounding or fundamental principles, the *Grundsätze*, can be undermined or overridden in the country by means of its vivacity, its spiritedness, its *Lebhaftigkeit*.

The power of 'enthusiasm' to distort and manipulate the mind had indeed already been recorded by Kant in his *Critique of Judgement*. He states there that the freedom of the mind is 'abrogated [rescinded, cancelled out: *aufgehoben*]' when a passion like hatred becomes dominant, but only becomes 'impeded [*gehemmt*]' when affection like enthusiasm develops (Kant 1952: 124n. [272:35]). While enthusiasm is thus related to feelings, it is not completely dominated by them, unlike passions, which belong solely to the faculty of desire. This allows Kant to assert, in the same section, that from an aesthetic point of view, enthusiasm *is* sublime, one of its most exemplary examples. This explains the promise *and* the danger of enthusiasm, its association with the idea of the good and also the dangerously excessive and far-reaching. For the source of the sublime is nothing less than the unbridled *imagination*:

> for though the imagination, no doubt, finds nothing beyond the sensible world to which it can lay hold, still this thrusting aside of the sensible barriers gives it a feeling of being unbounded; and that removal is thus a presentation of the infinite. As such it can never be anything more than a negative presentation [*Darstellung*] – but still it expands the soul. (Kant 1952: 127 [274:10])

The enthusiasm that shakes everything and goes beyond all bounds is inseparable from the sublime that takes place between imagination and reason, between the *feeling* of being unbounded and the *cognitive* awareness that one has overcome, in so doing, what belongs to the sensuous. The sublime, while thus an affect for Kant, is tied to reason, not to sensibility. The only thing enabling this alliance between the sublime and reason, and indeed, the only thing preventing enthusiasm from collapsing into something much more dangerous for Kant, is the purely negative character of the presentation (*Darstellung*) produced by it. Enthusiasm, unlike *Schwärmerei*, will not dare to include in its imagination the positive presentation of something like – to use Kant's own example – the idea of freedom. There can be no direct picture or positive presentation of the infinite, or the supersensible. But rather than limiting the emotional power of enthusiasm, this, Kant warns, only increases it.

The word 'enthusiasm' is also crucially the same word used by Kant to refer to the French Revolution in another text published in the same year as the *Anthropology*, namely, his 1798 *The Conflict of the Faculties*. Yet though these two texts were published in the same year, the particular essay which mentions enthusiasm in *The Conflict of the Faculties* – 'An Old Question Raised Again: Is the Human Race Constantly Progressing?' – was written, according to Howard Caygill, in 1795, the year before Kant finished teaching and assembling the manuscript of the *Anthropology*. In this essay, Kant posits something that 'borders closely on enthusiasm, the very expression [*Äusserung*] of which is fraught with danger', not in the participants of the revolution, that is to say, its actors, but in its outside observers, its borderless, or rather, international 'spectators [its onlookers, or audience: *Zuschauer*]' (Kant 1979: 153).

There is thus not only enthusiasm in the actors of the French Revolution as Kant would claim in the *Anthropology*, but something which resembles this feeling in the spectators of this revolution, and it is made public (*öffentlich*) even when making known this enthusiastic response is a danger to the spectators themselves. But it is not the same form of enthusiasm, or rather, the *Anthropology* and *The Conflict of the Faculties* show the ambiguous function of enthusiasm – and indeed, the *Gemüt* as a whole – in the work of Kant: the problem that enthusiasm is at once attached to the expression of freedom as a moral idea *and* the violence of an uncontrollable affect. As Peter Fenves declares, 'from his earliest writings onward Kant is drawn into the critical project of distinguishing an empowering enthusiasm from a debilitating *Schwärmerei*' (Fenves 1998: 122). *Schwärmerei* is often translated as 'fanaticism', and unfortunately, with even more confusion, as 'enthusiasm' in Robert R. Louden's Cambridge University Press translation of the *Anthropology*. Fenves gives good reasons for *Schwärmerei* to be translated as 'exaltation' in his introduction to *Raising the Tone of Philosophy*, though he notes it has its own drawbacks (Fenves 1998: xi–xii).

As Kant himself warns when referring to the enthusiasm of the spectators, even if enthusiasm is the 'passionate [*Affekt*] participation in the good . . . [it is] not to be wholly esteemed, since passion [*Affekt*] as such deserves censure' (Kant 1979: 155). The enthusiasm of the actors, those revolutionaries in France – which we take for Kant not to be censured due his language of tremors and vibrations – should thus not only be differentiated from the more genuine, purely moral and unselfish (*uneigennützige*) enthusiasm of the observers of the revolution, it must be seen as its more dangerous originator, nothing less than the unleashing of a more troubling side to an affect that is, if laudable, still 'blind' (Kant 1952: 124 [272:10]). This unstable side of enthusiasm, we might remark, stands not only opposed to the disinterested outlook of the spectators, but also to the universality of that outlook. It was indeed the 'universal' quality of that disinterested outlook – that it was purportedly shared by all – that was supposed to prove that the character of mankind was a moral one, that cosmopolitanism was being furthered, and that a state of affairs was being gradually achieved whereby 'war (the source of all evil and corruption of morals) is deterred' (Kant 1979: 153).

Kant's reading, by emphasising the purely *moral* nature of the enthusiasm in the spectators, suggests that the enthusiasm in the French nation, the revolutionaries, was more problematic, precisely because it was *not* motivated by this pure moral reason, but by empirical causes, that is, by self-interest (*Eigennutz*). Indeed, his reading suggests that the consequence of an infectious spirit of freedom, *Freiheitsgeist*, is that it allows one to be vulnerable to a feverish enthusiasm, to a certain kind of derangement – Kant goes so far as to say in section twenty-nine of the *Critique of Judgement* that despite the importance of enthusiasm, it is comparable to 'delirium [*Wahnsinn*]' (Kant 1952: 128 [275:15]). Kant, the philosopher-clinician, no longer speaks of the enthusiasm in the spectators by the time the *Anthropology* is published, but only in the actors and in relation to understanding the French national character.

What this reading of enthusiasm purports to represent then is nothing less, we might say, than a philosophical *diagnosis* of nationalism.[3] A philosophical diagnosis because it claims that the source of enthusiasm, as one of the exemplary examples of the sublime, was the imagination of that which was beyond the sensible – thus even if French enthusiasm was impure, even if it was mixed with empirical causes and was not motivated by purely moral causes, its unbridled power was for Kant derived partly from non-empirical causes. The fervour of the French Revolution, in other words, is to be placed between the sensible and the non-sensible, its structure follows that of the schematism, it advances by a mediation between the empirical and the non-empirical.

This national enthusiasm bears a certain resemblance to what Kant, in his *Reflexionen* on Anthropology (Refl. no. 1353), called 'national delusion [*Nationalwahn*]', the kind of devotion, he further notes, which should be replaced by proper '[constitutional] patriotism and cosmopolitism' (Kant, cited by Kleingeld 2003: 299). This more proper civic, patriotic and cosmopolitan attitude we have every reason to believe was thus for Kant to be found in the international audience and onlookers of the French Revolution, specifically, the Germans, rather than the French who were blinded by their own involvement and self-interest. Kant's reading of the French Revolution, or rather, his revised reading of it after the Terror, since he returned to the issue in many texts (not all considered here), thus claims to explain the failure of the event in terms of national delirium. For if enthusiasm manifests itself politically, as a form of national political affectation, as it did for Kant in the case of the French, this always led from the beginning to the risk of political excess insofar as enthusiasm as a blind affect always threatens to take its unbounded origins to extremes. The resulting political excess is thus no accident for Kant; it is inherent in the ambiguous functions of enthusiasm. The French people are both 'rich in spirit [*geistreichen*: gifted]' and dangerously flawed, or rather, as we will see in the next section, their sense of spirit – *esprit* rather than *Geist* – while admirable, is also their downfall (Kant 1979: 153).

In fact, the word 'enthusiasm' has an even earlier reference in the work of Kant, for he had already differentiated 'fanaticism [*Fanatizism*]' from 'enthusiasm [*Enthusiasmus*]' as early as the *Observations*. He states there, in a footnote, that enthusiasm means 'the state of mind [*Zustand des Gemüts*] which is inflamed beyond the appropriate degree by some principle, whether it be by the maxim of patriotic virtue [*Maxime der patriotischen*], or of friendship, or of religion' (Kant 2007: 58n. [2:252]). The very examples Kant uses to illustrate 'enthusiasm' are telling. Enthusiasm seems dangerous for Kant not only because it can be popular among the participants, among the multitude, among the crowd, but also because the object of enthusiasm can be the nation itself. The danger of enthusiasm is that it always risks the rise of a national-populism, a national enthusiasm *about* the nation.

The danger such an enthusiasm posed was thus, according to this logic, already to be found in such texts as the 1789 *Declaration of the Rights of Man and the Citizen*, with its famous third claim that 'the source of all sovereignty resides essentially in the nation; no group [*corps*], no individual, may exercise authority not emanating expressly therefrom' (cited by Kramnick 1995: 467). Kant's vigilance regarding this claim about the nation, about the people, is evident in his 1795 essay *Perpetual Peace*, when he states that unlike the majesty of a 'State [*Staat*] [. . .] it would be absurd to speak of the majesty of a people [*denn Volksmajestät ist ein ungereimter Ausdruck*]' (Kant 1991: 103). The implicit rejection of the idea of popular sovereignty, that sovereignty resides only in a people, is apparent when we remember, as Derrida observes, that

> *majestas* has always been a synonym of *sovereignty* [. . .] [as is evident by the fact that in] Roman political law, *majestas*, the grandeur of what is absolutely grand, superior to comparative grandeur itself, a grandeur most high, higher than height itself, more elevated than magnitude itself, is the word most often translated as *sovereignty*. (Derrida 2005d: 81, 139)

## KANT AND THE FRENCH ESPRIT

But what is the source of this concern about France, about the exercise of reason in France? If we return to the *Observations*, we find Kant saying that to a Frenchman, 'a *bon mot* [written in French in Kant's text] does not have the same fleeting value with him as elsewhere; it is eagerly spread about and preserved in books, as if it were the most momentous event' (Kant 2007: 54 [2:246]). That *bons mots* are nothing less than the opposite of rigorous science for Kant is revealed in the *Critique of Judgement*, when he writes in section forty-four that

> as for a beautiful science – a science which, as such, is to be beautiful [*schön*], is a nonentity [*Unding*]. For if, treating it as a science, we were to ask for reasons and proofs, we would be put off with elegant phrases [tasteful witticisms: *geschmackvolle Aussprüche*] (*bon mots*) [sic; again written in French in Kant's text]. (Kant 1952: 165 [305:10])

Metaphysics as a systematic science cannot be beautiful; any philosophy that is presented by means of *bons mots* is thus debarred from being a true science – it is relegated to the level of beauty, for it does not deal with reasons and proofs, but only elegance. We will even see, in a moment, that the very expression *bons mots* is an obstacle to science for Kant, because of its resistance to translation. It seems then to be a question of language and the way books in the French language are written, the cultivation of a certain 'style', one no doubt involving and invoking a poetic and literary tradition, the kind associated, we might imagine – and it is a question of *imagination* – with the *roman* and the history of romance.

The question is indeed how to *present* philosophy, what the *Darstellung* of philosophy should be – for philosophy must not be a *roman*; it must not present itself as a *roman*. The possibility that Kant's own work, or at least his cosmopolitical outlook, may appear at times to be a romance itself, nothing less than a novel, a piece of fiction, is enough of a threat for Kant to rebut this suggestion in the ninth proposition of his aforementioned essay *Idea for a Universal History with a Cosmopolitan Aim*. He admits, 'it appears that with such an aim only a *novel [Roman]* could be brought about'. But Kant insists that the 'system', even if it is not given or constructed – since Kant only provides the *premises* for a universal history, one which would have to be *completed* by an as yet unknown philosopher of the future – is not a fiction, it does not belong to fiction, the genre of fiction. Though we do not possess the 'system', we know in *advance* that it could not be a '*novel [Roman]*' (Kant 2007: 118 [8:29]; original emphasis).

In fact, in the seventh proposition, Kant had already warned that his idea of universal history might even appear 'enthusiastic [novel-like: *schwärmerisch*]' (ibid. 114 [8:24]). Derrida, in one of his UNESCO lectures, notes the German word *schwärmerisch*, having quoted the French translation of the Kantian passage by Stéphane Piobetta, which renders the German word using the French word *Romanesque*. Derrida adds that it could be more accurately translated as 'exalted, enthusiastic' (Derrida 2002b: 7). But as we have seen, it is perhaps better to separate *schwärmerisch* from *Enthusiasmus*, the former being an illness, a *mania*, which could not, unlike enthusiasm, be praised for Kant under any circumstance. The *schwärmerisch*, whose etymology Fenves notes derives from 'swarm', and in particular, the swarming of bees, represents we might say, the breakdown of civil society, the kind of civil society envisaged by Kant in the *Anthropology*, when he states that man 'was not meant to belong to a herd, like cattle, but to a hive [*Stock*], like a bee' (Kant 2007: 425 [7:330]). The appearance of the *Roman* and *schwärmerisch* together is thus no accident; those who present philosophy as a novel are likely to be deluded about the 'system', they do not understand how to properly present philosophy. This is the problem *bons mots* present.

If this gives credence to Kedourie's claim that 'Francophobia may well have started as a theory of literature', it also foresees that the issue of translation, at least from the French language, will become unexpectedly philosophically pertinent for Kant (Kedourie [1960] 1993: 54). While this chapter will show that the French words Kant invokes in his works are not arbitrary or philosophically unimportant, there is one passage in Kant's *Lectures on Anthropology* from 1784–5 – the so-called Mrongovius set of lectures – that sums up Kant's attitude much more explicitly. Kant writes:

> The German language is very rich in synonyms; it is therefore more suited to philosophy than French, for the latter has many words with multiple meanings. It [that is, the German language], is very pure and every mixing from foreign languages is immediately noticeable, e.g. *Genie*, from *ingenium* or *genius*. It is not like this in other languages. The French take, e.g. a Latin word, add a French ending, and immediately it sounds completely French. (Kant 2012: 495 [25:1411])

That the question of language is pivotal with regard to France is revealed by the fact that Kant, when speaking of the French language in the *Anthropology*, will write that it 'has become the universal language *of conversation* [*Konversationssprache*], especially in the feminine world' (Kant 2007: 407–8 [7:312]; original emphasis). Kant thus acknowledges the universality of French, the kind that inspired Bayle to advance it as the philosophical language *par excellence*, but he does so by relegating it to the level of conversation, to the 'feminine world'. He continues this gendering of the French language – something already registered in fact with his association of the language with the genre of romance – at a more surreptitious level when he adds that the

> words *esprit* (instead of *bon sens*[4]) [and it is crucial to note that Kant once again leaves these and the following words *in French* in his German text], *frivolité, galanterie, petit maître, coquette, étourderie, point d'honneur, bon ton, bureau d'esprit, bon mot* [an expression that we saw Kant use in the *Observations* and that he would reuse in his *Critique of Judgement*], *lettre de cachet*, and so forth, cannot easily be translated into other languages, because they denote more the peculiarity of the sensibility of the nation that uses them [*die Eigentümlichkeit der Sinnesart der Nation die sie spricht*: note the recourse to what is *eigen*, what is proper, what is particular to oneself] than the object that the thinking person [*der denkende*] has in mind. (Kant 2007: 409 [7:314])

This suggests that for Kant, not only is the power of reason, of *Vernunft*, in France called into question, but the French language itself is thought to possess a particular challenge to philosophy insofar as some of its words – we may note the sparseness of explicitly theoretical terms in Kant's list – resist transparent translatability and absolute univocity. The emphasis is indeed on *words*, on the lexematic, not on the syntactic. Kant, unlike Hamann for instance, does not discuss syntax, French or otherwise. Moreover, Kant does not close the list of terms or words, but with the abyss of the 'and so forth' leaves it open *without* criterion or limit. Nothing in the French language *is in principle* excluded from appearing as an obstacle to pure reason, that is, thinking free from the sensibility of a nation.

Following the logic of this, it means that since one cannot escape using a so-called natural language to articulate philosophy, since every philosophical discourse *must* retain an irreducible connection to natural language for Kant, it is philosophy in and through the French language that one is being warned about, above all, in that little word *esprit* – that word which speaks of the 'mind', 'spirit', 'breath', 'wit', and a certain 'enthusiasm' as well as the figure of the 'spectre' or 'ghost', together in the one breath. As Derrida notes in his aforementioned second philosophical nationalism seminar devoted to Adorno, and which briefly considers Kant, 'the characteristic is properly philosophical [*proprement philosophique*]: French people are not sufficiently philosophical because of their language [*langue*]'.[5]

The French language, in other words, is something Kant thinks is inherently too susceptible to the play of language, to its various tropes and turns. The problem with French is that it cannot always be fixed, policed or settled at the level of *proper* sense (and we might remember here the analogy of the Kantian critique regarding the police in the prefaces to the *Critique of Pure Reason*). If Kant dreams of a language beyond translation, a language without need of translation, he also thinks something like a metalanguage already exists, something that would guarantee the orderly flow between the 'natural' languages. What ensure this universality beyond a given language, as we will see shortly, are the objects of thought that stand beyond any language, the *ideal* content of the mind. As Derrida comments, Kant strives for

> a secularization of language [and we might here remember Babel and the *Semitic idiom*, one in principle inimitable *not only* because it belongs to the idiomatic, *but also* because it is a sacred language], the sort of transparency of universal language in an abstract and technical sense. (Derrida 2002b: 44)

Yet, if Kant believes that the French language presents itself as a hindrance to the classical model of transportable univocality, he also feels that he need not comment on his conception of language, that he need not formulate or make his philosophy of language explicit – beyond noting the existence of objects of thought – in order to makes his case legitimate.[6]

The tropology of the French language, in other words, condemns itself, precisely because it gives due place to place itself, it gives thought a place, a country, a topology, that should not be present at the level of the intelligible. The scandal of the French language is that unlike all other 'natural' languages, which totally efface their cultural particularity at the level of thought, which eradicate any trace of the sensible when dealing with the intelligible, the French language allows its particular *national sensibility* to breach the bastion of *reason*. The abstract universality sought by philosophy, the logic of the proper which is most proper to it, is rendered susceptible once again to the babel of languages, or rather, the babble of *one* language. While the *Critique of Pure Reason* need not have been written in German and Latin according to this line of thought, it could not, it seems, have been written in French.

This is so despite the fact that Kant was also fundamentally wary of Herder's manner of writing, as is witnessed in his reviews of parts one and two of Herder's *Ideas for the Philosophy of the History of Humanity* in 1785, the year after Kant's *Idea for a Universal History with a Cosmopolitan Aim* was published. In the second review, he notes that

> instead of there being neighbouring passages from the domain [*Gebiet*] of philosophical language [in fact, Kant does not mention, and he will never mention, 'philosophical language' as such, but simply the philosophical: *das Philosophische*] into the precinct [*Bezrik*] of poetical language [*poetische Sprache*], the boundaries [*Grenzen*] and proper dominions [*Besitzunger*] of both have been completely displaced [*verrückt*]. (Kant 2007: 138 [8:611])

If one is to write, as Herder does, *about* so-called natural languages, national literatures and the genius of languages, one needs to keep rigorously separate all that belongs *properly* to philosophy, and so, what might be thought to be philosophical language, and all that belongs to poetical language. Kant says this despite claiming that with regard to Herder's theories of 'natural' language, he cannot judge, for this

> reviewer [i.e. Kant], when he sets foot outside nature and reason's path of cognition, does not know how to proceed any longer, since he is not versed in the learned study of languages [. . .] hence does not understand at all how to make use philosophically of the facts narrated and thereby also preserved in them; hence he admits that he can have no judgement here. (Kant 2007: 140 [8:63])

This is all the more significant since Kant does not consider the usage of a natural language in philosophical discourse more generally. He does not, in other words, consider the paradox of presenting philosophy as a universal project in one or more natural languages. This is despite the fact he claims that philosophy by necessity *cannot* present itself as a mathematical demonstration. The claim that the mathematical mode of presentation is not fit for philosophy is in fact made a few passages after he alludes to the story of Babel, in the first section of 'The Discipline of Pure Reason'. He claims there that '*philosophical* knowledge is the *knowledge gained by reason from concepts*; mathematical knowledge is the knowledge gained by reason from the *construction* of concepts' (Kant 1933: A713, B714; original emphasis). The difference for Kant is that the former uses the 'discursive [*diskursive*] employment of reason', which because it does so cannot attain apodictic certainty, while the latter uses the separate 'intuitive' employment of reason, which by means of *a priori* intuition (e.g. spatial figures) can attain apodictic certainty (ibid. A719, B747). While mathematics thus *begins* by means of clear and lucid 'definitions', philosophy, in contrast, begins by means of '*exposition* [*Exposition*]' so as to *attain* clarity (ibid. A729, B757).

So despite the fact that Kant takes mathematical demonstration as an *ideal* means of presentation, philosophy for him must be presented as exposition, it is essentially discursive, providing

> *acroamatic* (discursive) proofs, since they may be conducted by the agency of words alone [*nur durch lauter Worte*] (the object in thought [*der Gegenstand in Gedanken*]), rather than *demonstrations* which, as the term itself indicates, proceed in and through the intuition of the object. (Kant 1933: A735, B763)

That is, in philosophy, there is no room for demonstration, but only for argumentation. As Jean-Luc Nancy notes:

> (Transcendental) philosophy thus does not define itself in any way in relation to literature. It defines itself – or rather, *presents* itself – by way of exclusion from mathematical construction [. . .] We are thus brought back to the partition between the philosophical and the mathematical . . . in the guise of their surreptitious identification. The renunciation of elegance and the critical position it forces Kant to occupy – or the reverse: the critical position and the renunciation of elegance it demands – repeats itself with a desire for elegance. Elegance is the term substituted for the presentation of the mathematical opus, and the desire for it is the desire to write a book. 'Literature' will be the name of the object of desire of the lost opus. (Nancy 2008: 34, 44; original emphasis)

That the essential discursive mode of philosophy concerns not only language and literature, but at some level the division of languages, is revealed when Kant declares that while he strictly will not say philosophy presents 'definitions' – because it can never make those definitions comprehensive, unlike in mathematics – he has to admit that

> The German language has for the [Latin] terms *exposition, explication, declaration*, and *definition* only one word, *Erklärung* [a word, moreover, as the translator Norman Kemp Smith notes, that Kant usually employs in the sense of 'explanation', but which can also be rendered as 'declaration']. (Kant 1933: A730, B758)

So despite the equation of the ideal content of the mind with language, not all languages will be equal to the task of philosophical exposition.

Moreover, one of the very words which unveils this is the *Latin* word 'exposition'. So as a concept, exposition has the distinguished role of distinguishing between philosophy and mathematics, but as a word, it has the distinguished role of distinguishing 'natural' languages – that is, Latin and German. The word 'exposition' exposes, that is, makes public, that not all languages will be equal to the task of philosophical exposition. In short, it professes that the place of the philosophical ex-position will matter, that philosophy will sometimes be explicated differently in different languages, explicitly or not. Philosophy will thus have to be sensitive to the boundaries of language and place. The significance of this – especially when we recall Kant's essay 'An Answer to the Question: "What Is Enlightenment [*Aufklärung*]?"' – is captured by Derrida when he asks:

> What to make of the German language [*langue*] as a philosophical language [*langue philosophique*], once it behoves every enunciation [*énoncé*] of philosophical rationality (it is the essence of the *Aufklärung*) to be produced, to be published, to be made public [and we might recall here the emphasis that Kant clearly places on the German word *Öffentlichkeit* – the public, the public sphere, publicity – with regard to reason *and* the enthusiasm of the international spectators of the French Revolution] in a universal and limitless fashion?[7]

It is precisely because of such a crossing of philosophy with the so-called natural languages that Derrida in his philosophical nationalities and nationalism seminar will propose to investigate 'philosophical idioms' and what constitutes a 'national idiom in philosophy' (Derrida 1992a: 3–4). For rather than finding this idiomatic situation unique and deplorable to the French language, Derrida insists that idiomaticity is the very *chance* of universality – 'the only possibility for a philosophy, for a philosophy itself to speak itself, to be discussed, to get (itself) across, to go from one to the other' (ibid. 3–4).

Rather than seek a process of universalising which would erase the differences of idiom, Derrida elaborates how any articulation of universalism must always be inscribed in the proper body of a singularity. He thus does not relinquish a process of universalising altogether, but rather seeks one that would respect the idiom, that would not crush it or seize it in the name of a given nation. The question of seizing on idiomaticity in the name of a given nation will be pursued at further length in the next chapter when we examine Fichte and how he advances what he thinks to be a national philosophical German idiom, one beyond the issue of linguistic competency. At issue will be the question of whether the *proprius* – that is, the order of property, purity and propriety – can be dissociated from the idiom, whether an idiom can be possessed and owned, or whether 'the idiom is always and only for the other, in advance expropriated (exappropriated)' (ibid. 227).

But if the *discursive* mode of philosophy is what is most proper to it, and if what is supposed to make language transparent is the object of thought in the mind (*der Gegenstand in Gedanken*), perhaps the most alarming word Kant mentions in his list of French words is none other than his first, the word *esprit*, the very word that 'translates' – among other things – 'mind' in the French language. For if the very word which names the entity that divides the intelligible from the sensible is itself contaminated with sensibility, the French *esprit* is flawed. The French mind is impaired when it thinks of itself in the French language, it can no longer be assured that the object it names – the mind – is immune from the very sensibility of the nation (*Sinnesart der Nation*) it must at times critique and delimit. The word *Sinnesart* in the passage is crucial, for

> *Sinnesart* refers to mental and emotional attributes, inclinations, states as these are empirically evident in physical and linguistic forms of expression. In Kant's account these belong to human sensible (as contrasted with intelligible) nature and the literal 'conduct of the sensibilities [*Sinnesart*]' parallels its counterpart, 'conduct of thought [*Denkungsart*].' (Munzel 1999: 25)

The act of thinking in French is thus corrupted by the very name of the entity that enables one to think, to think about thinking and to think about names. The sensibility of the nation will always interfere with the French mind as soon as the *esprit* is named. In fact, earlier in the *Anthropology*, at the end of section eight, Kant had compared 'sensibility [*Sinnlichkeit*]' to a 'mob [*Pöbel*], because it does not think' (Kant 2007: 256 [7:144]). The French mind as *esprit*, as a word that denotes more the sensibility of a nation than the object the thinking person has in mind, thus seems susceptible to the mob, not only historically, but also structurally. The mob is embodied for Kant in nothing less than the French language, in the French *esprit*. If the French mind is not quite a mob, it will always remain susceptible to its forces and tactics.

The use of the word *Pöbel* by Kant suggests why the French *esprit* will never fully recognise the *law of reason*, why it will always seek to exempt itself from reason – the accordance of reason as the highest *legislative* power. For the word *Pöbel* is the very same word used by Kant in the first passage of 'The Character of Peoples' to describe that part of the people which exempts itself from the law. Let us not forget that for Kant the ideal philosopher is a legislator. He defines the 'ideal [*Urbild*] of a philosopher' as a 'legislator of human reason [*Gesetzgeber der menschlichen Vernunft*]' in distinction to an 'artist of reason [*Vernunftkünstler*]' (Kant 1933: A839, B867). The excess of the French Revolution and the French *esprit* are thus inseparable for Kant. The political revolt is already to be found in the susceptibility of the French *esprit* to the mob, to the sensibility of the nation that does not think, that lets itself be carried away by means of an infectious spirit of freedom, *Freiheitsgeist*.

But the sense of *esprit* as wit (as in *mot d'esprit*) also comes into play for Kant. This is registered in the *Anthropology* when he writes that 'In the French language, *spirit* [*Geist*] and *wit* [*Witz*] bear one and the same name, *Esprit* [French in Kant's text]. In German it is different' (Kant 2007: 329 [7:225]; original emphasis). But the association of humour and wit with the French – already marked with the *excessive* use of the *bon mot* for him in the writings of French philosophy – can also be seen to be evident in the *Observations*, when Kant details that the French philosopher 'likes to be witty, and will without reservation sacrifice something of the truth [*Wahrheit*] for the sake of a witticism. By contrast, where he cannot be witty, he displays just as thorough an insight as someone from any other people' (ibid. 54 [2:246]). Kant, in his *Lectures on Anthropology*, continues this association of wit with the French, connecting both to what is fashionable. As Kant writes:

> Wit gives rise to fashion, or an object of imitation for the sake of it being new. Fashions are thus witty because they delight through the representation of novelty [. . .] – One mental ability suits one nation better than another; for example, wit suits the French, the power of judgement better suits the English and Germans. (Kant 2012: 388 [25:1264])

As Jean-Luc Nancy observes in his essay '*Menstruum Universale*', the *Witz* is nothing less than the 'product of a peculiar nationalist quarrel' (Nancy 1993: 253).

The quarrel is indeed national, demarcated in this case by the figure of the French philosopher, the one who is seen as being in danger of negating or sacrificing the very aim, or perhaps even the *duty* that makes him or her a philosopher, the search for truth. He or she replaces what Kant calls 'the tone

[*Ton*] of truthfulness [*Wahrhaftigkeit*]' in his 1796 short essay 'Announcement of the Near Conclusion of a Treaty for Eternal Peace in Philosophy', with what might be described as a *fashionable* tone, perhaps even, a *bon ton* (Kant 1993: 93). The French philosopher, no doubt because of his or her language, too often uses a *bon ton* at the expense of a more properly philosophical tone – the tone of truthfulness. The importance of this more properly philosophical tone is that it befits the hearing of philosophy, a hearing free from the kind of sensibility marked and remarked in the very language of the *bon ton*. This expression, which is inextricably linked to the sensibility of the French nation for Kant – even if it is not perhaps reducible to it – marks out the intonation of the French language. The affect of the French language, its danger, is tied up with its tone. The *bon ton* signals, in its very untranslatability, that French is a language of tone, that tone matters to it, that one cannot escape tone in the French language, and that this can only *obstruct* philosophy as the systematic arrangement of concepts free from affection and tonal difference. As Jean-Luc Nancy observes:

> Philosophy installs itself thus not as merely another tone – the tone of the shopkeeper as opposed to the tone of the superior [*grand-seigneur*] [that Kant invokes and analyses], but as the absence of tone, the absence of the seductive, contagiously affect-laden voice, the absence of the veiled voice – and thus atonal exposition that can only be modelled on the book conceived as a well-armored treatise. Prose is the palliative of the mathematical shield. (Nancy 2008: 78–9)

In sum, the significance of the tone of truthfulness is that it is 'itself an index of a properly philosophical affect, not merely the absence of all affect but the trace of this absence as affect itself' (Fenves 1991: 207n.).

In fact, the object of interest for the French philosopher, according to Kant, is the very figure of affect for him – the woman. For 'In France, the woman gives all society and all intercourse their tone [*Ton*]' (Kant 2007: 54n. [2:246]). Indeed, if we return to Kant's *Lectures on Anthropology*, he states that 'In France the women set the tone, and the woman who usually sets the tone is called the woman of good tone [Kant once again uses the French term in his German language text: *de bon ton*]' (Kant 2012: 490 [25:1401]). This is no doubt tied to the fact that the French language is the universal language of the 'feminine world'. It is the language that deploys, above all else, the very techniques of so-called high society, of courting, of seduction, of eloquence, to advance its aims. If gallantry (*galanterie*), flirting (*coquette*), frivolity (*frivolité*) and wit (*esprit*) are present in French philosophy, Kant warns that it will always be partly at the sacrifice of truth. He thus concludes in the *Observations* that 'The object to which the merits and national capabilities of this people are most devoted is woman [. . .] because she provides the best opportunity for displaying in their best light the favourite talents of wit [*Talente des Witzes*]' (Kant 2007: 54–5 [2:246–7]).

The logic of these passages is undeniable; French is the language of the woman, 'the feminine world', because it is the language of wit, nothing less than the mother or maternal language of *esprit*. If French philosophy remains tied to the *spirituel* in its outlook, too closely tied to wit and to spirit, unable in the end to differentiate them, it is because of the association of the French language as the mother tongue of France, the language of fashion and of the feminine world. This gendering of the French language is of course no accident when one remembers the history of French *salons* in the seventeenth and eighteenth centuries, something itself recalled by Kant when he cites the *bureau d'esprit* – another name for the salons, clubs and societies frequented famously by both males and females – as an example of a French term that reflects the sensibility of the nation. The expression *bureau d'esprit* that Kant had earlier stated was difficult to translate reappears in his *Lectures on Anthropology*, where he defines it as 'a meeting of beautiful minds', invoking the name of Marie Thérèse Rodet Geoffrin, a leading figure of the French salon scene (Kant 2012: 391 [25:1267]). Indeed, as Erica Harth states in her *Cartesian Women*, '*esprit*, or natural wit was supposed to be the particular virtue of salon women' (Harth 1992: 38; my emphasis).

But the association of philosophy written in French with the figure of the woman, with the frivolous, the ladies of the *salons* rather than the School, is of further import when we recall the politico-pedagogical history of the 1637 *Discourse on Method* (*Discours de la méthode*), a text that was not only first published in French, unlike Descartes' other texts, which were originally written in Latin and then subsequently translated into French, but one which tries to justify the choice of choosing a 'vulgar tongue [*langue vulgaire*]' over Latin by stating that this would make it easier to appeal to 'natural reason [*raison naturelle*]', the same force that makes philosophy potentially universal. This 'natural reason' is present again when Descartes describes the choice of language in the *Discourse on Method* as an attempt to write – as he put it in his famous letter to Père Vatier on 22 February 1638 – 'a book which *I wished to be intelligible even to women* while providing matter for thought for the finest minds' (cited by Derrida 2004a: 27; Derrida's emphasis).

If Descartes wishes to be understood by women, he can only do this, facilitate this, he believes, by writing in French. He thus wishes women to be at some level conversant with philosophy. If he does not call for their unlimited access to philosophy, it is because, as he states in the same letter, the arguments and rhetoric of scepticism would too easily sway them. In an earlier letter, written to Silhon in 1637, he had in fact spoken of his fear that he would be read as if he were trying to bring in scepticism, rather than defeat it, and that this would 'disturb weaker *minds [faibles esprits]*' (cited by ibid.: 25; my emphasis). He is thus still wary of the 'feminine world'. However, he still believes that since women as a whole are denied access to Latin, the language of the school, yet possess 'natural reason', they should have some access to philosophy. Descartes does this, crucially, Derrida notes, by writing in a language that was at the time gaining power in the court of France, with the monarchic State administration, as it extended its power by enforcing linguistic unification over the country. Descartes thus 'secures a certain clientele in the foreign courts where the use of French was fashionable [*à la mode*]' (ibid. 17). Moreover, as Freeman G. Henry notes, 'the degree to which France had successfully exported its language and its culture was nowhere more evident than in nearby Prussia' (Henry 2008: 47). Indeed, the international power of French can in fact be measured by the Berlin Academy's essay contest for 1782–4, which was entitled *Qu'est-ce qui a rendu la langue française universelle*, a title that 'took the *fact* of its universality completely for granted: only the causes [of the universality of French] were to be discussed' (Rickard 1989: 118; original emphasis). The influence of the French language in this time period is indeed registered by Kant, who notes in his *Lectures on Anthropology* that a Frenchman, even though 'he rarely learn[s] to speak German properly', 'thinks his language [i.e. French] is the best and believes everyone has to learn it' (Kant 2012: 490 [25:1402]).

The vogue of the French language, its association with all things fashionable, its use, for example, in the Potsdam court of Frederick the Great and the Academy in Berlin, no doubt only increased the danger of this language for Kant, especially when *la mode* (fashion) and *le mode* (form, manner, mode, method, the *way* of doing something, that is, *methodos*) cross paths in the French language, as is evident in the *Discours de la méthode*.[8] As Kant wrote in the *Anthropology*, France can be thought of as 'the land of fashion' (Kant 2007: 408n. [7:313]). The problem for Kant, if we may put it this way, is that in French *la mode* too often dictates *le mode*. The gender difference, in other words, makes all the difference.

Kant's association of French philosophy with the figure of the woman thus not only brings into question the matter of who should have access to philosophy and so questions regarding the pedagogical structure of philosophy, philosophy 'outside' of the school, but also the politico-linguistic dimension of writing philosophy in one 'natural' language above another, especially when philosophy is written in an 'official' or 'national' language of a State and when that language may also have predominance at an international level. That this dispute around genre and around language circulates and traverses the name of Descartes, or rather, his legacy, is also telling. We might recall, for example, Victor Cousin in the 1840s stating that the teaching of philosophy in France must derive from the Cartesian tradition, since, as Derrida puts it, for Cousin what is '*true* and [what is] *French* coincide, natural truth is also national; Descartes *is* France' (Derrida 2002c: 122; original emphasis). Indeed, as François Azouvi points out in a work which studies the multiple and warring receptions of Descartes in France, Descartes has come to embody the French, to represent or incarnate France *herself* to such a degree that he has been claimed by such conflicting camps as French positivists, French republicans and French Catholics (Azouvi 2002). The legacy of Cartesianism is thus also a distinctly national legacy, as we will see further in Chapter 5 when we consider how Tocqueville claims Descartes as the embodiment of the 'American philosophical method'.

## KANT AND THE PHLEGMATIC GERMAN

While for Kant the Frenchman has the benefit of having a certain international language at his side – however flawed that language may be for Kant – it is really the German who exemplifies the critical spirit of the times, the *Aufklärung*, that is, the Enlightenment that he himself so famously wrote about. For as Kant writes in the *Anthropology*, the German

> is the man of all countries and climates; he emigrates easily and is not passionately bound to his fatherland [. . .] he has no national pride, and is also too cosmopolitan to be deeply attached to his homeland [*der Mann von allen Ländern und Klimaten, wandert leicht aus und ist an sein Vaterland nicht leidenschaftlich gefesselt* [. . .] *er hat keinen Nationalstolz, hängt gleich als Kosmopolit auch nicht an seiner Heimat*]. (Kant 2007: 413 [7:318])

The German is thus the exemplary example of the cosmopolitan for Kant; he represents the ideal insofar as he belongs to a non-nationalist nation, a nation devoid of *Heimat* and associated troubling passions.

The reasons for this national-cosmopolitical identification in the German national character are also not external for Kant, as is revealed when Kant discusses the 'phlegmatic' character of the German mind. For phlegm '(taken in its good sense) is the temperament of cool reflection [*kalten Überlegung*]', the kind of temperament that ensures that

> one can expect as much from the talent of the German's correct understanding [*richtigen Verstandes*] and profoundly reflective reason [*tief denkenden Vernunft*] as from any other people capable of the highest culture; except in the department of wit and artistic taste, where he perhaps may not be the equal to the French, English and Italians. (Kant 2007: 413 [7:318])

Kant's aim in this passage is thus ostensibly to place Germanic culture as something on par with what he takes to be the highest cultures achieved in his own age – England and France. Yet, in the terms Kant chooses, he also reveals that it is not only equal to England and France, but is in surreptitious ways, superior to them. In the example above, we may note that the *only* way a German may not exceed France and England in terms of culture is in wit. But as we have already seen, this capacity was analysed mostly as a danger for Kant, above all, when it appeared *in* philosophy, that is to say, when it transformed philosophy proper into spiritual philosophy, to a philosophy dependant on the *esprit* and the *spirituel*. Even more importantly, Kant advances the German by always taking the French and the English as opposites, but not just as any opposites, but also as the best opposites, privileged opposites – opposites of the highest culture – and then maintaining that the German has sides of both, that it *unites* them in a certain way. The German thus participates in two terms of opposition at the same time. It is the German that embodies the very schema of universality.

If the French mind can be all too easily inflamed (*erhitzt*) with enthusiasm, above all, when it concerns itself with a political state of affairs, with a spirit of freedom (*Freiheitsgeist*), the German mind is equated with a profoundly reflective reason (*tief denkenden Vernunft*), a mind which is cold (*kalten*) and phlegmatic and so free of dangerous affection. The German mind, in other words, is inherently philosophical, it is best suited to philosophy, to the requirements of philosophy. Indeed, Kant had already noted in the *Critique of Judgement*:

> even freedom from affection (*apatheia, phlegma in significatu bono* [apathy, being phlegmatic in a good sense]) in a mind that strenuously follows its unswerving principles [*Grundsätze*] is sublime, and that, too, in a manner vastly superior [to an affect like enthusiasm], because it has at the same time the delight of pure reason [*reinen Vernunft*] on its side. Such a stamp of mind is alone called noble. (Kant 1952: 125 [272:25])

The German mind is noble, stamped as noble, not only because it partakes of the sublime, but also because it does so by remaining free of the dangers of enthusiasm, by annulling it and thus always remaining on the side of reason. But the true force of Kant's example is only revealed when we compare it not only with the French, but with the English. For if England is not the example it takes itself to be, especially in terms of its supposed ability to combine 'civil freedom [*Freiheit*] internally with power [*Macht*] against outsiders', Kant maintains that the German is not only the most exemplary example of the cosmopolitical citizen, but the one who 'in his own country [. . .] is more hospitable to foreigners than any other nation [*Nation*]' (Kant 2007: 407, 413 [7:311, 7:318]). If freedom takes on dangerous forms in France, it is erroneously thought to be best distributed in England, yet, as we discover, it is in fact the German who exemplifies the spirit of hospitality and thus who most keenly understands what freedom, under its cosmopolitical guise, really entails.

The same logic of an advancement can already be observed in the *Observations* when Kant writes that the German

> has a happy mixture in the feeling of the sublime as well as the beautiful; and if he is not equal to an Englishman in the former or to a Frenchman in the latter, he surpasses them both insofar as he combines them. (Kant 2007: 56 [2:248])

If the German plays a pivotal role for Kant, in terms of heading a certain national-cosmopolitical identification, in terms of providing the best example of reflective reason, in terms of uniting the best of French and English culture, it should also be recalled that he declares in the *Idea for a Universal History with a Cosmopolitan Aim* that Europe 'will probably someday give laws [that is, legislate] to *all* other [continents]' (ibid. 119 [8:30]; my emphasis).

If Europe is the very example of an advancement for Kant, a heading for the rest of the world to follow, the German stands at the tip of this advancement, leading the way, not due to any national pride, but because he represents the *best* cosmopolitan, the *most* cosmopolitan figure possible. As Derrida declares:

> there is a praise of the German as the least national or nationalistic nation among others, as the cosmopolitan *par excellence*. Kant locates himself, as well as Germany, as the invariant centre from which to evaluate the variations [*écarts*] and measurements of national excesses.[9]

As John Dewey observes, in his *German Philosophy and Politics*:

> It is perhaps worth while to recall that Kant lived, taught and died in Königsberg; and that Königsberg was the chief city of east Prussia, an island still cut off in his early years from western Prussia, a *titular capital* for the Prussian kings where they went for their coronations. (Dewey 1915: 37; my emphasis)

The place of this invariance we might say is thus not only Germany at the 'centre' of Europe for Kant, but Königsberg – it is the cosmopolitan city *par excellence* – it is the heart of Europe, its cosmopolitan core, a city where one can experience the world, as Kant puts it, 'without even travelling', without leaving its boundaries (Kant 2007: 4 [7:121]). This city, and Germany as a whole, would therefore be situated at the head of the history of the world, and be an essentially philosophical centre, because both nation and city call for an understanding of the national and its excesses that is *not* exclusively an empirical task. If Germany – the *Deutschland* Kant spoke of in a footnote in the *Anthropology* – is the bearer of this responsibility, the responsibility of measuring national differences (*écarts*), it is because it is at the centre of philosophy, because it lays claim to be a philosophical capital, a point of concentration for philosophy, the place where the national and the regional may be monitored, surveyed and measured, precisely because Germany is above, in a certain way, the national and regional dimensions it can recognise in others, for example – and these are not just any examples, as we have seen – the French and the English. It does this, moreover, not by denying its Germanic nature, but by being German.

The paradox is thus that Germany becomes the most cosmopolitan nation not by renouncing its national character, but by emphasising it, keeping true to its particular nature. The gesture is thus at once a cosmopolitical and a nationalistic gesture; it secures a certain privilege for Germany, even as it tries, no doubt, to undo the danger this privilege creates at the same time. If more aggressive forms of nationalism were not compatible with Kant's Germanic cosmo-national schema, it was not because they emphasised the nation, but because they emphasised the wrong nation or the nation in the wrong way, because they misunderstood the cosmopolitan underpinning of the German nation. More aggressive forms of nationalism, be they German or non-German, would thus be denounced for not sufficiently appreciating the unique place Germans occupy, for not understanding that Germans need not emphasise the privilege of Germany in terms of national superiority, but only by defending its claim to be the nation that best advances a national-cosmopolitical spirit. If that spirit is devoid of the kind of national fervour witnessed in the French Revolution, it is, above all, because it does not pursue the impure enthusiasm of the French, but rather acts on behalf of mankind as a whole. Though Kant does not speak of a national mission, we might say the German national mission is to advance, like Fichte would later say, the cosmopolitical spirit.

The question of the German language is also not entirely absent from this central position, even if Kant makes no explicit remarks on the German language in the *Anthropology*, as he will do on the French and English languages. As we have seen in the previous section though, in his *Lectures on Anthropology*, Kant does mention the superiority of the German language, especially in contrast to the French language. Kant's praise of German can also be found in another set of anthropology lectures, the so-called Menschenkunde lectures (1781–2), when Kant states that the German language has benefited from Germany being a land obsessed with titles, for 'titles, which serve as distinction to things, give rise to a language which is very extensive and has a great richness of words for intellectual concepts, wherein consists precisely the great beauty of the German language' (Kant 2012: 317 [25:1183]). Indeed, Derrida, in his nationalism seminars, comments that while Kant does not discuss the German language in the way Fichte and Hegel would shortly after, there is nevertheless already a conscious problem forming around the fact that 'the philosophical words of the German language which are indispensable to characterising Germanity [*la germanité*] also pose the same problems of translation'.[10]

It is perhaps instructive to recall that Kant had already taken an interest in the possibilities of German language in the *Observations*, as when he states that the

> sentiment for honor in the Frenchman is **vanity** [*Eitelkeit*], in the Spaniard **haughtiness** [*Hochmut*], in the Englishman **pride** [*Stolz*], in the German **pomp** [*Hoffart*], and in the Dutchman **conceit** [*Aufgeblasenheit*]. At first glance these expressions seem to mean the same thing, but in the richness of our German language they mark very noticeable differences. (Kant 2007: 56 [2:249]; original emphasis)

It should also be noted, however, that unlike Fichte and Hegel, not only did Kant's interest in German waver, but the resources he finds in it will also never be tantamount to a simple privilege, for whatever relationship Kant's philosophy has to the German language, this language will always be marked by its co-presence with Latin – if this presence is not in fact often a subordination to Latin – especially when Kant comes to write the three *Critiques*.

Moreover, even though he wrote the *Critique of Pure Reason* mostly in German, following the example of Thomassius and Wolff, and to a lesser degree, Leibniz, in using German as a language for philosophy, he did importantly sanction its translation into Latin by Friedrich Gottlob Born soon after it first appeared. In fact, Born wrote a revealing letter to Kant on 7 May 1786, when he asked permission to translate Kant's works, starting with the first *Critique*. In the letter, he gives the following reasons for the urgency of his proposed translation, noting that works such as the *Critique of Pure Reason*

> are certainly not brought forth by every century, and from which one may expect the most important revolutions in the domain of philosophy, are not only worthy of being introduced to foreigners but cannot indeed be made available to them too soon. Rarely do foreigners possess enough knowledge of the German language to enable them to read such profound works in the original and to understand them correctly. The usual translators have, on the whole, only a very limited knowledge of the language, especially when it comes to rigorous philosophy. Their translations are therefore shallow, incorrect, puzzling and not infrequently

patent nonsense. But old classical Latin is easily comprehensible to *everyone*. (Born writing to Kant, in Kant 1999: 253; my emphasis)

Born's note of inclusion, 'everyone', is needless to say, restricted to meaning everyone who 'matters', that is, those in the scholarly community. He also, it is important to note, finds no inherent reason why philosophy cannot be written in German. The problem, rather, stems from the lack of German that most foreigners – that is, foreign scholars or philosophers – possess. The problem is made worse, Born implicitly notes, by the fact that philosophy in particular requires close attention to language, not because language plays some pivotal role in philosophy, as Hamann or the so-called German Romantics would later claim, among others, but because it must – as Kant himself noted in the *Critique* – avoid confusion, that is to say, the confusion that the event 'Babel' names, which it has come to announce in its very name.

The problem for Born will thus be that translations will be made by those incompetent to translate philosophy written in the German language, especially when they translate from German into other 'vernacular' or 'national' languages. What is thus needed for Born is a language that would not confuse other languages, which would allow everyone in the scholarly community to climb the edifice of the *Critique* without confusion descending upon them. This language, is of course, Latin, or rather, old classical Latin, a specific kind of Latin. Not that Kant agreed to simply translate his *Critique* into this kind of Latin. As he stated in a letter in 1787 to Christian Gottfried Schütz, he preferred that the translation not be dominated by 'style', since it 'might aim too much at elegance'; rather, Kant preferred a translation that would 'be more or less scholastic if not quite old Latin in its precision and correctness' (Kant writing to Schütz, in ibid.: 261).

But to acknowledge the central importance of Latin here, we do not in fact need to know that Kant agreed to the translation, as we know he did. The *Critique of Pure Reason* thus appeared in Latin between 1796 and 1798 under the title *Opera ad philosophiam criticam*. (If 'translation' is indeed still the right term for a work that has already been fundamentally influenced and constituted by the language it claims to be translated into for the 'first' time.) As Foucault observes, the fact that 'Kant never fails to assiduously note the equivalent word in Latin throughout the three *Critique*s shows that the universality of his argument is at one with a certain implicit Latinity. The Latin referencing is systematic and essential' (Foucault 2008: 98). Foucault goes on to note that in the *Critique of Pure Reason*, Kant is even embarrassed by his German, and considers it a limitation. If this is undoubtedly the case, Foucault fails, however, to observe that Kant is also occasionally embarrassed by his use of Latin, and that elsewhere in the *Critique*s, Kant will utilise the resources of German above Latin. An example of the former is when Kant states in a footnote in the first *Critique*:

I have to apologise for the Latin expressions which, contrary to good taste, have *usurped the place of their German equivalents*, both in this section [namely, 'Paralogisms of Pure Reason'] and in the work as a whole. My excuse is that I have preferred to lose somewhat in elegance of language rather than to increase, in however minor a degree, the reader's difficulties. (Kant 1933: B403; my emphasis)

An example of the latter can be found in the *Critique of Practical Reason*, when Kant declares that there

> is an old formula of the schools, *nihil appetimus, nisi sub ratione boni; nihil aversamur, nisi sub ratione mali* [we desire nothing except under the form of the good; nothing is avoided except under the form of the bad], and it has a use which is often correct but also very often detrimental to philosophy, because the expression *boni* and *mali* contain an ambiguity [*Zweideutigkeit*], owing to the poverty of the language, by which they are capable of a double sense and thus unavoidably involve practical laws in ambiguities [*auf Schrauben stellen*]; and the philosophy which, in using them, becomes aware of the difference in concepts in the same word but can still find no special expressions for them is forced into subtle distinctions about which there is subsequently no agreement inasmuch as the difference cannot be directly indicated by any suitable expression. The German language has the good fortune to possess expressions which do not allow this difference to be overlooked. For what the Latins denominate in a single word, *bonum*, it has two very different concepts and equally different expressions as well: for *bonum* it has *das Gute* [good] and *das Wohl* [well-being]; for *malum* it has *das Böse* [evil] and *das Übel* [ill, bad]. (Kant 1997: 188 [5:60])

If Foucault's emphasis on the overall and implicit Latinity of the *Critique*s is correct though, his claim that the *Anthropology* has a different relationship to Latin is all the more important (especially since that is the first 'post-critical' text that mentions the German word *Nation* rather than the Latin *natio*). For Foucault, 'the real work, the path taken by the thinking in the *Anthropology*, does not pass through this Latinity, rather it is directed by the German system of expression' (Foucault 2008: 99). The examples Foucault gives of this are the lexical field of *Sagen* (*Wahrsagen*, *Vorhersage* and *Weissagen*) and *Dichten*, but what can be noted for our purposes is that this is linked to the 'popular' dimension of the work, that the *Anthropology* describes itself as a 'systematically designed and yet *popular* [work]', one which is popular because it allows 'reference to *examples* which can be found by every reader' (Kant 2007: 233 [7:121]; my emphasis). The examples Kant gives in the *Anthropology* are thus recognised in the text not to be exhaustive. Moreover, they are not presented in this model as irreplaceable examples: the reader can find his or her own examples and this will cause no deficiency in the work; on the contrary, it will provide further proof, strengthen the argument of the *Anthropology*. This view can be usefully compared to the preface of the *Metaphysics of Morals* where Kant explicitly deals with the question of a 'popular philosophy' when responding to Garve. As Kant remarks:

> Philosophic treatises are often charged with being obscure [*Vorwurf der Dunkelheit*], indeed deliberately unclear, in order to affect an illusion of deep insight. I cannot better anticipate or forestall this charge than by readily complying with a duty that Garve, a philosopher in the true sense of the word, lays down for all writers, but especially for philosophic writers. My only reservation is imposed by the nature of the science that is to be corrected and extended. This wise man rightly requires [. . .] that every philosophic teaching be capable of being made popular [*Popularität*] (that is, of being made sufficiently clear to the senses to be communicated to everyone [*einer zur allgemeinen Mitteilung hinreichenden Versinnlichung*]) if the teacher is not to be suspected of being muddled [*Dunkelheit*] in his own concepts. (Kant 1996a: 3–4 [6:206])

Kant thus makes a distinction between the writer and the writer-philosopher: if both have a *duty* to be clear, to avoid obscurity and attain *Popularität*, the philosophic writer – who is also, importantly, depicted as a teacher (*Lehrer*), someone involved in pedagogy and communication – is the one *most* bound by this duty to clarity. However, Kant then makes a further distinction between those philosophic writers who engage in a systematic critique of the faculty of reason, and those who do not. The latter can popularise their works – teach them to everyone – because their work can be made clear to the senses; the former cannot, however, since what they deal with goes beyond the senses. As Kant states, he gladly admits that philosophic writers must be clear, but

> with the exception only of the systematic critique of the faculty of reason [*Vernuftvermögens*] itself, along with all that can be established only by means of it; for this has to do with the distinction of the sensible in our cognition from that which is supersensible but yet belongs to reason. This can never become popular – no formal metaphysics can – although its results can be made quite illuminatingly for the healthy reason [*gesunde Vernunft*] (of an unwitting metaphysician [*eines Metaphysikers, ohne es zu wissen*]). (Kant 1996a: 4 [6:206])

Thus for Kant, a philosopher should indeed avoid obscurity unless that philosopher is critiquing the power of reason itself, because the system capable of thinking the supersensible can never become popular. Only the results drawn from metaphysics and not the process of metaphysics itself can be presented to the public. The sensible and intelligible distinction cannot be made popular, since the distinction *involves* what can and cannot become popular. What is popular for Kant belongs to sensibility and only to sensibility, thus the popular cannot properly speak of the intelligible. As he puts it:

> popularity [*Popularität*] (common language [language of the people: *Volksprache*]) is out of the question here; on the contrary, scholastic *precision* must be insisted upon, even if this is censured as hair-splitting (since it is the *language of the schools* [*Schulsprache*]); for only by this means can precipate reason be brought to understand itself, before making its dogmatic assertions. (Kant 1996a: 366 [6:206]; original emphasis)

The sensible and intelligible distinction – which all Kantian metaphysics rests upon – cannot thus be made accessible outside of the language of the school (*Schulsprache*). The scholastic language employed when discussing metaphysics is not accidental for Kant; there is thus an intrinsic and immutable limit to how available philosophy can be for him. Moreover, he states:

> if *pedants* presume to address the public [*Publikum*] (from pulpits or in popular writings [*Volkschriften*]) in technical terms that belong only to schools, the critical philosopher is no more responsible for that than the grammarian is for the folly for those who quibble over words (*logodeadalus*). Here ridicule can only touch the man, not the science. (Kant 1996a: 4 [6:206])

But, however determining this linguistic factor is in philosophy or the national characteristic for Kant, it is, in spite of the importance he assigns to language at various places, not the decisive factor, as it will be for Fichte, though not simply or entirely in an empirical way, as we will see in the next chapter. For Chapter 4 deals with Fichte's *Addresses to the German Nation*, a series of addresses that no doubt present a challenge to Kant's distinction between *Volksprache* and *Schulsprache*, since they not only address the *Publikum* in technical and metaphysical terms, even going so far as to discuss our apprehension of the supersensible, but they also constitute an entire tract on what a national education should consist of, and how one can educate a public on matters of the intelligible. They are also, at the same time, a series of addresses attacking words like *Popularität* in the name of a German national philosophical idiom.

## NOTES

1. Derrida (1984–8), Box 19, Folder 14, pp. 7–8; trans. Joseph Adamson.
2. This would include the 'reception' of Kant in various national contexts, for example, France, Germany, the USA, etc. Derrida strangely omits the name of 'Kant' in his Frankfurt Address 'Fichus', when he details an imaginary or 'virtual' book that would interpret the history of the Adorno prize. Though he states its first chapter would be 'a comparative history of the French and German legacies of Hegel and Marx', he gives no place to the different legacies of Kant. This is strange not only because of the pivotal role of Kant for Adorno, especially as a place of resistance to nationalism, but because Derrida complicates Adorno's faith in Kant's ability to counter forms of nationalism in his own nationality and philosophical nationalism seminars of 1984–5. It should, however, be recalled that Derrida in 'Mochlos' did speak of 'the whole history of French post-Kantianism, the modes of appropriation, translation, exploitation of Kantianism, of this Kant or that Kant, in philosophy and literature, in "French Ideology," in the "French school." This history is under way, more restless than ever; our interpretations of it would come to be inscribed in that history and perhaps inflect it' (Derrida 2004a: 174). Concerning Kant's legacies, one would, at the very least, have to consider which texts of Kant were translated and which were not, the timing of those translations, which were more important to a certain 'nation', which were neglected, etc. A telling example is the speed at which certain texts, for example, the *Observations* and *Perpetual Peace* were translated and published into French (1795 and 1796 respectively). This, of course, has everything to do with the relations of Kant with the French Revolution. For a detailed account of the French reception of Kant between 1788 and 1804, see Azouvi and Bourel's *De Königsberg à Paris: la réception de Kant en France* (1991).
3. It should be noted that commentators like Pheng Cheah would not agree with this assessment because for them it is anachronistic. They note that cosmopolitanism, including Kant's vision of it, arose not against nationalism, but against the absolutist dynastic States. Cheah, in his *Inhuman Conditions*, states, for example, that 'Kant's vision indicates that it is formulated prior to the spread of nationalism in Europe [. . .] Kant's idea of the cosmopolitical is formulated too early to take into account the role of nationalism in the transition between the age of absolutism and the age of liberalism. It is more a philosophical republicanism and federalism designed to reform the absolutist dynastic state than a theory opposing the theory of modern nationality' (Cheah 2006: 23). My project can be said to complicate these kinds of assertions, by showing that Kant, while not necessarily reacting to 'the theory of modern nationality' as we know it, is certainly not limited to engaging with the absolutist dynastic States that Cheah emphasises. Cheah, like most commentators on Kant, does not engage with Kant's comments on national character, his linking of the *natio* and the *Stamm* with the State, or Kant's contrast of the cosmopolitical with national delusion (*Nationalwahn*). It should also be noted that Cheah does not mention the French Revolution, or Kant's reaction to it, and just as significantly, the French Revolution's role in the rise of nationalism.
4. Kant had earlier in the *Anthropology*, in section six, named '*sound* human understanding', that is, knowledge of the application of rules to cases, as '*bon sens* [in French in his German text]' (Kant 2007: §6, 250 [7:139]; original emphasis).
5. Derrida (1984–8), Box 18, Folder 2, Seminar 2, p. 13.
6. Michael N. Forster makes the case in 'Kant's Philosophy of Language?' (2014) that there are three distinct phases in Kant's attitude towards language. There is the pre-critical

phase, where Kant thinks language and thought are closely related; the critical phase, where he thinks they are more independent of one another; and the post-critical phase, which Forster links above all to the *Anthropology*, which once against posits a much closer relationship between language and thought than Kant held during the critical phase. Forster's case for three distinct phases is ostensibly persuasive, in that it highlights that Kant did not always have the same attitude towards language, and so changes his mind on the subject, but it does forget to factor in that Kant taught lectures on the *Anthropology* for many years prior to its publication in 1798. The *Anthropology* and the three *Critique*s cannot thus be so easily divided from one another in terms of distinct phases. While Kant thus does not simply have one consistent philosophy of language in his career, neither does he have a clear phase – the so-called post-critical phase – where he returns to being interested in language. This becomes evident when one takes on board not only Kant's explicit remarks on language as such, but his remarks on specific so-called natural languages, such as French, German or Latin, something Forster does not discuss. The three phases that Forster offers thus seem overly simplistic.

7. Derrida (1984–8), Box 19, Folder 16, Seminar 1, p. 7; my comments in parentheses.
8. Jean Luc-Nancy, in his *The Discourse of the Syncope*, also utilises the difference between *le mode* and *la mode* to investigate Kant's relationship to writing, language and literature. He writes, for example, that 'What can set off a trend [*des effets de mode*] is thus not without its necessity, but this necessity does not belong to fashion [*la mode*] as such. By contrast, fashion *as such*, or, to be more precise, thinking of something as *fashion* [*la mode*], should not be separated from the thought of mode [*du mode*], to which it is tied by a bond that is as much metaphysical as it is etymological and semantic. In other words, the thought of substance. Fashion [*la mode*] and mode [*le mode*] are twin figures of the idea of variation on the basis of an underlying truth, nature, or substance. There is probably no mode [*pas de mode*] properly speaking – with everything this word connotes about aesthetics, society, and economics – except in a society structured by Western metaphysics. And fashion trends consist precisely in that they hark back to the system of substance' (Nancy 2008: 3).
9. Derrida (1984–8), Box 18, Folder 2, Seminar 2, p. 15.
10. Ibid. p. 14.

CHAPTER 4

# The Metaphysics of Nationalism: Fichte and the German Language as a National Philosophical Idiom

> It is characteristic of the Germans that the question 'what is German? [*Was ist Deutsch?*]' never dies out with them.
> Friedrich Nietzsche, *Beyond Good and Evil*, section 244

It has become commonplace to take J. G. Fichte as one of the prophets of nationalism. Indeed, the dominant tendency in nationalism studies is to view Fichte's *Addresses to the German Nation*, delivered in 1807–8, as one of the founding documents of German nationalism. It is, moreover, taken as the primary example of a work declaring an *ethnic* nationalist viewpoint, something that not only defines the German nation in terms of an *Urvolk*, but which advances a notion of the nation defined in terms of a genealogical myth of common or shared descent. This view has become enshrined in nationalism studies, especially since Elie Kedourie and George Armstrong Kelly wrote on Fichte in the 1960s. This is despite the work of Hans Kohn, in the same decade, who at least acknowledged that if the German nation was sometimes treated as a concrete entity by Fichte, and sometimes as an ideal entity, his guiding principle was nevertheless 'not a historical and even less a biological reality, but a metaphysical idea' (Kohn 1967: 241).

However, if Kohn underscores Fichte's guiding principle as a metaphysical idea, he also claims that Fichte simply made a mistake when he confused the ideal and the real, and that he made this blunder because his philosophical reasoning was *overcome* with national fervour. As he puts it, 'under the stress of the times and of his own emotions, the rational philosopher, the disciple of Kant, rejected the power of reasoned argument. The intensity of individual emotions seemed to him a sufficient foundation for truth' (ibid. 238). He thus dismisses Fichte's *Addresses* as merely confused; lacking a rigorous philosophical system, it does not stand for Kohn beside Fichte's earlier philosophical works. The danger of Fichte's work for Kohn is thus not ultimately its metaphysics, but its *lack* of a rigorous and systematic metaphysics. There has since been little work done on Fichte's *Reden an die deutsche Nation* in the Anglophone world, and the little that has been written tends to endorse Kedourie's belief that the text declares an ethnic nationalist viewpoint.

The reception of Fichte in France after World War II, in contrast, depicts Fichte as a leading democrat and cosmopolitan. Leading scholars and commentators such as Xavier Léon and Martial Guéroult, or more recently, Alain Renaut and Luc Ferry, have argued that Fichte advocates not a form of ethnic nationalism, one dependant on some notion of race or ethnicity, but a cultural form of nationalism, one facilitated and promoted by means of *Bildung* – a word widely recognised to be difficult to translate, especially since it is connected to *Bild* and *bilden*, but which is often translated as 'education', 'cultivation' and 'formation' – and so *open in principle to anyone*. Both the dominant Anglophone and Francophone views of Fichte will be challenged in this chapter, not by denying or ignoring the cosmopolitan or national ambition of the *Addresses*, but by arguing that it is both nationalist *and* cosmopolitan in its outlook – that the national mission it outlines is one drawn in cosmopolitical terms.

In philosophy, even among readers of Fichte, the text is usually ignored or marginalised; indeed, it is usually treated as *distinct* from Fichte's philosophical writings insofar as it deals with a 'regional' ontology – one in pursuit of the question 'What is German?' – and not the foundational science or fundamental ontology pursued in his *Science of Logic* (*Wissenschaftslehre*). Edmund Husserl, for instance, delivered three lectures in Freiburg entitled 'Fichte's Ideal of Humanity [*Fichtes Menschheitsideal*]' in 1917 and 1918 to soldiers returning from the war, but he only mentions the *Addresses to the German Nation* insofar as it is a 'social-pedagogical' piece of writing (Husserl 1995: 131). This is despite Husserl discussing the heights which German Idealism achieved as a specifically 'German' phenomenon, and how distant that landscape now is from the contemporary world dominated by 'exact sciences and the special technical culture deriving from them' (ibid. 111). In fact, Husserl states:

> we would in vain page through the millennia in a book on history or study the most remote cultural regions in order to find a philosophy which would appear more unintelligible [*unverständlicher*] to us Germans and moderns [modern humanity: *modernen Menschheit*] than this philosophy of German Idealism which is indigenous to our people [once again, it is a matter of propriety, of one's own, of self-sufficiency, that which refers only to itself: *unserem Volk eigenwüchsige*]. (Husserl 1995: 111)

Thus, while Husserl avoids confronting the issue of how we are to understand the national character of philosophy, he still claims that German Idealism is 'indigenous [*eigenwüchsige*]' to the German people, even though it transformed what he calls 'world-culture [*Weltkultur*]' and is now, in the modern world, unintelligible to the German people (ibid. 111). Moreover, Husserl suggests it is not unintelligible to them because of its technical or scholastic language, that is to say, because they lack the training to decode what is found 'inside' the texts, but because of a change in 'spiritual life [*Geistesleben*]' (ibid. 111). He can thus only avow, in the end, how Fichte 'awakens in the German people the faith that, if they fulfil in freedom their higher determination, salvation must thereby come for all of humanity. The Fichte of the war of liberation speaks also to us' (ibid. 131). The significance of Husserl's charged words can be highlighted by recalling that, as Étienne Balibar has observed, the phrase 'war of national liberation' was first coined during Prussia's uprising against Napoleon in 1813, and that in 1915, the German general staff printed hundreds of thousands of copies of Fichte's *Addresses to the German Nation* and placed them in soldiers' backpacks (Balibar 1994: 232).

The year 1915 was also the year that the neo-Kantian Hermann Cohen published the first edition of his essay 'Germanism and Judaism [*Deutschtum und Judentum*]', a text that discusses Fichte and the idea of German Idealism alongside Judaism, but which does not discuss the *Addresses* explicitly. Derrida, in 'Interpretations at War: Kant, le Juif, l'Allemand', notes that while Cohen's nationalist text is a work that praises Kant's philosophical achievement as one that is 'unsurpassed' in modern times, it is also a text that at a certain crucial juncture praises Fichte for showing that philosophy is a 'national affair [*eine nationale Sache*]' (Cohen 1915: 283). Fichte demonstrated this, according to Cohen, by showing that the 'I' of 'I think' is not a formal norm, as Kant had thought, but something substantially and irreducibly national. Moreover, the fact that Fichte's philosophy of the self (*die Ich-Philosophie Fichtes*) was developed at the height of German Idealism was for Cohen crucial, since 'the national "I" of Germanness [*Das nationale Ich seiner Deutschheit*] is the true ethical-social realisation of the Idealism of humanity [*Menschheit*]' (ibid. 283; my translation).

As Derrida explicates, what Cohen claims is that

> the nationality of the ego is not a characteristic or an attribute that supervenes to a subject who was not national-social to begin with. The subject is originally and through and through, substantially, subjectally national. The *ego cogito* discovered by Fichte is national. It has universal form, but this universality does not come to its truth except as nationality. (Derrida 2008: 283)

In light of Husserl's and Cohen's readings of Fichte, and their emphasis on the concept of *Menschheit* in his philosophy, it is surprising that Adorno, in his 1965 broadcast 'On the Question: "What Is German?"', does not mention the *Addresses to the German Nation*, even though he discusses the dangers of German linguistic nationalism and Fichte's doctrine of action as an end-in-itself as embodying the ultimate Germanic resistance to 'commercialization' or the Anglo-Saxon 'mercantile spirit' (Adorno 2005: 207).

This chapter will thus examine what thinkers such as Adorno ignore, but it will also argue against the dominant Anglophone and Francophone views of Fichte. I claim that the notion of a national philosophical idiom that Fichte's thought presents, far from being a cover for its nationalism, is the vehicle of its nationalism. That Fichte's metaphysics, far from being separate from his nationalistic project, is constitutive of it at the most elementary level, so much so that the *Addresses* is a work of philosophical and not simply ethnic nationalism. It will thus be claimed that the nationalism of Fichte is not reducible to a set of claims regarding ethnicity or even the empirical world, even if a discourse on the organismic, on what counts as life, irreducibly haunts the *Addresses*.

One prominent exception to Kedourie's and Kohn's interpretation of Fichte is Arash Abizadeh. In his essay 'Was Fichte an Ethnic Nationalist? On Cultural Nationalism and Its Double', he notes that for

> those who wish to take Fichte's philosophy seriously, it [the *Reden*] is read in light of the fact that Fichte's nationalism is little to be seen in his earlier – or indeed, his later – works, thus inviting the easy dismissal of the text as inconsistent with these other, more 'serious' ethical and political writings, to which proper philosophical attention must be paid [. . . moreover,] what is tacitly taken for granted by many Anglophone scholars is that the ethnic character of the *Reden*'s nationalism is so obvious (and perhaps so obviously proto-racist) that the text's only interest is a historical footnote to one of human history's most shameful chapters. (Abizadeh 2005: 335)

However, if Abizadeh admirably scrutinises the *Addresses* in a manner not frequently witnessed in nationalism studies since Kohn and Kedourie, and does not take its ethnic point of view as a pre-established fact, he also never confronts the cosmopolitical ambition of Fichte, be it in texts like the *Dialogues on Patriotism and Its Opposite* from 1806–7 or the *Addresses* itself. Moreover, he treats the philosophical dimension of the *Addresses* as merely a screen for what he thinks is the surreptitious deployment of the nation as a 'natural' community defined in terms of blood and descent. Abizadeh thus believes that he can reassert the ethnic nature of the *Addresses* by reading it as a 'cryptic-ethnic' text, one that preserves its ethnic definition of the nation by initially conceiving the nation in terms other than ethnic, but which then advances surreptitiously towards the very ethnic definition it first seemed to avoid (ibid. 336). He therefore correctly notes, for example, the importance of the word *Geschlecht* in the text, but presumes it to be a word that can be solely determined in natural and biological terms within Fichte's text. He thus takes the term to have no, or little, philosophical importance. He does not, for example, consider how the meaning of *Geschlecht* is intertwined with the question of *mankind* for Fichte, of what humanity is taken to be in the *Addresses*.

This chapter thus compares Abizadeh's approach to Fichte with Derrida's, which does indeed focus on the philosophical dimension of the word *Geschlecht* and the metaphysical aspect of the *Addresses*. The chapter begins by focusing on whether Fichte was advancing an ethnic definition of the nation, cryptic or not.

## FICHTE AND THE QUESTION: 'WHAT IS GERMAN?'

In the first address, Fichte declares: 'I speak for Germans only, and Germans simply [*schlechtweg*], without acknowledging, indeed leaving aside and rejecting, all the divisive distinctions that unhappy events have wrought for centuries in this one nation' (Fichte 2008: 10). The Holy Roman Empire, which had dissolved as a union of territories in the Napoleonic Wars in 1806, will thus not, if it ever did, give the impetus to unite Germany, for Fichte – it will not bring Germany, this *one* nation, together. As he states:

> We shall show at the proper time that every other term of unity or national bond [*Nationalband*] either never possessed truth and meaning; or if they did, that these points of agreement were annihilated by our present situation [namely, the French occupation], have been torn from us and can never return; and that it is solely by means of the common trait [*der gemeinsame Grundzug*] of Germanness [*Deutschheit*] that we can avert the downfall of our nation [*Nation*] threatened by its confluence with foreign peoples and once more win back a self that is self-supporting and incapable of any form of dependency. (Fichte 2008: 11)

The national unity that Fichte strives for is thus not something to be simply achieved by him, or others like him, for he takes it to be *already* instantiated:

> In the spirit whose emanation these addresses are, I behold the concrescent unity [*durcheinander verwachsene Einheit*] in which no member [*Glied*] thinks the fate of another foreign to his own, a unity that shall and

must arise if we are not to perish altogether – I behold this unity [*Einheit*] as already existing, perfected and present. (Fichte 2008: 11)

But what is this unity that bonds Germans together? As we will see, the entire *Addresses* are occupied with this question. They begin to answer this question by differentiating the Germans from what they take to be the rest of Germanic Europe, even though, as Fichte declares, 'the German is in the first instance a branch of the Teutons [*der Deutsche ist zuvörderst ein Stamm der Germanier*]' (ibid. 47; translation modified). The German is thus descended from the Germanic tribes, but he is not identical to them. In the fourth address, entitled, 'The Principal Difference between the Germans [*Deutschen*] and Other Peoples of Teutonic Descent [*den übrigen Völkern germanischer*]', Fichte states that the latter group can be defined as those 'whose task it was to unite the social order established in ancient Europe with the true religion preserved in ancient Asia [which is, for Fichte, Christianity]' (ibid. 11). The Germanic tribes, the *Germanier* – for example, the Franks, Goths, Burgundians, Langobardi – are therefore distinguished by the fact that they brought something foreign, that is to say, Asian, into the heart of Europe; they Christianised Europe.

But in spite of their shared Christian heritage, there are major differences that Fichte notes between the Germans and the Germanic tribes, for

> the former remained in the original homelands of the ancestral race [the original place of residence of the ancestral people or principal stock: *in den ursprünglichen Wohnsitzen des Stammvolks*], whereas the latter migrated to other territories; the former retained and developed the original language of the ancestral race [*die ursprüngliche Sprache des Stammvolks behielten und fortbildeten*], whereas the latter adapted to a foreign language [*fremde Sprache*] and gradually modified it after their own fashion. (Fichte 2008: 48)

The difference between the German and the Germanic tribes – which were originally 'one stem [*Grundstamm*]' – is thus essentially one of language (*Sprache*), but this in turn has a relation to migration, the movement of peoples across Europe (ibid. 47). The fact that the Germans remained where they were thus ensured, according to Fichte, that the original language (*ursprüngliche Sprache*) that all Germanic tribes once shared is now possessed *only* by the Germans. But there is a further troubling aspect, namely, that Fichte's account at this point invokes the very thing that the citizens of Athens had to do to ensure that the autochthony of their first ancestor continued: to *stay in the same place*, to reside on the soil of their ancestors. But things are not so simple.

For Fichte immediately goes on to declare that, with regard to changes, the change of soil, is quite insignificant. Man makes his home [*Heimat*] without difficulty in every region of the earth, and national character [the *proper* character of a people: *Volkseigentümlichkeit*], far from being greatly altered by habitat [*Wohnort*], instead prevails over and alters the latter after its own image. (Fichte 2008: 49)

Like Kant then, Fichte seems to discount on the whole the importance of soil and geography on national character. Moreover, he declares that such intermingling of peoples due to migration or war has taken place in none other than the 'mother-country [*im Mutterlande*]' – that is, Germany – due to, for example, Slavs, and that this has meant that it is 'no simple task for any of the peoples who trace back to the Teutons to prove a greater purity of descent than the others [*eine größere Reinheit seiner Abstammung vor den übrigen darzutun*]' (ibid. 49). The privilege of the German is therefore not one of simple purity of descent (*Reinheit seiner Abstammung*). Whatever this privilege amounts to, Fichte accepts that there is no such thing as purity when it comes to lineage and descent. The unity of the Germans is not, in other words, simply a genealogical matter.

What is more important, Fichte claims, is language (*Sprache*). Indeed, he states that the German *Sprache* 'establishes a complete contrast between the Germans [*Deutschen*] and the other peoples of Teutonic descent [*Völkern germanischer*]' (ibid. 49). But this difference, according to him, emerged in time, it was not innate. He does not, in other words, claim that the German language has some special quality (*Beschaffenheit*) that other languages do not have; rather, he claims that in the case of Germans:

> something peculiar to them has been retained [something of their *own* has been properly retained: *dass dort Eigenes behalten*] and in the latter [i.e. the Germanic tribes] something foreign adopted [*hier Fremdes angenommen wird*]; nor is the issue the prior ancestry [*die vorige Abstammung*] of those who continue to speak an original language [*derer, die eine ursprüngliche Sprache fortsprechen*], but only the fact that this language continues to be spoken without interruption [*dass diese Sprache ohne Unterbrechung fortgesprochen werde*], for men are formed by language far more than language is by men [*indem weit mehr die Menschen von der Sprache gebildet werden, denn die Sprache von den Menschen*]. (Fichte 2008: 49)

Fichte thus opposes a historical link between linguistic continuity and biological continuity. It is merely the fact that the German language has been *continuously* spoken that is supposed to single it out. The privilege bestowed upon the German language is therefore not given due to any intrinsic value – for example, its distinctive syntax – but simply because it has not been interrupted in its development, and in doing so, has allowed its speakers to have something of their own retained. If German did not originate as the original language for Fichte, it did *become* the original language by being kept 'alive' when all other languages were 'dying'. As a consequence, he believes that because the German people have always *possessed* it, it is properly their own and it can be made *pure* – what is at stake is thus a logic of appropriation (*idion, proprius, le propre, Eigenheit*). We shall examine Fichte's philosophy of language later in this chapter, but for now, let us concentrate on why commentators have frequently found these passages to equate to the very thing Fichte seems to deny – a claim about the purity of descent and the positing of an ethnic definition of the nation.

## FICHTE AND THE 'SECRET IDIOM OF THE IDIOM'

For Kedourie,

> there is no clear-cut distinction between linguistic and racial nationalism. Originally, the doctrine emphasized language as the test of nationality, because language was an outward sign of a group's peculiar identity and a significant means of ensuring its continuity. But a nation's language was peculiar to that nation only because such a nation constituted a racial stock distinct from other nations. (Kedourie [1960] 1993: 66)

In other words, for Kedourie, language and race are nearly always found together; when one names language as the distinctive feature of a nation, one is also always invoking at the same time race, because language and race are often coupled together. Kedourie thus identifies a sleight of hand occurring with linguistic nationalism – it speaks of language but slips inevitably into a discourse on race. For Kedourie, then, linguistic nationalism always collapses into a form of racial nationalism. Abizadeh holds a similar view, for he argues that Fichte relies on the notion

> of a *people that persists over generations*: a nation that not only shares a language, but also one that shares it over time. This is what explains the *Reden*'s subtle slide from linguistic to ethnic nationalism, why Fichte begins with an uncompromising linguistic-cultural conception of the nation, but ends up speaking of descent (*Abstammung, Abkunft*). (Abizadeh 2005: 346; original emphasis)

The problem with these kinds of reading, as Derrida notes, is that they presume that what Fichte calls language – or rather, *Sprache* – merges with what the linguists call language or linguistic ability. While both Kedourie and Abizadeh outline Fichte's philosophy of language, they do not sufficiently acknowledge how Fichte differentiates an idiom *within* an idiom, what Derrida in his reading of Fichte aptly calls the postulation of a 'secret idiom of the idiom'. In other words, Abizadeh presumes that those people who persist over generations, who inherit the language and pass it on, must be those people who are ethnically German. But for Fichte, those who are said to speak German, and indeed, who may be born German, may in fact be 'strangers to this idiom of the idiom' (Derrida 2008: 29). The descendants of those who empirically speak German are therefore not necessarily the ones who inherit the true German idiom. As Fichte comments, 'there is little that is truly German left among the Germans themselves' (Fichte 2008: 85). Fichte believes this, crucially, because he does not equate the ability to speak German with the linguistic ability to speak the German language; rather, he equates it with the ability to understand the *Geistigkeit* that he thinks is internal to what is truly German. The ability to hear the national German idiom is thus different from attaining linguistic competency in a so-called natural language. There is thus something 'cryptic' in the *Addresses*, as Abizadeh notes, but the crypt is the secret idiom of the idiom, and not, as traditionally understood, some form of biologism. Fichte makes this pivotal distinction when he states that:

> Those who believe in spirituality [*Geistigkeit*: the emphasis is thus on the intelligible and the ideal] and in the freedom of spirituality, who desire the eternal progress [*die ewige Fortbildung*] of this spirituality through freedom [*Freiheit*] – wherever they were born and whichever language [*Sprache*] they speak – are of our race [*ist unsers Geschlechts*: as we will see, the problem is precisely how to translate this locution, if it is indeed translatable], they belong to us and they will join us. Those who believe in stagnation [*Stillstand*], retrogression [*Rückgang*] and circularity [*Cirkeltanz*: a round dance], or who even set a dead nature at the helm of world government[1] – wherever they were born and whichever language they speak [*Sprache*] – are un-German and strangers to us [*ist undeutsch und fremd für uns*], and the sooner they completely sever ties with us the better. (Fichte 2008: 97)

Abizadeh notes that there has been a series of French scholars of Fichte – like Martial Guéroult, Alain Renaut, Luc Ferry and Étienne Balibar – who have highlighted this passage and made it impossible in so doing to 'take for granted the text's unmediated ethnic character' (Abizadeh 2005: 335). He identifies their position as interpreting the *Addresses* as a text articulating not ethnic nationalism, but 'cultural nationalism', one which is *open* in principle to anyone by means of *Bildung* and which potentially 'avoids the pathologies of its ethnic kin' (ibid. 336). For Abizadeh, this 'French thesis', as he calls it, while a useful correction to the Anglophone caricature of Fichte as a blatant ethnic nationalist, goes too far. For while he readily admits that the text does not espouse what he calls unmediated ethnic nationalism, a form of nationalism defined directly in genealogical terms, he does believe that the text espouses what he calls mediated or cryptic ethnic nationalism, a form of nationalism that at first avoids genealogical definitions, but which draws upon ethnic types and models in the final instance.

The strongest point Abizadeh has against the recent reception of Fichte by scholars in France is that the latest translator of the *Addresses* into French, Alain Renaut (1992), renders *ist unsers Geschlechts* in this context as 'our species [*notre espèce*]', rather than 'our kin' or 'our race', thus effacing the other possible meanings of *Geschlecht*, just as a recent translator of the *Addresses* into English, Gregory Moore (2008), has effaced the other meanings of the German locution by rendering it simply as 'our race', even though the word 'race' (*Rasse*) itself does not appear in the *Addresses*. In fact, Moore notes that the word *Geschlecht* has in his translation been rendered 'as "race" or "generation", with no difference in meaning between the two' (Moore 2008: xlii). R. F. Jones and G. H. Turnbull followed a similar trajectory in their 1922 translation of the *Addresses* into English, having translated the locution as 'our blood'. Derrida, in contrast, notes that he will probably not translate the word *Geschlecht* at any point because he is unsure of whether it has 'a determinable and unifiable referent' (Derrida 2008: 51). Moreover, he notes that an earlier French translation of the *Addresses* by Serge Jankélévitch (1952) leaves out the locution *ist unsers Geschlechts* altogether – probably, Derrida says, because the text was translated after the war in a situation where the word 'race' was particularly dangerous.[2] The difficulty of the word *Geschlecht*, Derrida stresses, is that 'according to the contexts that come to determine this word, it can be translated by "sex", "race", "species [*espèce*]", "genus [*genre*]", "gender [*genre*]", "stock", "family", "generation" or "genealogy", or "community"' (Derrida 2008: 28).

Alongside the difficulty of the word *Geschlecht*, the logic of the passage that it appears in should be closely examined, for according to Fichte, someone can be born German and speak German, yet not be truly German if they do not acknowledge the infinite progress (*die ewige Fortbildung*) of spirituality (*Geistigkeit*) through freedom. For Fichte, the empirical ability to speak German thus does not make someone a true German or even a proper German speaker. Abizadeh argues that this interpretation cannot be correct since it cannot make sense of a large part of the *Addresses*, in particular, he notes, the fact that Fichte had earlier in the text differentiated the Germans from the *Germanier* – the Germanic tribes – by means of language. But this is to conflate the empirical distinction between the German (*der Deutsche*) and the

*Germanier* with the *further* metaphysical distinction that Fichte makes between what is essentially and inwardly *Deutsch* from what is merely empirically and outwardly *Deutsch*. Indeed, there is a continuous emphasis upon the *internal* in the *Addresses*, befitting the historical event that properly institutes and constitutes the German spirit in its exemplary mission for Fichte – the German Reformation.

What the German Reformation, and specifically Luther, achieved was 'not a matter of merely replacing the external intermediary between God and man but of dispensing with an external intermediary altogether and finding the bond of union within oneself' (Fichte 2008: 77). Ignoring this concern for what is internal and what is external, what is held to be inside and what is held to be outside of the German nation, as Abizadeh does, in fact *misses* a crucial strand of Fichte's nationalism. For his claim about the idiom within the idiom, as well as allowing non-German speakers to speak the German idiom, also allows Fichte to distinguish 'true' Germans from 'false' Germans. In other words, it allows him to locate internal enemies within German-speaking territories. As Fichte comments, the foreignism (*Ausländerei*) he is seeking to overcome can 'be found at home or abroad' (ibid. 78). The gesture of recognising an idiom within an idiom is thus as troubling as it is inclusive. Derrida's use of the word 'secret' hints at this, since the etymology of the word derives from the past participle of the Latin verb *secernere*, meaning 'to put or set apart', from *cernere*, 'to sift or separate', and *se*, 'one's own'. Hence, the secret idiom of the idiom, the secret *idion*, is what separates or severs; it is what cuts and separates the proper from the non-proper.

Fichte's gesture is not even as inclusive as it might first appear, for he only allows non-German speakers to become German; he does not allow German speakers, or indeed, speakers of any language, to possess the secret idiom of *other* idioms. There is only *one* secret idiom and that is German. It remains singular and pure. One can thus only properly become a German by this method. For it is only the true German idiom – the idiom that gives voice to *Geistigkeit* – that Fichte stipulates as having this quality. The privileging of the German *Sprache* therefore remains, if not as a conventional natural language, as an internal non-empirical idiom within all other languages. As a result, for Fichte, all other nations and national languages can only be defined *outwardly* and empirically. The French, for example, are those who simply are born French or speak the French language. Being French, unlike German, is *entirely* an empirical matter for Fichte. There is no secret idiom of the French idiom; one cannot speak German with a secret French idiom. It is thus possible, on this outline, to be, empirically speaking, a Frenchman, but philosophically, a German. This is the cosmopolitan strand of Fichte. However, the nationalist strand appears at the very same time as the cosmopolitan strand because while one can belong, empirically speaking, to *any* nation, one can *only* philosophically belong to Germany. The only national identity that is held to be essentially philosophical is German. The claim that Fichte is defining the German purely in ethnic terms, as found in Anglophone commentary on the *Addresses*, would thus paradoxically mean that Fichte is embracing the philosophy of the very people he would be contesting – the French. In sum, what should never be forgotten is that Fichte continually opposes French Materialism to German Idealism.

Moreover, Fichte's gesture is especially troubling not, as Abizadeh would have it, because it simply relies on making the German separate from the Germanic tribes by means of positing an 'original language', but because Fichte claims to *dispense* with the privilege of the German language while *reasserting* its privileged role as a secret universal idiom. While possession of the German language, according to Fichte in the seventh address, is thus not even a necessary condition for being German, he still relies on his earlier claim, made in the fourth address, that German has been continuously spoken, to privilege the secret idiom of the German idiom, the idiom that is supposed to remain separate from the German language. As a result, the secret idiom of the idiom, while not identical to German, will still share the destiny of the German language, and it *needs* to do so in order to claim its metaphysical privilege.

Nevertheless, for Fichte, this idiom does not vitiate its universality by being German, *but only becomes universal by being German*. The fact that the German language has not been historically interrupted for Fichte will therefore still have metaphysical consequences. Fichte thus *never* completely eradicates the privilege he accords to the German language, even when its possession is seemingly not needed in order to be identified as German. As Derrida comments, Fichte says *ist unsers Geschlechts* in German,

> and this *Geschlecht* is an essential *Deutschheit*. Even if the word *Geschlecht* acquires a rigorous content only from out of the 'we' instituted by that very address, it also includes connotations indispensable to the minimal intelligibility of discourse, and these connotations belong irreducibly to German, to a German more essential than all the phenomena of empirical Germanness, but to a certain German [*à de l'allemand*]. (Derrida 2008: 29)

In other words, Fichte still uses the indispensable resources of a certain German to articulate the claim that there is an idiom beyond German as a natural language. He therefore ultimately relies on the fact that one does not know how to translate the locution out of German; in fact, its untranslatability is *required* to produce the sought-after effect. As a result, Fichte relies on the fact that no translation of *Geschlecht* can be made that does not erase some meaning or connotations of the word, including its reference to mankind.

This is why, as we will see in the next section, to speak about the Germans, for Fichte, is to speak about all mankind, or rather *Menschheit*, and why, in turn, it is in the world's interest that Germany should fulfil its cosmo-national destiny. In short, the word *Geschlecht* needs to retain an irreducible connection to German in order to achieve Fichte's intention of identifying the German as the best representative of humanity.

## FICHTE AND COSMOPOLITANISM

There is thus an internal relation between the cosmopolitical and the German for Fichte – they are coextensive insofar as the true German can come from anywhere and speak any language. Accordingly, like Kant, Fichte believes that the German national character is the most exemplary figure of the cosmopolitan. The true German represents the *best* cosmopolitan, the *most* cosmopolitan figure possible, because unlike all other national groups, he is not bound by his empirical constitution, be it by his blood, his native soil or his language. His community, that is, the German nation, is formed by an intangible spirit – a belief in the infinite progress of spiritual freedom – and spirit alone.

In fact, Fichte had written – if not published – on patriotism the year before delivering the *Addresses* in 1807. The text, entitled *Dialogues on Patriotism and Its Opposite* (*Der Patriotismus und sein Gegenteil*), has two interlocutors speak of the place of patriotism within cosmopolitanism, one of them convincing the other that these views are not strictly opposed to one another, because:

> B: '[. . .] cosmopolitanism is the dominant will, that the purpose of existence, of humanity be really achieved by humanity [*Zweck des Menschengeschlechtes im Menschengeschlechte wirklich erreicht werde*]. Patriotism is the will, that this purpose [*Zweck*] be first fulfilled in that nation of which we ourselves are members, and that the result shall spread from it to the whole of mankind [*ganze Geschlecht*].'
> A: 'I shall accept that for the time being.'
> B: 'It should be clear to you if you look more closely at the conception I have just described, that in reality [*wirklich*] there cannot possibly be any cosmopolitanism, but that in the true world [*Wirklichkeit*], cosmopolitanism necessarily becomes patriotism.' (Fichte 1971: 228–9; my translation)

For Fichte, the promotion of cosmopolitanism is thus to be achieved not simultaneously and equally by all of mankind, but by one leading nation advancing the cause of cosmopolitical progress on behalf of mankind. The emphasis on a single nation, the postulation of a national mission, is thus justified in terms of a cosmopolitical and teleological framework. In other words, cosmopolitanism cannot become effective (*wirklich*) for Fichte unless it becomes a form of patriotism. This higher form of patriotism is possible only because of the *Wissenschaft* found in Fichte's *Science of Knowledge* (*Wissenschaftslehre*), which is written in German. This patriotism is therefore a *philosophical* vocation, as he states:

> philosophy [*Wissenschaft*] and its widest possible dissemination in our time must be the immediate purpose of mankind [*Zweck des Menschengeschlechts*], which can and must set itself no other goal [*Zweck*]. The German patriot [*deutsche Patriot*], in particular, wants this to be achieved first of all among the Germans and that from them it should then spread to the rest of mankind [*Menschheit*]. The German can desire this, because through him philosophy began and it *is set down in his language* [*in seiner Sprache ist sie niedergelegt*]. It may be assumed that in the nation which has had the power to generate philosophy there should also lie the greatest facility to grasp it. Only the German can desire this, for only he, through the possession of philosophy and through the understanding of time which has thus become possible, can comprehend that this is the immediate purpose of mankind [*Zweck der Menschheit*]. This purpose is the only possible patriotic goal [*Jener Zwek ist der einzige mögliche patriotische Zweck*]. Only the German can therefore be a patriot. Only he can, in the interests of his nation, embrace all of mankind. Whereas from now on, since the instinct of Reason has become extinct and the era of egoism has begun, every other nation's patriotism must become selfish, narrow and hostile to the rest of mankind. (Fichte 1971: 234, cited by Perkins and Liebscher 2006: 12)[3]

The German has therefore a special role to play for Fichte, for only he can ensure the progress of mankind (*Menschheit*); every other form of patriotism is selfish. As we will see in the next section, it is in fact because terms like *Menschheit* are German that Fichte will claim that the German language *is* the language of philosophy. An indication of this line of thought, however, is already found in the above passage, when Fichte declares that the necessary *Wissenschaft* has been grounded in 'his' language – the relationship of the *Wissenschaft* to German is thus held to remain essential and irreducible. The opposite of this higher form of cosmo-nationalism, indeed, a corruption of it, is for Fichte none other than France. While it was the leading cosmopolitan nation for him in the 1790s since it advanced the cause of republicanism through the French Revolution, in the 1800s it betrayed its mission with the rise of Napoleon and what he took to be the opposite of cosmopolitanism – French imperialism.

In fact, the distinction of the German nation, in contrast to the French nation, was for Fichte precisely its ability to avoid this kind of despotism. He states, for example, that the 'German nation is the only modern European nation that has for centuries shown by the deeds of its burgher class that it is capable of supporting the republican constitution' (Fichte 2008: 83). He goes on to argue that the continuous republican constitution of the German nation has thus 'been until now the pre-eminent source of German culture [*deutscher Bildung*] and the primary means of safeguarding its particularity [*Eigentümlichkeit*: what is most *proper* to the German]' (ibid. 115).

But even what first appears in the German nation, and is protected by it, eventually spreads to the whole of mankind, according to Fichte. He thus describes, for example, the German Reformation as 'the last great and, in a certain sense, complete world deed [*Welt-That*] of the German people' (ibid. 73). This worldly perspective, this concern for mankind, is why the German is 'imbued with a spirit not narrow-minded and exclusive, but universal and cosmopolitan' (ibid. 91). Therefore, devotion to one nation was not only compatible with cosmopolitanism for Fichte, it was in fact *necessary* in order to bring about cosmopolitanism. By serving the German nation, one was, according to this logic, serving humanity as a whole. Moreover, in doing so, wherever one was born and whatever language one spoke, one was *becoming German* – because the German nation, unlike other nations, defined itself in terms of a spirit of freedom, one that embodied the cosmopolitan project. This cosmopolitical strand of the *Addresses* is what Abizadeh underplays in his reading of Fichte and what the French scholars bring out in their interpretations. Indeed, Guéroult claims:

> it is no longer race that defines this 'absolute people', but rather its aptitude for liberty and its revolutionary mission. The word *German thus takes on an entirely cosmopolitan signification* [Guéroult proceeds to cite the *ist unsers Geschlechts* passage from the seventh address; it should be noted that Guéroult in fact follows the French translations of *ist unsers Geschlechts* into *notre race*, even though he will sometimes *insist* on a German word, as he does in the sentence immediately *after* the *ist unsers Geschlechts* passage, when he leaves the German term *Cirkeltanz* intact and in parentheses alongside the French translation] [. . .] As such spirituality is no longer a privilege resulting from Germanic ethnicity, but Germanness itself results from profound spirituality, independently of any reference whatsoever to ethnic, linguistic, or geographical characteristics [. . .] *Germanness* no longer designates anything but the character possessed by all those who recognize themselves as belonging to a single fraternal humanity (a people). (Guéroult 1974: 240–1; my translation)

One of the reasons Abizadeh opposes this kind of reading is that it treats the *ist unsers Geschlechts* passage 'as if it were a purely "philosophical" act, i.e. a conceptual clarification of the meaning of a key term', rather than something delivered as a '*political act* intended to "rouse" the German nation against the Napoleonic yoke'. However, the problem with this kind of objection is that Abizadeh himself seems to treat the political dimension of the text as an *addition*, something that comes *after* its philosophical constitution, as if the '"philosophical" act' were not already a 'political act' (Abizadeh 2005: 349; original emphasis).

This is all the more pertinent since Fichte himself affirms the primacy of the practical over the theoretical in philosophy. If, for Kant, practical and theoretical philosophy were separate but co-ordinated aspects of one discipline, for Fichte, all philosophy must be built on the foundations of practical philosophy. As Dieter Henrich notes, 'in Fichte's *Science of Knowledge* [*Wissenschaftslehre*], practical philosophy becomes for the first time a part of epistemology' (Henrich 2003: 208). Moreover, Fichte places the foundation of all philosophy on an 'act' (*Thathandlung*) – the act of positing the self. Indeed, activity and man are inseparable for Fichte, as he states, 'thought [*Gedanke*] and activity [*Tätigkeit*] are only apparently divergent forms ... science [*Wissenschaft*] is itself life [*Leben*], self-subsistent life [*in sich selbstbeständiges Leben*]' (Fichte 2008: 62). But Abizadeh seems to hold the nationalism of Fichte separate from his philosophy, including, pivotally, his philosophy of non-natural life (*Leben*). There is no rigorous examination of Fichte's metaphysics (e.g. on life or his definition of man), and moreover, Abizadeh treats the so-called philosophical clarification of terms – be it *Geschlecht* or *Geistigkeit* – as if it were an 'act' without the gravest of political consequences, or as if the meaning of these terms in Fichte were something separate or subordinate to the political act of rousing. Abizadeh, in other words, unwittingly continues the tradition of *dissociating* nationalism from philosophy – Fichte's metaphysical system is not condemned as such, but only the way it collapses into a 'political act'. The metaphysics it constructs is merely a screen to its nationalism; it plays no essential part in the formulation of its nationalism. The political, and in this case, the language of genealogy, of *Abstammung* and *Abkunft* in the *Addresses*, is thus taken as an 'act' distinct from philosophy, rather than something already inscribed within a series of concepts that as a chain have metaphysical value. The reading I have pursued has, in contrast, recalled that 'There is no such thing as a "metaphysical-concept" [...] The "metaphysical" is a certain determination or direction taken by a sequence or "chain"' (Derrida 1981a: 6). It is this metaphysical system, one that touches every single aspect of the *Addresses*, including its genealogical language, that is being ignored, allowing us to think, as Abizadeh does, that there is only one 'extended metaphysical discussion in the whole of the *Reden*' (Abizadeh 2005: 349). He thus discounts the possibility that genealogical terms – such as *Geschlecht* – may have a central role in the metaphysics of the *Addresses* due to their position in a chain of concepts. In fact, ignoring the metaphysics generated from this chain or constellation of concepts has led us, I have argued, to *overlook* aspects of Fichte's nationalism. Rather than separating Fichte's metaphysics and politics, I have thus demonstrated the political dimension of his metaphysics and the metaphysical dimension of his politics.

However, unlike commentators such as Guéroult or Renaut, I do not want to read Fichte's position as being simply cosmopolitan and republican in nature. As I have already shown, Fichte privileges German in a deeply problematic way, if not as a 'natural' language, as an idiom within all languages. But as well as this, my claim is that we need to be more sensitive to how the different strands of cosmopolitanism and nationalism function in the text – how Fichte's deployment of *ist unsers Geschlechts* remains ambivalent throughout. For if it is true that the German *Sprache* is privileged as the secret idiom of the idiom in Fichte, it is also true that this nationalism is paradoxically coherent with certain forms of cosmopolitanism that are democratic and republican in spirit. As Derrida states:

> The sole analytic and unimpeachable determination of *Geschlecht* in this context is the 'we', the belonging to the 'we' to whom we are speaking at this moment, at the moment that Fichte addresses himself to this supposed but still to be constituted community, a community that, strictly speaking, is neither political, nor racial, nor linguistic, but that can receive his allocution, his address, or his apostrophe (*Reden an . . .*), and can think with him, can say 'we' in some language [*langue*] and from a particular birthplace. (Derrida 2008: 29)

The cosmopolitical ambition of the *Addresses* is thus inscribed, we might say, in this 'we', the 'we' that can extend to all of humanity. But at the same time, this 'we' is never completely separated from what is essentially German, the potentially universal community of the 'we' is only made possible by the secret German idiom, even if it extends beyond the borders of the German nation and language – beyond what is empirically German. Thus Fichte's claim that the 'cultivation [*Bildungsmittel*]' of a 'new race of man [*Menschengeschlechts*] must first be applied by Germans to Germans [*von Deutschen an Deutschen*], and that it is a task that quite properly [*eigentlich*] and immediately pertains to our nation' (Fichte 2008: 47).

Derrida, in 'The Ends of Man', in fact analyses the use of the first person plural by philosophers. He claims that there is often a move from 'the we of the philosopher to "we-men", to the *we* of the total horizon of humanity [*l'humanité*]' (Derrida 1982: 116; original emphasis). This can be witnessed in Fichte when he discusses the choice of what sign or *Bild* should be used to designate the total horizon of humanity. For Fichte, the pivotal choice is between the Latin *humanitas* and the German *Menschlichkeit* and *Menschenfreundlichkeit*. The choice will *itself* for him determine who is most able to speak on behalf of mankind – who will usher in the next stage of progress for mankind as a whole. This is what Abizadeh forgets in his reading of Fichte; he neglects the pivotal question of man, of humanism in the *Addresses*. For the contrast with *ist unsers Geschlechts* is not simply and always *undeutsch* as Abizadeh would have it, but also includes mankind insofar as the German is identified *with* man, taken as the best example of what a human being is. For the question *what* is man and *who* is the privileged representative of humanity is grounded for Fichte most fundamentally in the question of what is German and what the German language – in contrast to the Latin languages – *names* when it names 'mankind'.

Those who can properly name mankind, according to Fichte, will be those who are most properly representative of man, those who best understand the spirit of infinite progress (*die ewige Fortbildung*). Moreover, he also thinks that the nation that can properly name mankind will be of crucial benefit for the *whole of mankind*.

## GERMAN AS A 'LIVING' LANGUAGE

Fichte believes this partly because the idiom within every other idiom for him is also essentially philosophical. The secret idiom of the idiom is thus philosophical *and* national, or rather, this national idiom is *equated* with the philosophical as such. It is held to be essentially philosophical because it is the only idiom that is truly *universal*. In other words, to speak German, true German, is, for Fichte, to speak philosophy. It is the secret idiom found in all languages, *including* the natural language called German. Indeed, for Fichte, philosophers who write in the German language and who write about the central role of language in philosophy, may themselves not be truly German. He denounces, for example, J. G. Hamann, writing that 'an un-German spirit among us [*undeutscher Geist unter uns*]' has expressed the nature of 'a dead language [*einer toten Sprache*] [. . .] in loftier-sounding terms', namely, 'a metacritique of language' (Fichte 2008: 63–4).

Similarly, philosophers who write in the German language with an essential recourse to Latin may still be truly German for Fichte – as none other than Kant was to him. In fact, Fichte unequivocally states that Kant, his former teacher, is 'the real founder of Modern German philosophy [*neuen deutschen Philosophie*]', even if Leibniz also struggled with 'foreign philosophy [*ausländischen Philosophie*]', as Kant in his *Critiques* managed to break the dominance of the sensuous in philosophy – the kind extolled, for example, in French materialism. What Kant did, according to Fichte, was to locate the supersensuous in reason itself, thus inaugurating a form of idealism into philosophy that would, for Fichte, overcome all forms of materialism. Kant, in other words, was the thinker of *schematism*. Hamann, in contrast, sought the origin of reason in language itself, going so far as to equate language with reason in his metacritique. For Fichte, this was a debasement of reason, something fundamentally 'un-German' insofar as it understood language merely outwardly and empirically. This linguisticism, according to him, forgot what underlies all natural languages, namely, the secret German idiom, the idiom that makes it possible for anyone – no matter where they were born and what language they speak – to become German.

This secret idiom is paramount not only because of its non-empirical nature, but because it is a 'living language [*lebendige Sprache*]', or rather, because access to the non-empirical – the supersensible and the spiritual (*Geistigkeit*) – is what constitutes 'life' for Fichte, it is 'living' insofar as it is non-empirical (ibid. 57). He thus opposes any equation of life with biology; the equation for him in fact constitutes one of the signs of a 'foreign philosophy of death [*todgläubigen Philosophie des Auslandes*]' (ibid. 88). Life is held, rather, to be a non-natural property. This is crucial, as it shows that Fichte links death with biologism, and all that which is fixed, limited and stagnant; and that he links life with spirituality (*Geistigkeit*), and all that which fosters eternal progress and originality.

The German language is therefore opposed to the French language not on empirical and philological grounds, but because, for Fichte, French can no longer have clear access to the non-empirical, that is, the supersensible and the spiritual. It is for him a dead language (*die tote Sprache*). It cannot even be considered to be a 'mother tongue [*Muttersprache*]' by those who speak it, since it can only name phantoms like *humanité* – like the Latin-influenced German *Humanität* – rather than concrete entities like *Menschheit* (ibid. 88).

The significance of this can be measured by Theodor Adorno's insight that the word *Menschheit* in Kant means the sum of all existing men *and* the human potential in men – the abstract principle of humanitarianism. As Adorno states in his *Negative Dialectics*:

> Kant must have noticed the double meaning of the word 'humanity [*Menschheit*]', as the idea of being human and as the totality of all men [. . .] His subsequent usage vacillates between ontical manners of speech and others which refer to the idea [. . .] He wants neither to cede the idea of humanity to the existing society nor to vaporize it into a phantasm [*phantasma*]. (Adorno 1983: 258)

We might state that Fichte's concern is also with warding off phantoms, that the superiority of the term *Menschheit* is for him linked to the fact that it is not associated with a philosophy of death. For Fichte, what *humanité* names is nothing but a spectre; this is why no tongue that utters it can be a 'living language', or indeed, a 'mother tongue'. It is inconceivable for Fichte that a 'living language' could house a ghost.[4] The term *humanité* thus has shades of meaning unacceptable to Fichte. He concludes that because French is a ghostly language, since it speaks of ghosts and ashes, it is where language comes to die. The opposite of this is the German language and German philosophy, which is 'opposed with earnest and unrelenting rigour to every foreign [*ausländischen*] philosophy with a belief in death [*todtgläubigen Philosophie*]' (Fichte 2008: 97).

Fichte believes in the superiority of the German language because he holds that language as a whole does not depend on arbitrary decrees or conventions. He in fact deploys a philosophy of language to differentiate the Germans from the Germanic tribes of Europe – like the Franks. His fundamental claim is that there is a one-to-one relation between sensible and supersensible (or supersensuous) objects designated in language, and that this relation must be maintained *over time* to have transparent access to the supersensible. This is because he holds that all language begins by naming objects of *immediate sensuous perception*. There is no unmediated access to the supersensible; language will at first name only objects that can be observed in sense experience. But because the supersensible cannot be observed by means of the senses – since it lies outside of what is given by means of sensibility – the supersensible world will be designated only *indirectly* by language. 'Language [*Sprache*] cannot do more in this sphere; it presents a sensuous image of the supersensuous [*ein sinnliches Bild des Übersinnlichen*]' (ibid. 51).

For this to have happened, according to Fichte, the first individual who wished to communicate about the supersensible must have designated a *self as part of the supersensible world*, as opposed to the sensible world. They must, in other words, have opposed 'a soul [*Seele*], a mind [*Geist*], and so on to a physical body' (ibid. 51). Supersensible objects – like the self – thus always have a corresponding relationship to a sensible object for Fichte; they depend on a sensuous *Bild* in order to be articulated. Words designating the supersensible are thus symbolical (*sinnbildich*) in character. What is named indirectly by means of a sensuous *Bild* are thus secondary and derivative terms, they are dependent on the sensuous objects, even if they are more significant because they do not belong to the sensuous world.

Moreover, because the sensuous world is not the same for all, because humans are dispersed across the world, and environment and locality differ, it is impossible, according to Fichte, for all peoples to acquire language in the same way, since they will have access to different sensuous objects. By adopting a 'foreign language', one is thus closing oneself off from the supersensible objects it names since one has not shared the sensuous *Bild* that make up the language. This explains the divergence of languages for him, for

> it is clear that this symbolic designation [*sinnbildlichen Bezeichnung*] of the supersensuous must in each case conform to the stage of development reached by the faculty of sensuous cognition in a given people [. . .] thus] this symbolic designation will take a very different turn in different languages, according to the difference in the relation that obtained and continues to obtain between the sensuous and spiritual [*geistigen*] development of the people [*Ausbildung des Volkes*] speaking a language [*Sprache*]. (Fichte 2008: 51)

For Fichte, it is thus impossible to acquire another language and have access to the supersensible objects it designates. By adopting a 'foreign language', one is, according to Fichte, closing oneself off from the supersensible objects it names since one has not shared the sensuous *Bild* that makes up the language.

This is why the name 'mankind' is so different for him in German from the Latin languages, because for the German, 'humanity [*Menschheit*] in general has remained only a sensuous concept [*sinnlicher Begriff*] in his language and has never, as it did with the Romans, become the symbol of a supersensuous idea [*Sinnbilde eines übersinnlichen geworden*]' (ibid. 55). Consequently, while *Menschheit* can either mean the sum of all men, the ontic human species as a whole, or the human potential in men, the German word *Humanität* or the French word *humanité* – both deriving from the Latin *humanitas* – signify solely the *idea* of humanity, humanity as a regulative idea. These Latin-influenced words are thus without a sensuous *Bild*.[5]

The reason this has such an impact on spiritual development (*Bildung*), for Fichte, is that he identifies the spiritual (*Geistigkeit*) with philosophy. As he states, 'when we are speaking of spiritual character [*geistiger bildung*], this should be taken to mean first and foremost philosophy [. . .] For it is philosophy that grasps scientifically [*Wissenschaftlich*] the eternal archetype [*Urbild*] of all spiritual life [*geistigen Lebens*]' (ibid. 61). But if spiritual cultivation is philosophy, it is not just any sort of philosophy. It must reflect the secret idiom of the idiom – the German idiom, the idiom that is essentially philosophical and living. Fichte thus redefines what 'natural' means in terms of a 'natural language'. For him, the opposition of a natural to an artificial language is not between a language that has arisen in an unpremeditated fashion and a constructed premeditated language, but between a 'living' language and a language of 'death'.

Moreover, this language of 'death' need not be a dead language; in fact, for Fichte, ostensibly all languages bar German in his own time were languages of 'death'. German is thus the only 'living' language left, and because of this, the only language *devoid of any possible confusion*. Fichte thus paradoxically *reinstates* the Cartesio-Leibnizian dream of a language without equivocation or confusion, but he finds this dream within a tongue *already* spoken. Fichte thus aligns a natural language with a universal language, and makes this *the* language of philosophy. German philosophy is thus the only philosophy worthy of the name for Fichte. This is so even if 'German philosophy of the present day is not German, but a foreignism [*deutsche Philosophie nicht deutsch, sondern Ausländerei*].' For

> true philosophy, which is complete in itself and has penetrated *beyond appearance* to its very core, proceeds from the one, pure, divine life [*göttlichen Leben*], – from life simply as such [*als Leben schlechtweg*], which is what will remain for all eternity, ever one; but not from this or that particular life. It sees how this life endlessly closes and opens again only in the world of appearance, that only by reason of this law is there a being and a something at all. For this philosophy being arises, whereas the other assumes it as a given. And so this philosophy is *properly* German [*Philosophie recht eigentlich nur deutsch*], that is, original [*ursprünglich*]; and inversely, if someone were a true German [*wahrer Deutscher*], then he would not be able to philosophise in any other way. (Fichte 2008: 87; my emphasis)

German philosophy thus brings itself into being for Fichte as it is essentially concerned with being, or rather, the act of something becoming the being it is. This is why the German is identified with the project of universality and cosmopolitanism. For Fichte, while one can be born French, one can only *become* a (true) German. Observable, brute facts can never thus make one a 'true German'; one has to, instead, follow a certain way of life. For him, this act of becoming German is nothing less than the manifestation of life itself. One is never a German to begin with; it is an act, something to be performed (like the positing of the self). This act of becoming German, for Fichte, is nothing less than the manifestation of life itself, the entity that brings all beings to life. German philosophy is thus opposed to foreign philosophy on the grounds that the latter concerns itself solely with what is already given, with what already exists – sheer materiality. German philosophy, in contrast, is a philosophy of life, derived from nothing less than life itself. It stands opposed not only to foreign philosophy, like the famous French Materialism of the eighteenth century – such as Helvétius' 1758 book *De l'esprit* – but a philosophy of the inert, a philosophy of death. As Fichte states:

> the intrinsic nature of the foreign [*innere Wesen des Auslandes*] – that is to say, non-originality [*Nichtursprünglichkeit*] – is the belief in something

final, fixed, immutably permanent; the belief in a limit [*Grenze*] [. . . it] necessarily believes in death as the first and the last, as the original source [*Ursprüngliche*] of all things – even of life. (Fichte 2008: 86)

In the end then, for Fichte, all true philosophy is a philosophy of life, and because the German idiom is the only 'living language' (*lebendige Sprache*), the German idiom is the only language of philosophy. It is the only idiom that is intrinsically philosophical. As Derrida states, this is why Fichte's *Addresses* 'wants to be both nationalistic, patriotic and cosmopolitan, universalistic. It essentialises Germanity to the point of making it an entity bearing the universal and the philosophical as such' (Derrida 2007a: 312).

If *Addresses to the German Nation* is taken to be one of the founding texts of German nationalism, my claim is that we should recognise this work not as an instance of ethnic nationalism, but as a novel kind of philosophical nationalism, one that presents an understanding of language and national identity in non-empirical terms. Hence, the claim is that although the *Addresses* – like nationalism as a whole – is not entirely or simply philosophical, its nationalism is rigorously comprehensible only on a philosophical basis. The claim that Fichte is implicated within nationalism is thus not advanced as a historical claim within the history of ideas, but as a *methodological* point regarding the non-empirical structure he provides for understanding German nationality as a form of philosophy – if not the bearer of philosophy itself.

## NOTES

1. As the editors of the 2005 *Gesamtausgabe der Bayerischen Akademie der Wissenschaften* (part I, vol. 10) edition of the *Addresses* point out, this claim about a 'dead nature' is a reference to Schelling and his *Naturphilosophie*.
2. The *Addresses* has been translated into French four times: in 1895 by Léon Philippe, in 1923 by Jacques Molitor, in 1952 by Serge Jankélévitch, and lastly, in 1992 by Alain Renaut. The first two translations render *ist unsers Geschlechts* as 'our race [*notre race*]', the third, as mentioned above, leaves out the locution all together, and the last, three years after the fall of the Berlin Wall, translates it as 'our species [*notre espèce*]'. The French reception of Fichte is detailed by Michel Espagne in *Les Transferts culturels franco-allemands* (1999), as well as in the journal *Fichte-Studien: Kosmopolitismus und Nationalidee* (1990).
3. I have used the English translation provided by Mary Anne Perkins, who cites this Fichte passage in her introduction to her and Martin Liebscher's *Nationalism Versus Cosmopolitanism in German Thought and Culture, 1789–1914: Essays on the Emergence of Europe* (2006).
4. Pheng Cheah explores the spectral languages invoked by Fichte in *Spectral Nationality*. For Cheah, Fichte articulates 'a discourse of exorcism aimed at Kant, whose ideas of the cosmopolitan federation and humanity [. . .]' Fichte regards 'as phantoms that need to be concretely grounded or chased away. For Fichte, cosmopolitanism cannot be actual (*wirklich*) or effective unless it becomes a patriotism' (Cheah 2003: 116).

5. David Martyn, in his essay 'Borrowed Fatherland: Nationalism and Language Purism in Fichte's *Addresses to the German Nation*', argues that Fichte remains blind to the borrowed origins of certain German words. 'For example, when Fichte approves of expressing the concept *humanitas* with the word *Menschenfreudlichkeit*, he is clearly under the impression that the latter is not a "borrowing"; he says it is a translation into "genuine true German". But *Menschenfreud*, it turns out, is a loan translation of *philanthropos*. What Fichte sees as a genuinely and truly German concept is really not German but Greek. The error is made possible by the phenomenon of the loan coinage, for it is difficult to imagine how Fichte would have made this mistake if German had, like English or French, adopted *philanthropos* not as a loan coinage but as a foreign word (*philanthropy*). Loan coinages [. . .] look domestic. They are assimilated in such a way that their foreignness, while always potentially discoverable, is easily forgotten or repressed, even by speakers who are well versed in language history' (Martyn 1997: 312).

CHAPTER 5

# Philosophical Rights-of-Way: Tocqueville and the American Philosophical Method

> Although the inhabitants of Europe have for the past three or four hundred years overrun the other parts of the world and are constantly publishing new collections of travels and reports, I am convinced that the only men we know are the Europeans; what is more, it would seem that, judging by the ridiculous prejudices that have not died out even among Men of Letters, very nearly all anyone does under the pompous heading of the study of man is to study the men of his own country [*les hommes de son pays*]. Regardless of how many individuals come and go, it would seem that Philosophy does not travel [*la philosophie ne voyage point*] and each People's Philosophy is ill-suited for another [*celle de chaque peuple est-elle peu propre pour un autre*].
>
> Jean-Jacques Rousseau, 'Discourse on the Origin and Foundation of Inequality Among Men *or* Second Discourse' (Note X, part 8)

In this chapter, I analyse a text that not only claims that 'philosophy travels', but that the philosophy of one people can also quite properly or appropriately *be* the philosophy of another – that travelling is not improper to philosophy – namely, Tocqueville's *Democracy in America* (*De la démocratie en Amérique*). It is a text, moreover, that not only describes a *national* philosophical method, but which uses this method to describe a *national character*. The opening chapter of the second volume published in 1840, entitled 'Of the Philosophical Method of the Americans' (*De la méthode philosophique des Américains*), will in particular be singled out for analysis, since it asserts that the USA, while not occupied by philosophical schools, has an implicit philosophical method due to its democratic social condition, namely, Cartesianism – that none other than Descartes is the Christopher Columbus of this new philosophical continent.

In examining the traffic between France and America that Tocqueville presents, I highlight the *political* role that Tocqueville assigns to Cartesianism in his analysis of America, and the way he uses the Cartesian method to underscore his ideas on American national 'prejudice', and the three dogmas that Tocqueville invokes, including the dogma of 'sovereignty'. Central to this is the opposition of national traditions Tocqueville draws between, on the one hand, a 'popular' (Franco-American) philosophy derived from the social and democratic conditions of modernity, and, on the other hand, an 'elite' (Germanic) philosophy derived from the social and scholastic conditions of aristocracy.

It should also be noted that professional philosophers have not traditionally read Tocqueville as a philosopher, since his observations are often thought to be primarily empirical and socio-political in approach and thus external to philosophy. This is as true in France as it is in the Anglophone world. Pierre Manent, for instance, notes that it has only been since 2002 that Tocqueville has been included in the syllabus for the French *agrégation de philosophie* (this was also the same year that Derrida, notably, discussed Tocqueville for the first time in public, his talk, derived from a conference at Cerisy, being published later in *Rogues*). As Manent pointedly asks, 'What are we to think of this belated promotion of Tocqueville to the rank of philosopher?' (Manent 2006: 108).

Indeed, in the USA, it can be claimed that it is only with Harvey Mansfield's recent introduction to his and Delba Winthrop's translation of Tocqueville's *Democracy in America* (2000) that Tocqueville has been read with significant and rigorous philosophical import. For in his lengthy introduction, Mansfield places Tocqueville's claims not alongside other socio-political observers of America, but alongside such thinkers as Aristotle, Montesquieu and Rousseau. In fact, Mansfield in a later essay notes that Tocqueville's writings are 'often denied the name of philosophy', since 'although he speaks of philosophers, he does not analyse their thoughts but confines himself to describing their *influence*, which he generally denies' (Mansfield 2004: 109). However, Mansfield himself ignores the large influence of Descartes in Tocqueville's work, linking him instead with such thinkers as Rousseau. This chapter thus also outlines what has long been neglected – the pivotal role that Descartes plays in Tocqueville's thought.

## CARTESIANISM ON THE ROAD

The first aporia in Tocqueville's description of this universal method can be noted straight away: Tocqueville speaks of an *American* method. A method, by definition, is a general means or manner of procedure and it deals with generic objects and not singularities. That is to say, a method traditionally involves rules or procedures that a 'subject' should be able to apply on more than one occasion and to a multiplicity of 'objects' external to itself. While a method might be applied on some occasion to only one object, it should not be defined by that one object. In other words, a method must be repeatable, and it must be able to be reapplied to other 'objects' in the same field to be held valid. As Derrida notes in 'La langue et le discours de la méthode', which discusses the history of the idea of method in Parmenides, Descartes and Heidegger:

> there can be no method [or a methodological step: *pas de méthode*] without, necessarily, an advance [*cheminement*], a step [*pas*], progress [*marche*], or an approach [or procedure: *démarche*], that is to say, without a course [*cours*], without a sequel or result [*suite*], without sequence [*séquence*], so many things that also form the structure of any history [*histoire*]. (Derrida 1983: 36; my translation)

What Derrida emphasises in this passage that discusses the very possibility of passage, of progress, of moving from one thing to another, is that a method is only a method when it can be applied in a non-singular fashion, applying itself to a *series* of objects in a recurrent manner. In short, there is no such thing as a method that can only be applied once, or that treats only one singularity – any method must potentially be *re*applied, 'iterability' being built into the very idea of method (*iter* being the Latin for 'again' or 'to repeat').

Tocqueville's analysis of this American *methodos* or *metahodos*, this literal following of the route, this becoming-road of a path – from the Greek *meta* (along, with, after) and *hodos* (path, way, journey) – constitutes what Derrida calls 'a philosophy of the method', one where the method in question is a 'methodologism', a 'procedural technology of thought [*technologie procédurière de la pensée*]'.[1] The vehicle by which Tocqueville will understand philosophy in the USA will thus be found on the road. Derrida drives home his point by declaring that this method constitutes 'the very machinery' of Tocqueville's interpretation of America.[2] It is thus no surprise that *Democracy in America* retraces the footsteps of one of the most famous philosophies of method – Descartes' previously invoked French-language publication *Discourse on Method*.

Tocqueville in fact opens the chapter by professing, or rather – since he intentionally avoids, as we will see, the mode of a professor – acting out his allegiance to Cartesianism. He states:

> I think that in no country in the civilized world is there less interest in philosophy than in the United States [*Je pense qu'il n'y a pas, dans le monde civilisé, de pays où l'on s'occupe moins de philosophie qu'aux États-*

*Unis*]. The Americans have no philosophical school of their own [*Les Américains n'ont point d'école philosophique qui leur soit propre*], and they worry very little about those that divide Europe; they hardly know their names. (Tocqueville 2010: 698)

His opening words, as Derrida notes, thus invoke and *repeat* the Cartesian locution, the *Je pense* made so famous by the *Discourse on Method*. He thus cites without citing, without showing his schooling, without mentioning names, like the Americans he is describing. Tocqueville, in other words, partakes of the very method he is describing. In fact, his very first words not only remind his readers of France and the Cartesian method, but they also straightaway place an emphasis on the self, on the power of the self to decide, to choose, to judge (*Je pense* . . .). In other words, what is at stake but unuttered in the *Je pense* is the sovereign power to determine something for oneself by self- or auto-determination.

But the '*Je*' of '*Je pense*', the Tocquevillian *cogito*, is not introduced, *à la* Descartes, as either an ego that faces the sceptical problem of solipsism, or *à la* Kant, as a formal subject of apperception; instead, it appears to itself, from the beginning, in relation to others. In short, the *Je* of Tocqueville is not a solitary *cogito*; rather, it is a communal *cogito*, indeed, a *cogito* with a national identity. But the nation it is associated with is not portrayed as one amongst others, one among a sample, but as the very model of the philosophical insofar as it is the exemplary source of Cartesianism. That is to say, Tocqueville manages to convey that he belongs to one of the countries *most* occupied by philosophy by comparing it to a country that he judges to be the *least* preoccupied by philosophy.

However, if Tocqueville claims that the philosophical establishment of the USA has yet to be established, it is not because he says it lacks philosophers, as he did in the first volume of *Democracy in America*, but because it lacks a *school* – professional philosophers. It does not have, in other words, what Europe has, a scholastic tradition. It does not have its own philosophical institution, its own philosophical property. Crucially, the logic of *le propre*, the logic of appropriation, is the driving force behind Tocqueville's claim – it is a matter of what is one's own, a matter of property, of propriety, in short, of *proprius*. Moreover, not only does America not have its own school, it is not even occupied – let alone dominated – by the schools of Europe, according to Tocqueville. While the logic of this claim and not its empirical accuracy is what will be examined in this chapter, we might note that its description is to a large degree confirmed by Bruce Kuklick, for as he notes, it was only by the 1830s that German philosophical ideas 'were making *inroads* at the American colleges. Many Germans immigrating to the USA had read German philosophy directly. Additionally, a trickle of American students returned from Germany with Kantian theories, and translations of German work were periodically published' (Kuklick 2003: 64; my emphasis).³

But even though Tocqueville notes the lack of an American (European-style) philosophical school, the schools of Europe are not united for Tocqueville – philosophy is not one. He does not, unlike Pierre Bayle, for instance, speak of an international scene, a republic of letters where intellectuals corresponded with each other from great distances using letters and pamphlets, that is, 'the traditional pathways of communication [or transportation routes: *les voies de communication*]' used between philosophers in the preceding centuries.⁴ Rather, Tocqueville suggests, philosophy is divided, it is splintered between the schools of Europe. The subject of philosophy has been divided by the national curricula, each housing its own approach or set of methods.

However, if America has no (European-style) philosophical foundation or fortification – a building, say, like the University of Berlin from 1810, to house its national philosophy – it does not imply it is completely bereft of philosophy. For as Derrida points out, Tocqueville is not saying that 'philosophy does not occupy and is not occupied with the USA'. Rather, Derrida sees Tocqueville as underlining that philosophy

> occupies the nation at a fundamental level, so that they do not even need to be occupied by it [*la philosophie n'occupe pas, ne s'occupe pas des USA. Elle occupe assez fondamentalement cette nation pour qu'ils n'aient même pas besoin de s'en occuper*].⁵

The inhabitants of the USA, in other words, do not need to take the famed Cartesian step of saying *Je pense* in order to be occupied at the most fundamental level by philosophy, since they live out their Cartesianism *as* an occupation. We might say, they have turned Cartesianism into a *viable* occupation – transformed it from a theoretical stance into a *way* of life. As Tocqueville writes in an earlier, unpublished draft of this section, available in the historical-critical edition:

> A nation can have a philosophy of its own and have no philosophical system *strictly* [*proprement*] speaking [. . .] you can say that the people in general have a philosophy even though no one has yet taken on the task of reducing these common notions to a body of knowledge, of specifying these general ideas spread throughout the crowds and of linking them methodically together in a logical order. (Tocqueville 2010: 706f.; original emphasis)

What is the national philosophy that is followed in the USA without academic support? Unbeknownst to Americans, it is Cartesianism. As Tocqueville states:

If I go still further and, among these various features, look for the principal one and the one that can sum up nearly all the others, I discover that, in most operations of the mind [*je découvre que, dans la plupart des opérations de l'esprit*], each American appeals only to the individual effort of his reason. So America is one of the countries of the world where the precepts of Descartes are least studied and best followed. That should not be a surprise. Americans do not read the works of Descartes, because their social state [*état social*] diverts them from speculative studies, and they follow his maxims because the same social state naturally disposes their mind to adopt them [*ce même état social dispose naturellement leur esprit à les adopter*] [. . .] So the Americans did not need to draw their philosophical method from books, they found it within themselves. (Tocqueville 2010: 699–701)

Americans thus do not need to read or cite Descartes in order to be Cartesians. Note Tocqueville does not claim that their avoidance of reading Descartes – or, indeed, any philosopher – is accidental. They do not pursue speculative studies because their democratic social condition (*état social*) encourages practical applications above theoretical science. The mention of 'speculative studies' in opposition to a 'philosophical method' once again cites Descartes without citing him. For in *Discourse on Method* we find Descartes writing of 'gaining knowledge which would be very useful in life and of discovering a practical philosophy which might replace the speculative philosophy taught in schools' (Descartes 1988a: 47). The logic of the claim by Tocqueville is thus that Americans follow Descartes by following his *own* example. Their method of acquisition is consistent with the method itself. They thus do not need to take the detour of studying the *Discourse on Method* to inherit his method, for they have a more *direct* path to Descartes – they can go *straight* to the method, the method that speaks of *le droit chemin*.

Rather than reading him, they implement or facilitate the rules of the mind, the French *esprit* so clearly and distinctly outlined by Descartes, by means of private judgement. That is to say, they draw opinions from themselves, and not from some external source of authority – for example, the school, including the school of Descartes. They thus follow the Cartesian precept to undertake 'studies within myself' to discover their own, so to speak, inner Cartesianism (ibid. 25). While they are therefore materialistic and anti-speculative according to Tocqueville, Americans make self-scrutiny and introspection, not scholasticism and reading, the sources of Cartesianism in America.

As Tocqueville puts it, the social condition of America makes its inhabitants naturally disposed to Cartesianism. We thus discover a second aporia. The condition that gives rise to Cartesianism operates in the junction between two senses of 'naturalness'. The condition that *naturally* disposes Americans to be

Cartesians is their *society*. The condition has thus come about through artifice, but it is an artifice that henceforth is allied with natural and paternal forces. The claim by Tocqueville therefore joins, on the one hand, the determination of natural found in 'natural language', the 'natural' understood as the historical and the particular, and on the other hand, the natural found in 'natural reason', the 'natural' understood as the ahistorical and the universal. The method is 'natural' in both senses. A *singular* set of historico-socio-economic conditions has thus given rise to a method that is *generalisable*, that appeals to 'the individual effort of his [that is, the "natural" Franco-American Cartesian's] reason [*l'effort individuel de sa raison*]' (Tocqueville 2010: 699). But this historicity is not external to the method or to method as such. Reflecting on the historicity implied by history and the history of method in 'La langue et le discours de la méthode', Derrida states:

> History, it is said, is that which is not repeated; it is the singularity of the event. But no history would be constituted as such without a certain iterability, without iteration, without recurrence, without the possibility of forming a tradition, of giving itself over to, of keeping for itself – of gathering or of accumulating – so many forms of repetition, in the widest sense of this word. [*L'histoire, c'est ce qui ne se répète pas, dit-on, c'est la singularité de l'événement. Mais aucune histoire ne se constituerait comme telle sans une certaine itérabilité, sans itérativité, récurrence, sans la possibilité de former une tradition, de se livrer, de se garder, de se rassembler ou de s'accumuler, autant de formes de répétition, au sens le plus divers de ce mot.*] (Derrida 1983: 36–7; my translation)

In this passage, Derrida conveys that history must maintain repetition. One can therefore only provide a history of the method due to the historicity already in-built into the method. What interests Derrida is the way this 'national-philosophical characterisation' can be compared with Fichte. For if Tocqueville speaks about a national techno-scientific method, Fichte, on the other hand, '[speaks] about a nature or a primordial philosophical essence proper to a people [*propre à un peuple*]'.[6] In other words, if Fichte equated the German nation with the natural 'gift' for the philosophical *as such*, Tocqueville speaks of a method that must be inherited, for:

> to speak of a philosophical method is another thing, it is to speak of a sort of technical historical given, of something that, to belong to a whole assembly of inhabitants or citizens [*pour être propre à un ensemble d'habitants ou de citoyens*], does not really constitute a native character, national in the sense of the native, related to birth or naturalness, or if you prefer, a natural *tekhnē*, a second nature that, besides, guards against

national prejudice. In any event, it is inherited. When Fichte speaks about the essence of German people, he ultimately refers to origins [*originarité*] and thus non-heritage. Here, the method being a *tekhnē*, it is inherited [. . .], anchored by heritage, by a Cartesian-democratic complex which would be constitutive of the USA – and which would distinguish essentially the philosophical method of this country from the English method. It would make American philosophy something more fundamentally continental than Anglo-Saxon.[7]

Tocqueville's method thus does not define for Derrida – unlike Fichte's philosophy, which concerns what is truly proper or naturally originary – what is naturally American or French in terms of what is native or originary to them. Derrida invokes the Greek notion of *tekhnē* to elucidate his point, for *tekhnē* – commonly translated as 'craft' or 'art', or even sometimes 'know-how', but related to the idea of appearing and disclosure – essentially revolves around the concept of *repetition*. As soon as something is repeatable, as soon as it can be detached from its origins, it becomes instrumentalisable, affected by technology. In short, it becomes amenable to a method. Hence, whereas Fichte aims for a purely non-instrumental language, an originary language free from the machinal, from *tekhnē*, from what he calls 'dead repetition', Tocqueville aims for 'a natural *tekhnē*', a *tekhnē* that while natural is not native – something acquired, but practised so long, repeated so often, it seems innate.

While France is thus claimed by Tocqueville to be the 'arch-fatherland' of the Cartesian method, the method being passed on via 'patrimony' or 'heritage [*patrimoine*]', the method is not inborn in the French, nor is it native to them.[8] Instead, it is transmitted or reborn constantly from one people to another from the Renaissance onwards. Indeed, it is destined to travel from one people to another since it is, as a philosophical method, made to travel: it is the 'open road' *par excellence*. On the other hand, if it has travelled to America, it is not through the standard form of transmission of philosophy; it did not, according to Tocqueville, come about through some form of 'academic exchange'.

America has thus expressed itself philosophically for Tocqueville, but it has done so *out-of-school*, out of earshot of the classroom. Accordingly, the philosophical method found amongst the Americans is acquired without formal tuition – the method is not and, as the method of avoiding authority, cannot be learnt or taught. It is pursued and found by one's own intuition, or it is not found at all. Indeed, not only is the method located outside of the precincts of any school, it in fact belongs, Tocqueville claims, to the inhabitants of America as a whole – or as Derrida stresses, *almost* all its inhabitants. Tocqueville states:

> It is easy to see [*Il est facile de voir*], however, that *nearly* all the inhabitants of the United States direct their mind in the same way [*dirigent*

*leur esprit de la même manière*], and conduct them according to the same rules; that is to say, they possess, without ever having taken the trouble to define its rules, a certain philosophical method that is common to all of them. (Tocqueville 2010: 699; my emphasis)

In sum, the inhabitants of the USA have their philosophy even though they do not have professional philosophers. They have a philosophical method – they conduct their mind with a Cartesian *esprit* – simply by means of their social condition, by the fact that they reside in the USA. The very *mœurs* of the nation produce a 'national philosophy'; or rather, they *repeat* a philosophy that came from elsewhere. They are thus 'Cartesian and democratic without effort, without reading, and almost without knowing it [or unwittingly: *quasiment sans le savoir*]'.[9] That is to say, they are almost unconscious of it, almost unconscious of possessing the very philosophy that denies the unconscious as such. The acquirement of the method is thus, in a certain sense, passive – but it is not dependent on race or language, but residence, national ('cultural') residence. Such a 'condition' is to be distinguished, Tocqueville hints in the most subtle fashion, from the intellectual or academic equivalent found, for example, in Germany, where philosophy is guarded, taught and espoused by an elite minority, a privileged few, those situated inside a university. In contrast, in America, at issue is a philosophy *practised en masse* by the people, a philosophy common to all. In other words, it is the difference between what we might call a philosophy fit for aristocratic and for democratic cultures; indeed, an 'aristocratic philosophical nationality' and a 'democratic philosophical nationality'. The Franco-American philosophical method is thus inherently democratic for Tocqueville since it can be practised as a way of life by all. This is in contrast to German scholastic philosophy, which due to its necessary expertise, training and instruction, is inherently aristocratic.

Having examined the role that the idea of method plays in Tocqueville's thought, it is now necessary to consider the politicisation of Cartesianism that Tocqueville develops. For a further aporia in Tocqueville's work is that he uses a thinker (the 'thinker', Descartes) who not only did not write on America, but who is renowned for not writing on politics, in order to discuss a method that Tocqueville claims is indissociable from the rise of democracy. Tocqueville thus takes, so to speak, the road less travelled, and proceeds not via an analysis of the founding fathers of America, or the authors of the *Federalist Papers*, both of whom he mentioned in the first volume, but via a thinker whose method was never meant to settle political matters and whose 'actual references to politics', as James V. Schall notes, are in fact 'scant', and *not* democratic (Schall 1962: 260). As a result, Tocqueville is led to ask, not surprisingly: 'Why did Descartes want to use it only in certain matters, although he made his method applicable to everything, and declare that only philosophical and not political things must be judged by oneself?' (Tocqueville 2010: 704).

Tocqueville's response is to suggest that the method was not in step with the times, that while Descartes' method was democratic, the age in which Descartes lived was aristocratic. Tocqueville thus suggests – in a rather Straussian manner – that Descartes could not, without endangering himself, *publicly* declare that men might judge for themselves in matters political. Descartes was mindful of what had happened to Galileo, and his decision to limit the scope of the method was a development of his decision not to publish *The World* (*Le Monde*) for fear of prosecution. According to Tocqueville, the method could, therefore, only be 'commonly adopted', that is, adopted *by* the community at large, and, indeed, applied *to* the community at large, when 'when men began to become equal and similar to each other [*à s'égaliser et à se ressembler*]' (ibid. 704).

Hence, he not only attributes to Cartesianism a *political* role that is revolutionary – indeed, he invokes the notion of analogous resemblance as a form of *egalité* alongside Cartesianism – he also transforms the Cartesian method into the idea of a political movement, a politico-philosophical *praxis*.

These claims about the political nature of Cartesianism are not advanced in a clearly thematised way by Tocqueville. Nevertheless, they can be seen to be at work in his various characterisations of American democracy. One can consider, for example, his claim about what he calls the democratic 'dogma of the equality of minds [or the equality of intellects: *le dogme de l'égalité des intelligences*]' – the belief that all men are *equal* when it comes to reasoning – to be an interpretation of the first sentence of *Discourse on Method* (ibid. 1146). For it is here that Descartes states that intellect is evenly distributed among all men, and hence that people err not due to lack of intellect, but due to lack of method, or the pursuit of the wrong method:

> good sense is the best distributed thing in the world [*Le bon sens est la chose du monde la mieux partagée*] [. . . hence] what we *properly* call 'good sense' or 'reason' – is *naturally* equal in all men, and consequently that the diversity of our opinions does not arise because some of us are more reasonable than others but solely because we direct our thoughts along different *paths* [*voies*]. (Descartes 1988a: 20; my emphasis)

The democratic method described by Tocqueville thus has two closely related aspects. First, it is not aristocratic; it is contrasted with systems or bodies of knowledge held by an *elite* cohort of intellects. This, we might note, is the usual form of the status of philosophy – Plato's philosopher kings, for instance, whose legitimisation for ruling is that they have access to non-empirical knowledge due to a unique kind of *schooling* undesired and unattainable by the rest of society (the 'masses'). Second, it is also contrasted with philosophy that can belong to a school of (schooled) thought: a system, a doctrine. The second aspect is foregrounded by Derrida who emphasises the distinction in Tocqueville 'between a scholarly philosophy and a philosophy which does not need a school, in the sense of the system, the doctrines, the scholasticism'.[10]

The method to be found in America is thus contrasted with the kind of doctrinal systematicity associated with an elite school, and hence also with elite schooling. Specifically, as Derrida hints in his use of the German word *Lehre* (teachings or doctrines) in this session,[11] with the (German) idea of *universitas*, the university 'system' of Kantian philosophy both dependent and reflective on the *faculties* that make philosophy possible. In other words, what is at stake is the Kantian depiction of the philosopher as 'purely a teacher of reason' or a teacher of pure reason (*reiner Vernunftlehrer*) – the teacher being the very archetype (*Urbild*) or ideal model of the philosopher. The Kantian border is thus breached; the topological figure Kant proposes for the teacher of pure reason is replaced by a figure outside of the school (Kant 2001: 64). Instead of Kant the university professor, we have Descartes the wanderer and sojourner, the young Descartes who wrote autobiographically about *leaving* rather than staying in the Jesuit college of La Flèche in Anjou, 'one of the most famous schools in Europe' as Descartes states, so as to discover true and certain knowledge (Descartes 1988a: 22).

The *esprit* that the inhabitants of the USA possess is thus subtly but unmistakably contrasted by Tocqueville with the Germanic system, the idea of philosophy *as* a system, that is, the *professional* philosophy of Kant or of the Kantian school. Most of the inhabitants of America thus have a philosophical method in common, but they have it without the need to posit it, without the need of turning it into a *thesis*. Its exposition does not take the form of a thetic presentation – it is not advanced by a position relating to *Setzung* or *Stellung*. The nationalistic framework of Tocqueville's claims can be measured by recalling Destutt de Tracy's 1802 *De la Métaphysique de Kant*, which had stressed the Cartesian 'method as *the* distinguishing characteristic of French [*le propre de la France*] as opposed to German philosophy, whose distinctive feature was *system*' (Azouvi 1998: 495, quoting Destutt de Tracy's term 'system').

De Tracy, in other words, appropriates the Cartesian method as something distinctly, or properly, French. It is something that is *owned* by them. Indeed, in the years following de Tracy, specifically, in the period 1815–40, and thanks to such figures as François Guizot and Victor Cousin, Descartes came to represent France to such a degree that he was identified with the nation itself, that is, he was in fact said to *be* France: the embodiment of France as such. In this regard it is worth stressing that Tocqueville's 'philosophical education' would have been steeped in this national lesson. Indeed, only two years before sailing to America, in 1828–9, he attended Guizot's lectures at the Sorbonne, and specifically, a course on the history of French civilization in 1828–9. Guizot had spoken about the civilised *bon sens* of the French in terms of the Cartesian rational genius in these lectures:

> Much has been said, particularly in recent years, about common sense [*bon sens*] as a distinctive feature of the French genius. This is true, but it is not practical common sense [*un bon sens purement pratique*] [. . .] This common sense is reason [*Ce bon sens, c'est la raison*]: the French spirit is at once rational and reasonable [*l'esprit français est à la fois rationnel et raisonnable*]. Therefore, gentleman, France possesses this honour: its civilization reproduces more faithfully than any other [. . .] the fundamental task of civilization. It is the most complete, the truest, the most civilized, so to speak. (Guizot, cited by Azouvi 1998: 503)

Tocqueville's choice of philosopher when discussing a national philosophical method in America is thus crucial, since it not only underscores that the method in question is a Cartesian method, but because the choice claims Descartes for America at a time when Descartes was being claimed in France not simply as one French philosopher among others, but as the embodiment of the national genius of France. Not that this went uncontested. Heinrich Heine, for instance, introducing 'German philosophy' to France in 1835 in his book *Religion and Philosophy in Germany*, claimed that while Descartes himself was French, his philosophy – that is, his method – was not. Crucially, Heine does not say this to counter the idea of a 'national philosophy', to counter the idea that one can speak meaningfully of the national character of philosophy, but to promote the idea that Cartesianism – or indeed, philosophy as such – was *foreign* to France. As he puts it:

> Réne Descartes is a Frenchman, and to great France belongs the fame of the initiative. But great France, the noisy, stirring, talkative land of the French, has never been a fitting abode for philosophy, which will perhaps never flourish on French soil. So assuredly felt René Descartes, who betook himself to Holland, to the peaceful, silent land of track-boats and Dutchmen. (Heine 1959: 60)

Heine's counterclaims to the, so to speak, Frenchification of Descartes, can therefore be seen as a response to Guizot, with Tocqueville in turn backing up his former teacher against German denunciators by declaring that Descartes was the embodiment not only of France, but of the American philosophical method as well, indeed of America itself. Moreover, it should be noted that Descartes during this period was not, as François Azouvi observes, claimed by a single group to be France, but equally by competing and rival French groups, for example, counterrevolutionary and 'antirational' figures in neo-Catholicism like Bonald and Lamennais; philosophical schools like the Saint-Simonians, who were led by Auguste Comte; and so-called *doctrinaire* liberals who wished to downplay the role of Cartesianism in the events of 1789. They all wanted Descartes for (their) France. Descartes thus came to exemplify, in the various strands of this emphatically nationalistic setting, a philosophy orientated around both the individual and the nation, a philosophy that was at once a philosophy of the individual and a national philosophy. The *Discourse on Method* was interpreted, in other words, as nothing less than the autobiography of France. While individuals in France therefore disputed what the heritage of Cartesianism meant, few disagreed on its national heritage. Descartes was *French*.

## THE BIRTH OF PREJUDICE AND THE PREJUDICE OF BIRTH

To this point, the focus has been on the nationalisation of the method that occurs in Tocqueville's work, as well as his mentors. However, it is also important to recognise that Tocqueville relates the method intrinsically to the national as such, that this essentially exportable French export – the Cartesian method – not only is not free of French national characteristics, but is compatible with the retaining or perhaps even the cultivation of certain national characteristics on the new terrain:

> To escape from the spirit of system [*Échapper à l'esprit de système*], from the yoke of habits, from the maxims of family, from the opinion of class, and, to a certain point, from the prejudices of nation, to take tradition only as information, and present facts only as a useful study for doing otherwise and better; to seek by yourself alone the reason for things, to strive toward the result without allowing yourself to be caught up in the means, and to aim for substance beyond form [*viser au fond à travers la forme*]: such are the principal features that characterize what I will call the philosophical method of the Americans. (Tocqueville 2010: 699)

The philosophical method of the Americans thus escapes the spirit of the system, rules of conduct emanating from the family, and the class-based – but only to some degree – prejudices which are or remain national. Tocqueville, in other words, qualifies his remark about national prejudices in a way he does not do with respect to class opinions and family maxims – America escapes *some* national prejudices, but it is *not* completely a-national, it is not completely devoid of national prejudices. This is crucial to note, for Tocqueville is often thought to have *downplayed* the role of the national in his analysis of America.

Eric Kaufmann, for instance, in his *The Rise of Anglo-America*, claims that Tocqueville saw the United States of America 'as a cosmopolitan civilization based on eighteenth-century liberalism' (Kaufmann 2004: 11). Kaufmann cites from a letter Tocqueville wrote to his friend Ernest de Chabrol whilst still travelling in America in 1831 – though he misattributes it to *Democracy in America* – accordingly, to prove this:

> Imagine, my dear friend, if you can, a society formed of all nations of the world [. . .] people [*gens*] having different languages, beliefs and opinions: in a word, a society without roots, without memories [*sans souvenirs*], *without prejudices*, without routines, without common ideas, *without a national character*, yet a hundred times happier than our own. (Tocqueville, cited by Kaufmann 2004: 11; my emphasis)

Kaufmann thus places Tocqueville at the head a tradition which thinks that Americans have no national character and are without national prejudice – the belief, in other words, that Americans have managed to create a truly cosmopolitical society devoid of nationality. I want to stress, in contrast, that by the time he writes *Democracy in America* Tocqueville does *not* exempt America from possessing national prejudices. Indeed, what I hope to show in this section is that the Cartesian watchword 'prejudice' is crucial to his reading of America – that Tocqueville changes his mind about the role of national prejudices on returning to France.

To understand this, one first needs to know that the gesture of *removing* prejudices is, as Derrida points out, a Cartesian one, not only because the Cartesian method 'casts doubt on prejudices' but because the very first prejudices it tries to remove – as described in the opening chapter of *Discourse on Method* – are 'natural and native prejudices', and thus to some extent, 'prejudices of childhood'.[12] It was these prejudices from childhood – above all, those taught at *school* – that, according to Descartes, misled the natural light of reason, taking it down the wrong path. While the topic of prejudice preoccupies the first section of *Discourse on Method*, the Cartesian principle about prejudice was explicitly formulated some years later, in section 71 of his 1644 *Principles of Philosophy*, since its very title is in fact the claim that 'The chief cause of error arises from the preconceived opinions of childhood'. It thus declares that:

> right from our infancy our mind was swamped with a thousand such preconceived opinions; and in later childhood, forgetting that they were adopted without sufficient examination, it regarded them as known by the senses or implanted by *nature*, and accepted them as utterly true and evident. (Descartes 1988c: 185–6; my emphasis)

The Cartesian method is thus concerned with one's deepest and earliest prejudices, those engendered by the territory where one was either born, grew up or schooled. In other words, those prejudices associated with birth – prejudices, in fact, both *about* birth (concerning your 'belonging by birth to a people, a nation') and prejudices which are given birth *to* in one's motherland or mother language ('German prejudices', 'French prejudices', etc.). Prejudices which disguise themselves as natural – 'implanted by nature', as Descartes states. Indeed, this is one of the reasons why Descartes recommends *travelling* in his *Discourse on Method*, and learning 'something of the customs [*mœurs*] of various peoples'. For travelling enables us to 'judge our own [customs] more soundly and not think that everything contrary to our own is ridiculous and irrational [*contre raison*], as those who have seen nothing of the world ordinarily do' (Descartes 1988a: 23). But the theme of one's birthplace resounds in other ways in Descartes' work. For, as Derrida puts it in an earlier seminar session from 1981–2 on 'La langue et le discours de la méthode', one of the most important aims of Descartes is 'to find [*retrouver*] a childhood or an origin without paternity, to think and invent all by oneself'.[13] In short, the Cartesian task is to find one's 'way' *without* paternal guidance – it is to raise oneself anew by reinventing oneself as a being without parentage, without schooling, without genealogy.

This logic of the child without parents resonates throughout *Democracy in America*, especially in the first volume. Indeed, in the second chapter of the first volume, the figure of the child and the problem of prejudice are once more to the fore. The chapter is entitled the 'Of the Point of Departure and Its Importance for the Future of the Anglo-Americans'. It opens like this:

> A man is newly born; his first years pass obscurely amid the pleasures or occupations of childhood. He grows up; manhood begins; finally the doors of the world open to receive him; he enters into contact with his fellow men [*contact avec ses semblables*]. Then, for the first time, you study him and think that the seeds of the vices and virtues of his mature years can be seen developing in him. If I am not mistaken, that is a great error. Go back to the beginning; examine the child even in the arms of his mother, see the exterior world reflected for the first time in the still dark mirror of his intellect; contemplate the first examples that catch his eye; listen to the first words that awaken his slumbering powers of thought [*les premières paroles qui éveillent chez lui les puissances endormies de la pensée*]; finally, witness the first struggles that he has to sustain. And only then will you understand the origins of the prejudices, the habits, and the passions that are going to dominate his life. The whole man is there, so to speak, in the infant swaddled in his cradle. (Tocqueville 2010: 45–6)

The theme of birth is thus central. The influence of infancy is not something that comes to an end upon maturity, but something that extends throughout one's life – birth is therefore political through and through, since it is the origin of a man's later *prejudices* and facility of thought. The concept of influence is, accordingly, broadened to include all experience, including the first words we hear from our mother – our mother language – and the first sights we see as infants. Moreover, Tocqueville associates the child's early exposure to prejudice explicitly with the figure of the mother, not the parent figure as such. Maternal influence is often ignored, Tocqueville suggests, in favour of *masculine* influence. We study man from 'manhood', not in his 'mother's arms', meaning we miss our earliest and most fundamental influences – the first words which *awaken* our potential reason and so our capacity to reason, to become beings that can say *Je pense*. We must be more vigilant, Tocqueville warns – we must recognise that the rational imperative of wakefulness is brought about by the same figure who unknowingly nurtures our first prejudices. We are prejudiced as to the origin of our prejudices, for our first prejudice, the mother of all prejudices, is in fact *about* our mother.

Tocqueville then extends his point to embrace nations as well. Nations are not invented or discovered, but *grow* like men; they all start as infants and mature over time. Tocqueville, in other words, describes the emergence of nation in terms of birth, following the meaning of the word 'nation' – *nasci* (to be born):

> Something similar happens among nations. Peoples always feel the effects of origin [*Les peuples se ressentent toujours de leur origine*]. The circumstances that accompanied their birth and were useful to their development influence all the rest of their course. If it were possible for us to go back to the elements of societies and examine the first memorials of their history [*histoire*], I am certain that we would be able to discover there the first cause of the *prejudices*, habits, dominant passions, of all that ultimately composes what is called the national character. (Tocqueville 2010: 46; my emphasis)

Nations are thus not only born, their origin plays a part in their future development; to understand a nation is partly to understand the *origins of its prejudices*. The only nation where we can witness this infant-like state on a national level is, for Tocqueville, the USA:

> America is the only country where we have been able to witness the natural and tranquil development of a society and where it has been possible to clarify the influence that the point of departure exercised on the future of States. At the time when European peoples descended upon

the shores of the New World, the features of their national character were already well fixed [*les traits de leur caractère national étaient déjà bien arrêtés*]; each of them had a distinct physiognomy. And since they had already reached the level of civilization that leads men to self-study, they have handed down to us a faithful picture of their opinions, mores, and laws. (Tocqueville 2010: 47–8)

What he calls the Anglo-Americans thus did not arrive on the shores of America without some shared origin – without some shared prejudices – which played a crucial role in their growth and expansion. Moreover, the figure of the mother in relation to America is particularly significant, for as Laura Janara observes, Tocqueville associated aristocracies with motherhood, but republics with fatherhood (Janara 2002: 12). The 'mother country [*mère patrie*]' of America is accordingly England, and the unspoken father, the implicit *patrie* – France (Tocqueville 2010: 50). Moreover, for Tocqueville, 'the novel spectacle of a thoroughly homogeneous society', with equal origins in Puritanism, in a democratic political culture, in the middle classes, and in the use of English language, gave the Anglo-Americans a singular historical experience to draw from in order for democracy to thrive (ibid. 59; my emphasis). The prejudices of the American national character are thus still to some extent transparent and widespread for Tocqueville, even centuries after the Anglo-Americans landed, since they can be traced back to a common origin. In other words, he contends we have all witnessed the birth of America – we can all trace its historical lineage, and obtain, so to speak, its birth certificate. We thus know its origins in ways we cannot with regard to other nations. We can therefore discern that the prejudices of the residents of the USA as a whole originated in the prejudices of its first settlers: the English.

In the above discussion, the role of the method and its relation to national prejudice was analysed. It is important, however, to also examine the relation of the method to the idea of family, and the way Tocqueville contrasts the 'natural' bond of family to the 'artificial' bond of society. For the fact that the growth of the nation was described as 'natural' in Tocqueville's depiction of infant-like nations is also telling. For in the chapter entitled 'Influence of Democracy on the Family' from the second volume, we discover an intimate connection between the natural and the democratic. Tocqueville states that 'In America, the family, taking this word in its Roman and aristocratic sense, does not exist' (ibid. 1032). While there is such a thing as the family in America, it does not resemble the Roman *familia* – it is not run by the *pater familias*, the traditional male head of the family and estate owner. This is the aristocratic model which passes itself on by means of *primogeniture*. In this model, 'the father is therefore not only the political head of the family; he is the organ of traditions, the interpreter of customs, the arbiter of mores' (ibid. 1036). He is the founder, the ruler and the law – the basis of family maxims and tradition. However,

> When the social state becomes democratic, and men adopt as general principle that it is good and legitimate to judge everything for yourself while taking ancient beliefs as information and not as a rule, the power of opinion exercised by the father over the sons, as well as his legal power, becomes less great. (Tocqueville 2010: 1036)

In other words, Cartesianism also revolutionises the family, insofar as the *general* Cartesian principle described – it is not named – is in fact the very same method Tocqueville had outlined earlier, the method that encourages one to judge for oneself and to treat tradition merely as a source of information about the past rather than as a source of authority.

The effect of this democratisation of the family is that the *legal* part of authority vanishes and is replaced by 'familial intimacy [. . . so that] it seems that the natural bond tightens, while the social bond loosens' (ibid. 1037). The democratic family persists not through the dominance of law, the juridical notion of *pater familias*, but through affection. If aristocratic social conditions thus made all relations, including familial relations, based on social (non-natural) bonds of *nomos*, democratic social conditions replace these with *natural* bonds – democracy thus naturalises what aristocracy conventionalises. However, the increasing power of natural bonds and the decreasing power of social bonds also has repercussions for society at large, since if 'The law can tie two citizens very closely together', like the vassal and the lord, it also means that if that law is

> abolished, they separate [and again become strangers]. There was nothing tighter than the knot that joined the vassal to the lord in the feudal world. Now these two men no longer know each other. The fear, the recognition and the love that formerly bound them have disappeared. You do not find a trace of them. (Tocqueville 2010: 1039)

Tocqueville thus concludes that 'Democracy loosens social bonds, but it tightens natural bonds. It brings family members closer together at the same time that it separates citizens' (ibid. 1040).

Democracy thus naturalises the family while at the same time weakening traditional customary relationships. But Tocqueville does not suggest that social bonds outside of the family in democracy will henceforth come to resemble natural bonds; he does not, in other words, invoke the notion of *fraternité*, of world brotherhood, the universalistic bonds of (spiritual) kinship. He thus avoids the French Revolutionary path *and* the Kantian Cosmopolitan path.

Indeed, both Cheryl B. Welch and Francesco M. De Sanctis have highlighted that Tocqueville avoided using the word *fraternité*, and that 'compared to equality and liberty, Tocqueville does not appear to be directly interested in the third principle of the Revolution. Fraternity is not an explicit theme in *Democracy in America*' (De Sanctis 1992: 114). However, the issue of national prejudice is further complicated in relation to the family since Tocqueville also speaks of a 'love of country [or patriotic attachment: *un amour de la patrie*]' in a chapter from the first volume entitled 'Of Public Spirit [*De l'esprit public*] of the United States' (Tocqueville 2010: 384). Issues related to the father figure *par excellence* – the *patrie* – will thus now be considered, with a focus on the tension between the different forms of patriotism that Tocqueville describes. For Tocqueville claims that there are two distinct kinds of attachment. There is the traditional form which is based 'in the unthinking [*irréfléchi*], disinterested and indefinable sentiment that binds the heart of the man to the places where the man was born'. This is based on 'instinct', memories of the past, attachment to soil, 'religious zeal' and the father figure, and is associated with monarchies. And there is a more modern form, which is 'more rational', 'less ardent perhaps', based on laws and civic rights, which 'arises from enlightenment [*naît des lumières*]', and 'ends up merging [*se confondre*], in a way, with personal interest' (ibid. 384–5).

Tocqueville states that because the inhabitants of the USA 'arrived yesterday on the soil that they occupy [. . .] the instinct for native land can hardly exist'; however, he notes, they do have an *interest* in the affairs of their 'town [*commune*]', 'district [*canton*]' and 'State', since they take an active part in the (regional) government of their society. In fact, using the verb *se confondre*, Tocqueville suggests that their patriotism would not be merely intermingled with that of their personal interest, but that it would be *indistinguishable* from their personal interest. The inhabitants of the USA thus do not possess an instinctive patriotism for their fatherland (*patrie*) nor do they possess a rational and reflective patriotism for the USA as a whole. Their affective attachment, one built on the rational model of the 'social contract' advocated by Rousseau, is localised, limited to their own State, not the Union as such.

However, Tocqueville also names a third kind of patriotism, a bastard formed from the two, which appears in periods of transition from aristocracies to democracies, and which he thinks is lamentable. He gives no name to it, and he states that the main problem with it is that it is not attached to the fatherland (*patrie*) by either traditional *or* modern forms of attachment. It can no more return to the attachment associated with the father figure, because 'peoples do not return to the sentiments of their youth any more than men to the innocent tastes of early years' (ibid. 386). But neither has this third kind of patriotism progressed yet to being a form of attachment based on law and civic rights; it thus allows men to 'escape prejudices [*échappent aux préjugés*] without recognizing the empire of reason' (ibid. 386; my emphasis). What this suggests, however, is that the modern form of patriotism, civic or constitutional patriotism, the kind which is attached to a township or State is *also* without prejudice, that it has, even more surely than the hybrid type, escaped prejudices, since it embodies the empire of reason.

On the other hand, and in tension with this, an earlier section, one dealing with the federal constitution of the USA, states that 'the affections and prejudices of the people are in the bosom of the States [not the Union]'. That while the 'sovereignty of the Union is a work of art [*l'œuvre de l'art*]', the 'sovereignty of the states is natural; it exists by itself, without effort, like the authority of the father of a family', so that 'The sovereignty of the States rests on memories, on habits, on local *prejudices*, on the egoism of province and of family; in a word, on all the things that make the instinct for native land so powerful in the heart of man' (ibid. 269–70; my emphasis).

The patriotic attachment to a given State on this model – *contra* what Tocqueville outlines later when he discusses 'the public spirit' – is instinctive, based on the father figure and bound up with prejudice, and the attachment to the Union resembles more closely the rational form of patriotism associated with republics insofar as it is constructed by means of human artifice, like a work of art (*l'œuvre de l'art*). But this more rational form of patriotism is *not* entirely removed from the instinctive form, for Tocqueville also admits that:

> the public spirit of the union is itself only a summary [*résumé*: Goldhammer in his alternative translation renders this as 'concentrated form'] of the provincial patriotism. Each citizen of the United States transfers, so to speak, the interest inspired in him by his small republic [*sa petite république*] to the love of the common native land [*l'amour de la patrie commune*]. (Tocqueville 2010: 261)

Attachment to the common or shared fatherland – the USA – thus exists *insofar* as instinctive attachments to individual States exist. This more rational form of prejudice is thus not as totally devoid of national prejudices as it may at first appear to be. The account here is thus in accord with the suggestion that the philosophical practice of American people, their method, has escaped some – but not all – national prejudices.

The starkest prejudices which Tocqueville names are those connected with race. He warns in the last chapter of the first volume of *Democracy in America* that Americans, '*after* abolishing slavery, [. . .] still have to destroy three prejudices much more elusive and more tenacious than slavery: the prejudice of the master, the prejudice of race, and finally the prejudice of colour' (ibid. 552; translation modified). The end of slavery is thus not the end of prejudice; it is only the beginning of a conflict with more powerful and formidable prejudices.

Moreover, in the second volume of *Democracy in America*, in a chapter entitled 'Why Great Revolutions Will Become Rare', Tocqueville warns:

> I do not believe that it is as easy as you imagine to uproot the prejudices of a democratic people; to change its beliefs; to substitute new religious, philosophical, political and moral principles for those that were once established; in a word, to make great and frequent intellectual revolutions. (Tocqueville 2010: 1143)

While the prejudices of America are thus open for all to see, they are not as a consequence any easier to remove; in fact, due to the fact that their origins are democratic, *they are more difficult*. One of the reasons for this difficulty is due to the aforementioned Cartesian (democratic) principle of resistance to intellectual authority:

> When conditions are almost the same, one man does not easily allow himself to be persuaded by another. Since all see each other very close up, since together they have learned the same things and lead the same life, they are not naturally disposed to take one among them as a guide and to follow him blindly; you hardly believe your fellow [*semblable*] or your equal on his word. It is not only confidence in the enlightenment of certain individuals [*les lumières de certains individus*] that becomes weak among democratic nations [. . .] [but] the general idea of the intellectual superiority that any man can gain over all the others does not take long to grow dim [*s'obscurcir*]. (Tocqueville 2010: 1146)

Tocqueville thus believes that national prejudices will be more difficult to overcome in democracies since men will cease to be as influenced by public intellectuals as they had been in previous aristocratic times – as they were in the Enlightenment with the *philosophes*, for example. The achievements of the Enlightenment will therefore be at risk, all too likely in a democracy, Tocqueville warns, to be covered over and forgotten about. In short, it risks leaving men, once again, in the dark, like the prisoners in Plato's cave. Tocqueville's warning can thus be read as an interpretation of Descartes' claim that though men err due to lack of method and not intellect, 'a majority vote is worthless as a proof of truths that are at all difficult to discover; for a single man is much more likely to hit upon them than a group of people' (Descartes 1988a: 28). This reveals the paradox that is at the heart of Tocqueville's analysis of the American national character. Americans live out a method that *removes* national prejudices, but insofar as this method is itself inherently democratic, and hence internally related to the dogma of the equality of the intellect, it also *shields* and even *cultivates* national prejudices. In other words, the method casts doubt on prejudices, but at the same time, it paradoxically undermines the power of the group to undermine national prejudices, above all those deep-rooted prejudices promulgated – and disseminated – via public opinion.

The tyranny of the majority is thus inseparable from the formation and maintenance of national prejudice in America; the stronger the majority, the more virulent national prejudice can be, and the less chance an individual can successfully critique it. The problem that Tocqueville defines, in other words, is that the method is *both* a nullifier and a creator of national prejudices. The routes of national prejudice therefore spread as the method becomes ever more widespread in society. While the origins of the method thus originate in a small band of German and French intellectuals, the conditions which make the method prosper – democracy – prevent the method from being guided by other American intellectuals later. Tocqueville's analysis of the American philosophical method therefore reveals the uneasy relationship democracy has with the establishment of national prejudices.

This anxiety can be seen at play in Tocqueville's opening chapter, when he states:

> I admit that in America I saw more than America; I sought there an image of democracy itself, its tendencies, its character, its prejudices, its passions; I wanted to know democracy, if only to know at least what we must hope or fear from it. (Tocqueville 2010: 28)

The prejudices of America therefore become the prejudices of democracy, they are at the same time democratic prejudices *and* national prejudices, or rather, it becomes increasingly difficult to tell one from the other. This same uncertainty is also found in Derrida's engagement with Tocqueville in *Rogues* when Derrida states that he will be constantly turning from dealing with 'democracy *in* America' to 'democracy *and* America' (Derrida 2005d: 14). The problem is perhaps no more clearly visible than in the title of Tocqueville's book, *De la démocratie en Amérique*, which some have thought should be translated – due to the use of the particle *de* – as *Concerning Democracy in America*, with the emphasis on democracy rather than America (Pierson 1996: 3).

On the other hand, as we have seen, the relationship between democracy and the national (the *patrie*) is far from being straightforward in *Democracy in America*. The nation is thus weakened (in a certain way) by the very thing that makes it such a desirable place to live. As Tocqueville puts it in his introduction

> The nation taken as a body will be less brilliant, less glorious, less strong perhaps; but the majority of citizens there will enjoy a more prosperous

> lot, and the people will appear untroubled, not because they despair of being better, but because they know they are well-off. (Tocqueville 2010: 21)

Derrida – no doubt relying on the fact that the word *gloria* was used in biblical writing to translate several Hebrew words which had a sense of 'brightness', 'splendour', 'magnificence' and '*majesty*' – interprets Tocqueville to mean that:

> in a democracy the national principle is less strong, that there is between the democratic structure of a society and the force of its national cohesion a kind of inverse relationship. That the progress of democracy – and equality, the great principle of American democracy – comes at the detriment to the force or brilliance of nationality [*l'éclat de la nationalité*].[14]

Indeed, Tocqueville explicitly associates glory with the nation some chapters later when discussing American patriotism. Tocqueville states that 'by defending the Union' the American patriot

> defends the growing prosperity of his district, the right to direct its affairs, and the hope of winning acceptance there for the plans for improvement that are to enrich him himself: all things that ordinarily touch men more than the general interests of the country and the glory of the nation [*la gloire de la nation*]. (Tocqueville 2010: 261; my emphasis)

Democratic *self-interest* thus comes at a detriment to the glorifying of the nation. The only time an American 'glories in the glory of his nation [*la gloire de la nation*]' is when he 'believes that he recognizes his *own* work, and he rises with them; he rejoices in the general prosperity that benefits *him*' (ibid. 160; my emphasis).

Moreover, the word *éclat* appealed to by Derrida (*l'éclat de la nationalité*) not only emphasises the onto-theological language of luminosity and radiance that shines forth in Tocqueville's use of the word *brillante*, but it also underscores the forceful violence that is at stake in any national principle, since the word *éclat* can also be used, more literally, to describe the shrapnel or splinters of grenades, since the word derives from the French *éclater* ('to burst out'). The brilliance of nationality can thus act both as a buttress to the national community and as a weapon. Democracy – which is too easily read as supporting agitation and revolutionary violence, according to Tocqueville – thus weakens or impairs, rather than promotes the idea of national glory. Indeed, as we will see in the next section, due to the social conditions of democracy, people in conditions of democracy, according to Tocqueville, recognise each other as fellows (*semblables*) whatever their national background – democracy thus undermines nationalism by reducing the political significance of national community. It hence sidesteps or bypasses interest in national differences. This is what scholars on Tocqueville (such as Cheryl B. Welch and Françoise Mélonio) have emphasised when they have discussed the issue of nationalism in Tocqueville. In doing so, however, they have also ignored the fact that Tocqueville outlines the democratic method in national terms, that he claims it is properly or foremostly *French* since the method appeared *first* in France before it radiated outwards, even if the first 'democratic' colonists of the USA were English pilgrims.

Here we might draw attention – in the wake of Tocqueville scholars who have debated the relationship of the first volume of *Democracy in America* to the second – to the fact that the second volume, unlike the first, is orientated around the French origins of the USA; its 'point of departure' can thus be contrasted with the second chapter of the first volume, which begins with an analysis of what it calls 'Anglo-Americans'. The emphasis on the *English* origins of the USA in the first volume – the pilgrims and Puritans – is thus quietly downplayed in favour of its French origins by the time of the second volume. As Derrida notes, Tocqueville describes the inhabitants of the USA not so much as 'Anglo-Saxons' in the second volume as 'Franco-Saxons'.[15]

## FROM DESCARTES TO THE ENLIGHTENMENT

Having examined the nature of prejudice in the previous section in relation to the national, the familial and the racial, it is now necessary to consider the political role of dogma that Tocqueville describes. For Tocqueville's language of luminosity is even more important than it might first appear. As he describes it, one of the principal characteristics of the American philosophical method is 'to aim for substance beyond form [*viser au fond à travers la forme*]' (Tocqueville 2010: 699). Arthur Goldhammer, in his translation of *Democracy in America*, has perhaps translated this more accurately as 'to aim beyond form at substance', highlighting that the form is to be *bypassed* or at least passed without incident (Tocqueville 2004: 483). As Harvey Mansfield and Delba Winthrop render it in their translation, Americans aim 'to see through the form to the foundation' (Tocqueville 2000: 403). Forms are thus understood as *obstacles* in America, they do not facilitate knowledge or understanding – they block it. As Tocqueville puts it, the American philosophical method means that they 'scorn forms, which they consider as useless and inconvenient veils [*voiles*] placed between them and the truth' (Tocqueville 2010: 701).

Tocqueville reprises his discussion of forms in his chapter 'How, in the United States, Religion Knows How to Make Use of Democratic Instincts'.

He states there:

> I have shown, in relation to the philosophical method of the Americans, that nothing revolts the human mind more in times of equality than the idea of submitting to forms. Men who live during these times endure representations impatiently; symbols seem to them puerile artifices that you use to veil or keep from their eyes truths that it would be more natural to show them entirely naked and in full light of day [*plus naturel de leur montrer toutes nues et au grand jour*]. (Tocqueville 2010: 750)

Forms are thus associated with *artifice*, with human constructs rather than nature. Nature does not veil truths nor, indeed, does she love to hide – as was thought in previous aristocratic times – man is the being that veils things. Truths are therefore 'naturally' associated with light in democracies; for they are plain for all to *see*. But Tocqueville at this point declares that he himself believes 'in the necessity of forms; I know that they fix the human mind in the contemplation of abstract truths, and forms, by helping the mind to grasp those truths firmly, make it embrace them with fervor' (ibid. 750).

Tocqueville thus explicitly links 'forms' with a *type* or kind of truth, namely, those belonging to the abstract realm, the realm of the intelligible rather than the sensible. In other words, he recalls the philosophical connection between the concept of form and the concept of *eidos* – a term that derives from the term *eido*, which means 'to see' – the sensible figure that comes to mean, from Plato onwards, the figure that is non-sensible, the figure that is no longer apparent to the physical eye, but only apparent to the mind. The American philosophical method thus resists the philosophical lure of the *eidos*, the realm of the intelligible and the non-sensible. It therefore not only rejects the transcendent modality of the platonic forms (*eide*), it also retreats from a nexus of concepts that are among the most important to forms of idealism.

The American philosophical method is thus naturalistic, concerned primarily with practical and empirical methods for acquiring knowledge. As Tocqueville puts it in chapter entitled 'Why the Americans Are More Attached to the Application of the Sciences than to Theory':

> Equality develops in every man the desire to judge everything by himself; it gives him, in everything, the taste for the tangible and the real, scorn for traditions and *forms* [. . .] Those who cultivate the sciences among democratic peoples are always afraid of being lost in utopias [that is to say, visionary, yet meaningless, speculation: *se perdre dans les utopies*]. They distrust systems; they love to stay very close to the facts and to study them by themselves. (Tocqueville 2010: 776; my emphasis)

But even though Americans are more fond of practical beliefs, they do not dispense with intellectual dogmas altogether, for Tocqueville. In fact, according to Tocqueville, such dogmas are an *inescapable* part of human life – they are not part of both the aristocratic and the democratic social condition, indeed part of the human condition as such. As he states:

> Dogmatic beliefs are more or less numerous, depending on the times. They are born in different ways and can change form and object; but you cannot make it so that there are no dogmatic beliefs, that is to say, opinions that men receive on trust and without discussion. (Tocqueville 2010: 712)

The most famous dogma that Tocqueville describes is not in fact in the chapter where the epistemological status of dogmas is explicitly discussed, but in the first volume of *Democracy in America*, in a chapter entitled 'Of the Principle of the Sovereignty of the People in America'. In that chapter Tocqueville declares that 'When you want to talk about the political laws of the United States, you must always begin with the dogma of the sovereignty of the people' (ibid. 91). He then states that the principle of the sovereignty of the people,

> which is more or less always found at the base of nearly all human institutions, ordinarily remains there as if buried [or enshrouded: *enseveli*]. It is obeyed without being recognized, or if sometimes it happens, for a moment, to be brought into the full light of day [*au grand jour*], people soon rush to push it back into the shadows of the sanctuary. (Tocqueville 2010: 91)

However, in America, things are different, for

> the principle of the sovereignty of the people is not hidden or sterile as it is in certain nations [a vain show and a false principle as among certain others; it is a legal and omnipotent fact that rules the entire society; that spreads freely and reaches its fullest consequences without obstacles]; it is recognized by the mores, proclaimed by the laws; it spreads freely and reaches its fullest consequences without obstacles. If there is a single country in the world where the true value of the dogma of the sovereignty of the people can hope to be appreciated, where its application to the affairs of society can be studied and where its advantages and dangers can be judged, that country is assuredly America. (Tocqueville 2010: 91–2; Tocqueville's interpolation)

That is to say, it is America that *best* reveals the power and nature of sovereignty that underlies all forms of social life beyond the mere aggregate of men found in a primal horde; it is America where the *dogma* of sovereignty, the sovereignty of the people, best comes to light – America is, as Derrida notes in his seminar on Tocqueville, the *aletheia* of sovereignty. Moreover, this discovery is not fortuitous, since what distinguishes the American philosophical method is that it scorns and sweeps away *veils* of all kinds, that is to say, it prefers to view truths in broad daylight, in the light of the open day (*au grand jour*). Tocqueville thus uses the expression *au grand jour* to describe both the increased *visibility* of sovereignty in America and the mode which the American philosophical method uses to *uncover* truths.

Still, as Tocqueville stresses, America does not found the dogma of the sovereignty of the people, since the dogma has always been present in one *form* or another. It just reveals and exposes it – it makes it public. As Derrida puts it in *Rogues*, 'America is the moment when sovereignty comes fully into the light [*la pleine lumière*]. This light simply illuminates [*Celle-ci ne fait qu'éclairer*], in return, in a circular fashion, what turned out to have always been there' (Derrida 2005d: 164). But if America is the place which throws light on sovereignty, it is because it is the place where the sovereignty of the people 'goes public' for the first time. Accordingly, it transforms the very notion of the public by not only disclosing something *about* the public and popular nature of sovereignty, but by disclosing this visibly *to* the public.

Moreover, since this dogma lies, as Tocqueville puts it, more or less, at the bottom of all human institutions, it is the very archetype of the dogma, the dogma of all dogmas, the dogma that best reveals the inextinguishable nature of all dogmas. (The two other main dogmas Tocqueville discusses in *Democracy in America* are the dogma of the equality of the intellect that we have already come across – resistance to authority; and – one we have not discussed but will pick up when we deal with American religiosity below – the dogma of the immortality of the soul.) While the dogma of sovereignty might thus vary in strength from time to time and while it might have many forms throughout human history, it never ceased to exist.

But all dogmas have, for Tocqueville, a socio-political role. They are necessary in order to transform an aggregate of men into a 'social body [*corps social*]' (Tocqueville 2010: 713). Indeed, they are necessary, he claims, for the formation of any 'common' as such, for the *cum* ('with') of any community, the 'with' without which there would be no community: for 'without common ideas, there is no common action, and, without common action, there are still men, but not a social body (ibid. 713). Without dogmas there is thus no unified body of individuals; dogmas are essential for achieving social unity since they *embody* the collective as such. In short, dogmas are an ineradicable part of political ontology, for Tocqueville – they name the very possibility of being-in-common. Thus even in a society marked by what Tocqueville calls 'individualism', there is a dogma in common, a dogma that binds the aggregate of men into a community; namely, the dogma of the sovereignty of the people. But dogmas for Tocqueville do not exhaust the kind of beliefs that are crucial for politics, for he also includes under this heading, 'general ideas'.

If Descartes overthrew the 'authority of the master [or specifically the schoolmaster: *l'autorité du maître*]', Tocqueville states, his method was not immediately taken up – it did not immediately come into common or general use as a national method (ibid. 702). This is because the method 'was discovered in a period when men began to become equal and similar to each other [*les hommes plus semblables*]' (ibid. 704). He thus charts the history of what he calls this 'same method' from the German Reformation in the sixteenth century, which subjected dogmas to the scrutiny of each man, to Descartes in the seventeenth century, who destroyed the 'rule of traditions', to philosophers in the eighteenth century like Voltaire, who 'generalising' the same principle, submitted to 'the individual examination of each man the object of all his beliefs' (ibid. 703). In other words, the method become increasingly popular as the equality of conditions became more evident in society, when men were 'almost the same [*presque semblables*]' (ibid. 705). So once the method emerged from 'the schools to penetrate society and become the common rule of intelligence', it became 'popular among the French [*populaire chez les Français*]', and 'openly adopted or secretly followed by all the peoples of Europe' (ibid. 705). Tocqueville thus concludes that this shows that:

> the philosophical method of the XVIIIth century is *not only* French, but democratic, which explains why it was so easily accepted everywhere in Europe, whose face it so much contributed to changing. It is not because the French changed their ancient beliefs and modified their ancient mores that they turned the world upside down; it is because they were the first to *generalize* and bring to light [*lumière*] a philosophical method by the aid of which you could easily attack all things old and open the *way* to all things new [*ouvrir la voie à toutes les nouvelles*]. (Tocqueville 2010: 705; my emphasis)

The French, in other words, are democratic before all others because they opened the way to democracy, because they acted as the opening force for this new democratic method. The way they achieved this, crucially, was by means of the Enlightenment (*les Lumières*), and by *generalising* the method. Tocqueville thus relies on the double meaning of generalising – the French both popularised and abstracted the method, they at once made it more popular, more accessible, and, at the same time, less concrete, more abstract, more widely applicable – beyond the nation both in philosophy and in politics. This is what in fact makes the French so singularly capable of generalising the method, of being the best democratic representatives of humanity. As he puts it in the chapter on parliamentary eloquence: 'Our orators [i.e. French orators] often speak to all men, even when they are only addressing their fellow citizens' (ibid. 869).

The theme of generalising is in fact crucial, for Tocqueville goes on to define a 'general idea' two chapters later as the act of collecting 'a very great number of analogous objects under the same form' (ibid. 727; translation modified). The only way for a human to comprehend the human race collectively is thus through the 'general idea' of humanity, through analogy (semblance) rather than singularity (alterity). The divisions of humanity are therefore overcome by general ideas. Moreover, the very idea of humanity – which democracy enshrines and makes increasingly visible – is made possible by general ideas. General ideas are thus *cosmopolitan* in orientation, they mark the end of the march, that is, the march towards cosmopolitanism and the march that marks the borderland, the boundary, the frontier (*marche*) that cosmopolitanism necessarily crosses. As Tocqueville puts it (in a manner that echoes Kant) in the final pages of the first volume of *Democracy in America*:

> peoples seem to march toward unity. Intellectual links unite the most distant parts of the earth, and men cannot remain strangers to one another for a single day, or ignorant of what is happening in no matter what corner of the universe. Consequently, you notice today less difference between Europeans and their descendants of the New World, despite the Ocean that divides them, than between certain cities of the XIIIth century that were separated only by a river. If this movement of assimilation brings foreign peoples together, it is opposed with greater reason to the offshoots of the same people becoming strangers to each other. (Tocqueville 2010: 654–5)

Tocqueville thus emphasises the *place* of generality. General ideas – the possession of which is the very mark of man – are what make cosmopolitan likeness possible as a political reality – they name the possibility of a compeer, someone similar or *semblable* as a human being, a fellow citizen, a fellow creature and a fellow man, the other man, every other man, as the fellow man. The *most* general of general ideas, the most exemplary, is thus likeness, and democracy is *likeness* politically manifested. Crucially, general ideas also proceed in the same manner as a method, they are analogous since both general ideas and methods conceive objects as *similar enough* to be treated in a non-singular fashion. Tocqueville's claims about general ideas and the role of generalisation can thus be seen to play an analogous role to the function of schematism in combining the empirical with the non-empirical when the question of 'Man' is at stake.

However, the privilege that Tocqueville gives to French in this movement beyond the national extends beyond their role in the Enlightenment. For he declares that nations do not have an equal passion and aptitude for general ideas. He states that the English have the *least* aptitude and taste for general ideas, that the Americans have *more* than the English but less than the French, and that the French do not only have the *most* passion for general ideas, but also for general ideas relating specifically to politics. The Frenchman, in other words, can best think the general idea of humanity, he can best understand the *resemblance* that unites all men irrespective of national differences – he can best name humanity and the likeness that all men have. This is the democratic method, the French method. Democracy at its most general level is thus, properly, French, since it depends on the very method that makes thinking of the *semblable* possible. As Derrida puts it, the French, for Tocqueville, 'have a right to priority in the pathbreaking idea of a democratic method [*elle a un droit de priorité dans le frayage de l'idée de la méthode démocratique*]'.[16]

What is being declared in this 'right' of passage, in other words, is a philosophical right-of-way. The trafficking between America and France of a philosophical method will have been made possible by this right. While what is in question is the notion of 'right [*droit*]' in general, and in particular an equal right of all men, a right-of-way first and foremost declares who has the right to go *first*, who has priority on the road. It is, we might say, the democratic equivalent of primogeniture, the right of the first-born (*primus*). France for Tocqueville is thus privileged – it is in pole position – for it was the first to *arrive* at the method. The word *frayage* as well as the word *droit* is crucial in the above passage by Derrida, for it invokes not only the conceptual breakthrough, but the act of 'opening a path', the breaking (*rupta*) of obstacles. It thus links to what Derrida has elsewhere called the *via rupta*, the broken, cleared or opened way, the newly formed route that is broken by the travel of a wheel. *Frayage* thus names a kind of clearing, the kind of clearing which traverses a forest rather than the kind situated in a forest. The word *frayage* thus invokes not only the newly opened space of democracy, concrete or otherwise, but the force inherent in the democratic aspiration.

While the method might have landed on the shores of America, it is thus France, for Tocqueville, that is the *first* place in the world to see the light of the new day. France rather than America therefore ultimately names the dawn of a new age, it possesses the intellectual copyright over the democratic method, even if the method is now in the public domain, even if it is tied essentially to the public and to any public. Indeed, the 'method is followed more rigorously and applied more often among the French than among the Americans' (Tocqueville 2010: 705).

The Americans, Tocqueville states, are limited by two circumstances: the fact that religion plays so central a role in their society that they can neither attack nor defend Christianity, and the fact that they attained the democratic social condition without a revolution. It is the unique position and inheritance of France – from Cartesianism to the Enlightenment – that provides the means of revolution from an aristocratic to a democratic age. Its method thus leads the *way* – it advances a (democratic) programme for the rest of the world to follow by identifying the cause of humanity with its *own* national cause. As such, as Derrida remarks, this 'spontaneous philosophy [*philosophie spontanée*]', this philosophy embodied by the *will* of the majority (*sponte*: willingly), 'this philosophy of a people which has since become a nation is rather paradoxical', since it implies

> on the one hand, a strong organisation, and on the other hand, a procedural organisation [or litigious organisation: *organisation procédurière*], technical [*technique*], regular [*régulière*: a word that crosses several codes, including the juridical code, when rendered as 'lawful', the code of technical mobilisation when rendered as 'scheduled', and the code of social propriety when rendered more colloquially as 'straight'], a set of rules that allow one to forge ahead [*un ensemble de règles pour parcourir un chemin*], *odos, methodos, Far West* [written in English].[17]

The rules are thus embedded or fortified in a legal code. So on the one hand, the method is about an edifice, something erect, a fortification, and on the other hand, it is about the experience of passage and transportation. The rules thus both enable transport and govern it – they constitute, in other words, rules of the road. America is thus a *Kampfplatz* for Tocqueville, it names the place where the Franco-American 'method' as opposed to the German 'system' becomes entrenched and fortified, the place where the Cartesian method is both *yank*ed away from its French origins, and the place it goes from strength to strength. In short, the fortification of the method operates like a freeway.

## TOCQUEVILLE'S PHILOSOPHY OF LANGUAGE

As a final part of this reading of Tocqueville, I want now to turn from the language *of* method that Tocqueville uses, towards his analysis of language – his conception of language *as* method. In the chapter 'How American Democracy Has Modified the English Language', Tocqueville notes the importance of understanding 'what type of influence the democratic social state and democratic institutions can exercise on language itself, which is the chief instrument of thought [*le premier instrument de la pensée*]' (Tocqueville 2010: 818; translation modified). We thus discover that democratic institutions may have an impact on how one thinks, for Tocqueville, because they have the power to affect 'natural' language as an instrument of thought, that is to say, as a technoscientific 'tool'. However, as we will see, this power is also a *politi-*

*cal* instrument of the first order, for Tocqueville, and not only because it can influence thought itself.

Tocqueville begins by reporting a series of observations on English, stating that 'educated Englishmen' – that is, the very *exemplar* of the aristocratic class he contrasts with American democrats – have complained that not only have Americans introduced many new words into English, but that 'these new words were particularly borrowed either from the jargon of parties, or from the mechanical arts, or from the language of business' (ibid. 822). What seems to be at issue is thus the dominance of one kind of discourse in language itself. But Tocqueville is not content to merely relay empirical observations about what is spoken about in the language, for he also thinks that he can bring out the *internal logic* of American English. He deploys, in other words, a philosophy of language. His approach, as ever, is to compare aristocratic and democratic social conditions. He notes that in aristocracies,

> Few new words are made, because few new things happen; and if you did new things, you would try hard to portray them with known words whose meaning has been fixed by tradition [and thus . . .] the new expressions that are created have a learned, intellectual and philosophical character that indicates that they do not owe their birth to a democracy. (Tocqueville 2010: 822)

He cites, after mentioning the influx of new words deriving from Greek and Latin into French from the time of the Renaissance, the example of the influence of Milton on the English language, and in particular, how Milton introduced more than six hundred words into the English language, all derived, Tocqueville notes, from Latin, Greek or Hebrew sources.

In contrast, Tocqueville claims that in democracies many words frequently fall out of use and suddenly return without rhyme or reason, since 'Democratic nations moreover love movement for itself. That is seen in language as well as in politics.' As a result, amongst such a people 'the majority makes the law in the matter of language' (ibid. 823). That is to say, language ceases to be controlled, directed and policed by an elite group of scholars and literary writers – for example, writers like Milton or French institutions like the *Académie française*, which Tocqueville joined in 1841 – and instead becomes shaped by the will of the majority. Philosophers, poets and scholars cease to make the *law* with regard to language, and it instead becomes a popular matter. Political representation is thus inherently tied to linguistic representation – if language represents, it must be amenable to popular representation. Moreover, this change applies as much to the language of the courts as to the law which governs language. A natural language thus becomes, under democracy, Tocqueville suggests, a language of the people. Indeed, under the helm of the people, with no learned body or institution to guide the language, it becomes a truly popular language. It turns into a language which is not merely capable of being *read* by a majority, but which is capable of being influenced by a majority. As Tocqueville declares, 'People do not read in the same spirit and in the same way as among aristocratic peoples; but the circle of readers expands constantly and ends by including all citizens' (ibid. 773).

Moreover, Tocqueville does not merely claim that American English is more influenced by the *jargon* of politics, commerce and technology than British English, he also claims that mass literacy and democratic language in America has major repercussions for philosophical discourse in American English. As he states:

> the majority [by definition] is occupied more with public affairs than studies, more with political and commercial interests than with philosophical speculation or literature [*belles-lettres*]. Most of the words created or accepted by the majority will bear the mark of these habits; they will serve principally to express the needs of industry, the passions of parties or the details of public administration. Language will expand constantly in that way, while on the contrary it will little by little abandon the terrain of metaphysics and theology. (Tocqueville 2010: 824)

The language of trade, he thus predicts, will end up controlling the influence of natural languages in democracies to such an extent that it harms and impairs philosophical and theological discourse in those languages. In other words, as soon as a democratically influenced language – like American English – becomes dominated by commercial and business terms, it suffers from increasing philosophical paucity, since it ceases to be guided by men of learning, and instead comes under the control of the (unlearned) majority. In short, those ignorant of the languages spoken 'in Rome and in Athens' – those tongues that have been historically privileged and dominant in European philosophical discourse, namely, Greek and then Latin (ibid. 824). Tocqueville thus claims that a degree of scholastic precision is needed for philosophical discourse to take place, and that this scholastic language is inherently tied to a knowledge of Latin and Greek, and that a language open to influence of a majority, like American English, could never satisfy that requirement.

Tocqueville thus posits a strict economic relationship between philosophical and commercial interests: the privileging of one in a natural language will always be at the expense of the other. However, while he suggests that the philosophical potential of American English might wither, he does not seem to think this will impact the American philosophical method: as we have seen earlier in this chapter, the philosophical distinction of Americans is to be found in their method and not in their language. On the other hand, there is a danger in the democratic effect on language, for Tocqueville:

> The most usual expedient that democratic peoples employ to innovate with regard to language [*langage*] consists of giving an uncommon meaning [*un sens inusité*] to an expression already in use. This method is very simple, very quick and very easy. Knowledge is not needed to use it well; and ignorance even facilitates its use. But it makes language [*langue*] run great risks. By doubling the meaning of a word in this way, democratic peoples sometimes make it doubtful which meaning they are leaving aside and which one they are giving to it. [Alternatively: they sometimes cast doubt on both the retained meaning and the acquired one: *rendent quelquefois douteux celui qu'ils lui laissent et celui qu'ils lui donnent.*] (Tocqueville 2010: 824–5)

For Tocqueville, the worst danger that can befall language is thus, following *the* most classical philosophical axiology, *ambiguity*. Words should not be doubled in meaning. The state of univocity remains the essence of language; it names the proper *telos* of language, and this is what democracy undoes. The worst danger for philosophical discourse is consequently not an excess of neologisms, or Americanisms, or foreign terms, but a surplus of value in existing stocks. And this is what democracy creates. It meddles with language, encouraging a certain kind of inflation within a language over time. It coins new meanings, creates uncertainty over future transactions, and as a result, decreases the real value, the stock value of a stock of words. But philosophical discourse should not be susceptible to this kind of fluctuation in stocks and shares, these rises in the shares of what might be proper to a word. In other words, what is proper for the language of philosophy, according to philosophy, is a language that mostly closely adheres to the proper as such – the literal and properly singular meaning of a word (*le sens propre*). It is this proximity to the proper that guarantees the proper place of philosophical discourse. As Derrida comments in a reading of Descartes' *Discourse on Method*:

> the properly philosophical or scientific project: [is] to reduce the ambiguity of language. The value of clarity and distinctness in the understanding of words, in grasping significations, will at the same time be a juridical, administrative, police (and therefore political), *and philosophical value*. (Derrida 2004a: 11; original emphasis)

According to this classic philosophical programme, one which is outlined in Derrida's 'White Mythology', if a word is to have more than one meaning, its meanings must be sufficiently clear and distinct, each remaining *one* and identifiable. Democracy is therefore a threat to philosophical discourse insofar as it threatens to ruin the promised universal communicability and translatability that univocity would seem to herald. The so-called universal characteristic envisioned, for example, in Descartes' Latin text, 'Rules for the Direction of our Native Intelligence' (*Regulae ad Directionem Ingenii*), would not tolerate the kind of irreducible polysemia that American English seems to foster. For Descartes, what is needed above all is a *mathesis universalis*, that is, a science modelled on mathematics insofar as it would be 'a general science which explains *all* the points that can be raised concerning order and measure *irrespective* of the subject-matter' (Descartes 1988d: 5; my emphasis).

Democracy is, as a result, inherently perilous for philosophy because of its effect on languages; it endangers the transparent and univocal status needed for philosophical discourse to take place – and its capacity to go from one place to another, from one language to another. It disrupts universal translatability, and thus highlights that translation is in fact as much a political as a linguistic issue. The idea of the multitude contained in democracy (*demos*) is thus internally linked to the idea of polysemy, or perhaps what we could call, following Derrida, unmasterable dissemination, that is, an *irreducible* polysemia where one cannot count the number of meanings (Derrida 1982: 248). In other words, democracy, for Tocqueville, encourages a state of affairs whereby words cease to be ruled or mastered by one meaning or even by a determined number of countable meanings. In so doing, democracy dethrones the one-to-one relation that is supposed to hold between what we say and what we mean. For Tocqueville, the outcome of this is deplorable:

> Since there is no common arbiter, no permanent tribunal that can definitely settle the meaning of the word, the latter remains in a variable [*ambulatoire*] situation. As a result, writers almost never have an air of being attached to a single thought; instead they always seem to aim at the middle of a group of ideas, leaving to the reader the trouble of judging which one is hit. This is an unfortunate consequence of democracy. I would prefer that you sprinkled the language [*langue*] with Chinese, Tartar or Huron words, than to make the meaning of French words uncertain [since . . .] there is no good language without clear terms. (Tocqueville 2010: 825)

In 'How American Democracy Has Modified the English Language', Tocqueville thus switches to discussing the *French* language in order properly to judge the havoc and damage that democracy might do to a (national) language. Moreover, Tocqueville claims that he would be more willing to allow non-European importations from other languages, than to see French words become uncertain or ambiguous. The French language, he implies, must not give up on its Cartesian spirit – it is not primarily French because its words are French, but because each of its words is clear and distinct.

Tocqueville thus implies that the French language could import a number of non-French words but *still in fact be French* insofar as it holds true to its Cartesian spirit – the spirit of clarity. In other words, French words are not clear because they are French, they are French (no matter their linguistic source) because they are clear. Tocqueville thus harks back to Antoine de Rivarol's famous dictum, made in his 1784 prize-winning essay to the Berlin Academy, 'Discourse on the Universality of the French Language', that 'what is not clear is not French [*Ce qui n'est pas clair n'est pas français*]' (Rivarol [1784] 1968: 49; my translation). Clearly, for Tocqueville, as for Rivarol, the value of clarity defines what is most French. The privilege which Tocqueville gives to the French is consequently to be found in both the Cartesian method and in French discourse, the French discourse on method. Their method is in general the most popular and democratic philosophy possible, and their language is the most methodical, presenting the *straightest* path to clear terms.

A certain philosophical 'language politics' is evident in *Democracy in America* in other subtle ways. We can consider, for example, Tocqueville's comment on language in an individual nation riven by social differences:

> In aristocratic centuries, when each nation tends to hold itself apart from all the others and loves to have a physiognomy that is its own [alternatively: to have distinct characteristics of its *own*], it often happens that several peoples who have a common origin become very foreign to each other, so that, without ceasing to be able to understand each other, they no longer all speak in the same way [. . .] You then find in the same idiom a language of the poor and a language of the rich, a language of commoners and a language of nobles, a learned language and a vulgar language. (Tocqueville 2010: 825–6)

Tocqueville contrasts this sociolinguistic scenario, where social-class dialects come to divide those who speak the same natural language, with the circulation of language in democracies, where social mobility ensures that words are continuously intermixed and exchanged so as to create 'a common mass' (ibid. 826).

Indeed, he states that 'Nearly all the different dialects that divided the idioms of Europe are noticeably tending to disappear; there are no *patois* in the New World, and they are disappearing daily in the Old World' (ibid. 826). Hence Tocqueville moves from a discussion of social-class dialects in the *one* language to a discussion of *patois*. What is at stake is thus not only non-Parisian French, but the so-called regional languages of France, such as Breton.[18] The eradication of the *patois* – which had intensified as a state-sponsored project in France since Abbé Grégoire's 1794 'Report on the Necessity and Means to Annihilate the Patois and to Universalise the Use of the French Language' (*Rapport sur la nécessité et les moyens d'anéantir les patois et d'universaliser l'usage de la langue française*) – thus becomes, for Tocqueville, a natural extension of democracy. The French language becomes a *national* language not because its use had been imposed forcibly on the entire population, but due to the *irresistible* forces of democratisation. The existence of *patois* is therefore, for Tocqueville, the result of class division in the age of aristocracy, and their elimination is the result of the equality of conditions in the age of democracy.

The widespread use of French is thus a sign of democracy and not of force or violence – its increasing influence is tied to the success of democracy and not the success of the State in implementing its linguistic policy at home or abroad. As a result, Tocqueville suggests not only that French is the language of democracy, but that *national* unity is conditional upon linguistic unity. However, the relationship between democracy and language is further complicated within the chapter since Tocqueville speaks not only of 'the language of a democracy [*la langue d'une démocratie*]' but also of 'democratic languages [*les langues démocratiques*]' (ibid. 819, 827). Moreover, he does not use these expressions equally, the former appearing only once at the beginning of the chapter, the latter appearing four times. He thus moves from the genitive to the adjectival – from speaking about the language *of* a democracy to *democratic* languages, and from the singular to the plural. He thus associates the proper functioning of a democracy with one language. A propensity towards monolingualism is therefore internal to democracies, the logic of the *semblable* and that of monolingualism are indissociably linked – the more the Old World eradicates *patois*, the more they do away with difference, and so the closer they resemble each other, both nationally and internationally.

On the other hand, he also asserts that there are democratic languages. Here he uses democracy as an adjective rather than as a noun to convey the fact that a language is shaped by democracy. In other words, 'democratic languages' names the *effect* of democracy on language. One of these effects, as we have seen, is that democracy disrupts the social-class dialects developed by aristocracies. A democratic language is thus a language neither of the poor *nor* of the rich, a language neither of the commoner *nor* of nobility, neither a learned language *nor* a vulgar language. It is language that bridges, that unites, that bonds – in place of the classic aristocratic bond dependant on national glory examined earlier – the 'people' together in a new form of 'with': a with without the not-with-the-other of national difference. The visible 'sovereignty of the people' is therefore conditioned by the transformation of aristocratic British English into a democratic language. In fact, in the second chapter of the first volume of *Democracy in America*, Tocqueville had declared:

The emigrants who came at different times to occupy the territory that the American Union covers today differed from each other in many ways; their aim was not the same, and they governed themselves according to various principles. These men shared common features, however, and they all found themselves in an analogous situation. The bond of language is perhaps the strongest and most durable that can unite men. All the emigrants spoke the same language [*langue*]; they were all children of the same people. (Tocqueville 2010: 49)

It was thus the commonality of Anglo-Americans, their similarity with one another, the fact that they already shared the same language, the English language, which cemented their cohesion, and this minimal sharing-with-the-other bonded the emigrants, every emigrant, from wherever they arrived, into one. Language, at this point, is singled out as the *most* important bond that can unite men. Tocqueville, crucially, even though he is discussing Anglo-Americans, does not state that it is particularly the English language that unites and unifies; he instead makes a point of saying that it is *a shared language in general* that unites and unifies. His remark, in other words, is directed as much to France – or indeed, anywhere else in the world – as America. The profusion of tongues, the reign of *patois*, is thus dangerous, intolerable and an obstacle to political cohesion. It is better to have one language, he thus suggests. This is what has proved to be, in the end, durable and long-lasting. The end of monolingualism is the end of democracy.

## NOTES

1. Derrida (1984–8), Box 18, Folder 2, Seminar 4, p. 3.
2. Ibid. p. 1.
3. However, it should be noted that Tocqueville does not mention *professional* figures like Jonathan Edwards, or some of his later followers like Samuel Hopkins and Nathaniel Emmons, that is, some of the leading *academic* philosophers of the time. Hopkins and Emmons, for instance, were philosophers attached to the Congregational Yale Divinity School, which was itself the centre of the New Divinity Movement, the bastion of American Calvinism (which American Transcendentalism is seen to be a rebellion against). Tocqueville thus remains silent, or ignorant, of the institutional, professional and academic philosophy of America at the time. But there is perhaps a reason for this omission, for as Kuklick notes, these 'divines were insular and ignored European currents of thought. They were inbred and hired only within the narrowest of circles' (Kuklick 1985: 181). These institutions thus fit Tocqueville's description of American insularity. But it is also important to note that insofar as this academic philosophy was attached to schools of theology, to seminaries, one has reason to think that Tocqueville *discounted* them as schools of philosophy, especially since Tocqueville at the end of his chapter on the American philosophical method distinguishes the 'following' of the method in America from France by the role of religion in each society.

4. Derrida (1984–8), Box 18, Folder 2, Seminar 4, p. 13.
5. Ibid. p. 13.
6. Ibid. p. 6.
7. Ibid. p. 7; my emphasis.
8. Ibid. p. 15.
9. Ibid. p. 12.
10. Ibid. p. 2.
11. Ibid. p. 2.
12. Ibid. p. 6.
13. Derrida (1984–8), Box 16, Folder 12, Seminar 7, p. 1.
14. Derrida (1984–8), Box 18, Folder 2, Seminar 4, p. 1.
15. Ibid. p. 3.
16. Ibid. p. 16.
17. Ibid. p. 3.
18. The language of Breton is mentioned by Descartes in his *Discourse on Method*. However, for Descartes, as opposed to Tocqueville, what matters more than the language one speaks and one's scholastic training in rhetoric, is the matter of how one reasons – it is reason that *best* persuades and not scholastic knowledge or knowledge of languages like French. As Descartes states, 'Those with the strongest reasoning and the most skill at ordering their thoughts so as to make them clear and intelligible are always the most persuasive, even if they speak only low Breton and have never learned rhetoric' (Descartes 1988a: 23). In other words, neither rhetoric nor Latin or even French is needed to present clear and distinct ideas – one can do so in the *patois* of Breton and without knowledge of rhetoric. One can thus be an unschooled peasant from Breton and still be more persuasive than a schooled French- and Latin-speaking scholar.

CHAPTER 6

# The Transcendental Declaration of Independence: Emerson and American Philosophy

> Why has America never expressed itself philosophically? Or has it – in the metaphysical riot of its greatest literature? Has the impulse to philosophical speculation been absorbed, or exhausted by speculation in territory, as in such thoughts as Manifest Destiny?
>
> Stanley Cavell, The Senses of Walden

Ralph Waldo Emerson stands in a paradoxical situation with regard to the idea of national philosophy. On the one hand, a small band of literary critics led by Harold Bloom have declared that he is the definitive American philosopher, the one who sets the standard of what it is to be not only a philosopher in America but an American philosopher, one whose work serves as a conduit for articulating what it means to be an American. On the other hand, few professional philosophers, analytic and non-analytic, have engaged with him as a philosopher, labelling his work, and 'American Transcendentalism' as a whole, as too unashamedly 'literary' in presentation to sustain 'properly' philosophical argument. This latter group thus place his achievement and output not alongside the German Idealists, who inspired him to write in the first place, but instead, solely within literary circles. Ellen Kappy Suckiel, for instance, does not believe on the whole that Emerson deserves the title 'philosopher', stating that she thinks he is better described as a 'preacher', since Emerson

> rejects discursive reason as a means to truth. His supporters would say that he is able to make the most of his use of his highly evocative literary talent precisely because he does not restrain his insights with the fetters of critical rigour and proof. (Suckiel 1985: 152)

She thus repeats the well-known mantra that Emerson is not a philosopher because he does not argue, because he replaces tuition with intuition rather than reconfiguring the relationship between them both. The 'birth' of American philosophy is thus usually identified in academic philosophy, but also elsewhere, not with American Transcendentalism, which is seen primarily as a literary, religious and, more lately, a socio-political movement, but with the rise of American Pragmatism. As Douglas R. Anderson notes in his *Philosophy Americana*, 'for many argument-riffers and intellectual historians Emerson does not appear to be doing philosophy. For most of the twentieth century his work lived only in literature programs, never in philosophy programs' (Anderson 2006: 189).

One thus encounters two distinct kinds of claim about the idea of American philosophy and Emerson. On the one hand, Suckiel can declare that 'Emerson, along with several other figures, himself provides the *standard*' (this is a pointed word, especially since Stanley Cavell has drawn attention to the fact that Emerson uses this word as both a measure of comparison *and* a flag) for what it means to be an American philosopher – 'a standard against which other philosophers must be measured if they are to count as American' (Suckiel 1985: 149; my emphasis). On the other hand, Robert Denoon Cumming can state that one

> can refer without apology to American literature and even to the American language, but not with very much confidence to American philosophy. With the exception of pragmatism, no influential philosophies have been initially native American. They have been transplanted here. (Cumming 1979: 6–7)

The belief that pragmatism was 'native' to America, in ways American Transcendentalism was not, can also be seen to have ramifications for other contemporary commentators, like Harold Bloom and Cornel West, both of whom try to domesticate Emerson as a full-bodied 'American' by reading him as a precursor to American Pragmatism, a proto-pragmatist, one that foresaw or pre-empted the philosophy of John Dewey and William James, rather than a figure who contests it or departs from it in many significant ways, for example, with regard to the stakes of idiomaticity in philosophical discourse.

What this chapter will reveal is that Emerson's manner of writing is politically committed to a notion of the idiomatic that is against the idea that the idiom can be owned – against the idea that there is such a thing as a 'pure idiom', one which expresses where one finally belongs. It argues that Emerson shows it is the essence of language not to let itself be appropriated by any one user or community of users, and that, paradoxically, what is most idiomatic (*idion*), what is most proper to a so-called national language, cannot be claimed as uniquely national property. It thus argues that the Emersonian idiom is not a closure or enclosing of self, but an allocution, a passage to the other. Moreover, it is shown that Emerson is not only critical of such notions as Manifest Destiny, and the language of the national bond or racial determinism, but reveals how indebted and hospitable American thought is to 'foreign philosophy' (including non-European sources) when he writes of what constitutes the American difference to philosophy. Consequently, I argue against those who believe Emerson to be advancing a racialist concept of the nation, or to be advocating a form of racial nationalism. On the other hand, I also identify a cosmo-national strain of thought in Emerson that once again schematically identifies a single nation as the 'home' of 'Man'. It thus argues that while Emerson is not a proponent of Manifest Destiny or racial nationalism, he still problematically privileges what he takes to be the cosmopolitan underpinnings of the USA.

Emerson, in fact, briefly appears in Derrida's seminars on philosophical nationalities and nationalism, when Derrida unexpectedly interrupts, as he notes himself, his third seminar session to consider Harold Bloom's then recently published article 'Mr. America', a piece that was originally published in *The New York Review of Books* in 1984, and later republished under the title 'Emerson: Power at the Crossing'. In his article, Bloom, one of the foremost thinkers in terms of the concept of literary influence, seeks a tradition of thought that would resist foreign influences and be native to America. He tries, consequently, to defend a tradition that America could properly and purely call its own – following the logic of appropriation traced throughout this book – a tradition that had not been 'transplanted' to America. As Derrida writes, Bloom's essay 'believes it is necessary to awaken a tradition of properly American thought [*la tradition de pensée proprement américaine*]'.[1] Derrida notes his personal friendship with Bloom (they had, for instance, published essays together in a volume entitled *Deconstruction and Criticism*), but identifies Bloom's gesture of purifying and defending the American tradition from outside forces and foreign elements to be a quintessential nationalistic and xenophobic gesture. Moreover, Derrida notes that it is the kind of gesture Hannah Arendt thought it would be impossible to make in the USA since it had, according to her, achieved the condition of nationless statehood. Derrida subsequently cites and questions her claim in *On Revolution* that 'America was spared the cheapest and the most dangerous disguise the absolute ever assumed in the political realm, the disguise of the nation' (Arendt 1990: 195).

But though Derrida highlights that the USA is not entirely free from the spectres of nationalism, he does not pursue the matter any further. In fact, none of Derrida's seminars sets out to treat any writer born in America; he only examines thinkers who visited or lived in America, like Tocqueville, Adorno and Arendt – the latter two in fact becoming 'naturalised' American citizens

– as well as thinkers who wrote about America, but who never visited it, like Kant and Heidegger. This approach is surely not accidental, not only because the USA is often thought to be an 'immigrant nation', and not simply because Derrida is keen to understand the politico-philosophical effects of immigration and hospitality on philosophical nationalism, but also because his seminars constitute an early examination of the notion of hospitality that would occupy him more consistently in the 1990s. Nevertheless, it does mean that he fails to identify any forces primarily within America that might undo American nationalism. Derrida does not, for example, question Bloom's reading of Emerson, or investigate the possibilities that Emerson himself provides for escaping the notion of a 'properly' American tradition. Derrida, accordingly, does not consider the numerous concepts and ideas that Emerson provides for thinking through the question of the national character of philosophy and the philosophical character of the national.

One of the few commentators of Emerson to have read him as a distinctly American voice and yet still as a philosopher is Stanley Cavell. However, Cavell has himself expressed the belief that Derrida's fame – the cult of orthodoxy that surrounds Derrida in certain circles – may in fact continue to suppress the Emersonian voice that Cavell seeks to rehabilitate. As he states, if Emerson 'is a founder or finder of philosophy for North America', then Derrida's claims about writing contribute to 'America's repression of its difference in philosophy. I put this so as to suggest that it is Derrida's fame, not necessarily what I therefore have to call his thinking as such, that contributes to this repression' (Cavell 1996: 41). Though Cavell distinguishes between Derrida's fame and his thought, he does not pursue the ways Derrida's thought can in fact help lift rather than facilitate the repression that America places on Emerson. The present chapter thus investigates the ways in which Derrida's work alongside Cavell's can help us to understand Emerson's writing, and in particular, the latter's concepts for thinking through the idea of 'American philosophy', especially since, as Joel Porte observes, Emerson 'asks perpetually about the meaning of America itself' (Porte and Morris 1999: 2).

In this chapter I will therefore, in contrast to readers like Bloom, argue that Emerson's texts in fact present a philosophy open to the other, and so the other in philosophy, as well as the other of philosophy, and that these texts achieve this by converting and transfiguring our notion of idiomaticity in philosophical discourse. He will thus be read as a philosopher, someone who inherits philosophy from Europe and elsewhere, but also as someone who tries to transform our notion of philosophy, and the ways it may be presented. In short, that the form of inheritance he claims is a transformation, one that uses philosophy to transform our notion of philosophy in and outside of America, not in the name of 'post-philosophy', as Richard Rorty would have it, or in the name of evading epistemology-centred philosophy, as Cornel West would have it, but in the name of re-establishing the democratic authority of philosophy, and so, what Derrida would call 'democracy *in* philosophy', as well as 'philosophical democracy' (Derrida 2002c: 29; my emphasis). Along the way I will also explore the reasons why Dewey would have called Emerson 'The Philosopher of Democracy', even though Emerson is rarely thought of as a political philosopher as such (Dewey 1903).

## THE 'AMERICAN MIND' VERSUS THE 'GERMAN ALIEN'

The issue of how 'foreign' or 'native' American Transcendentalism is to America has been debated since, and indeed, before the term 'transcendental' was used by Emerson in a lecture of the same name in 1842. Its importance as a concept, one used to name a group of thinkers, was already reflected a decade earlier, when Frederic Henry Hedge (who had studied in Germany) discussed the significance of Kantian philosophy. He had stated in 1834, six years before Tocqueville had described the 'American philosophical Method' as Cartesian, that:

> [the] pre-eminence of Germany among the nations of our day in respect of intellectual culture, is universally acknowledged; and we do fully believe that whatever excellence that nation has attained in science, in history, or poetry is mainly owing to the influence of her philosophy [. . .] – in one word, to the transcendental method. (Hedge 2006: 24)

Similarly, George Ripley, when discussing the influence of Kantianism in America in 1838, stated that Victor Cousin, the famous statesman and translator of German philosophy into French,

> presents a favourable contrast to the most eminent philosophers of Germany . . . Called upon to exhibit the reasonings and conclusions of the German philosophy to a promiscuous audience in the metropolis of France, he has addressed the popular mind with singular success, and solved the cardinal problem of presenting the highest truths of speculation in a form adapted to the average intelligence of enlightened society. (Ripley 2006: 26)

The importance of Cousin's importation of 'German philosophy' into Parisian circles, his translations and expositions, therefore lay in the fact that it popularised its conclusions, made them accessible to the 'popular mind', that is to say, the national mind. It exhibited the German philosophical 'results' in way that was democratically accessible to all. But this same 'obscurity' regarding the scholastic difficulty of Kant's writings, and those of other 'German philosophers', Ripley notes, also exists in the Unites States of America as well as France:

> For this reason, the German philosophers, in their native costume, will never become extensively popular in this country . . . Their writings will be studied by all who love philosophy for its own sake [that is, professors and perhaps non-professional enthusiasts] [. . .] But they cannot be made the direct foundation of a philosophical culture in a country like our own. We must start with the freer, more popular, more concrete, and more finished productions of the great French writers who have been formed in the Germany school. (Ripley 2006: 26)

The USA should, according to this outline, import German philosophy via France; German writings should not be directly translated into American vernacular, but find their way to America through a more democratic and accessible language; in other words, they must be, paradoxically, translated from French. The discussion of philosophy in America was thus notably framed in *national* terms already by the mid-1830s. Moreover, figures like Andrews Norton attacked Emerson in the same decade for importing 'foreign philosophy'. This introduction of foreign elements, this bodily 'infusion', was criticised for meddling not only with the 'language of philosophy', but, just as crucially, the 'language of America'. Norton thus states that 'our common language is abused; anti-tricks are played with it; inversions, exclamations, anomalous combinations of words, unmeaning, but coarse and violent, metaphors abound, and withal a strong infusion of German barbarians' (Norton 2006: 148). Norton thus opposes 'our common language', the English language, to the 'barbarian tongue', the tongue influenced by German terms beyond the line – we might say, *limes* – of what is acceptable. As Lawrence Buell notes, this nationalised discussion led 'to the contemporary caricature of Transcendentalists as Germanized aliens' (Buell 2006: 146).

This reception of Emerson continued in the twentieth century with writers and critics like Perry Miller. For Miller, in his well-known essay 'From Edwards to Emerson', the question was once again whether 'New England's transcendentalism' was 'wholly Germanic or Hindu in origin?' He asks:

> Is there any sense, even though a loose one, in which we can say that this particular blossom in the flowering of New England had its roots in the soil? Was it foolishly transplanted from some desert where it had better been left to blush unseen? (Miller 1993: 14)

Miller's answer – framed, notably, in autochthonous terms – was that it was indeed native and home-grown, above all, due to the influence of Puritan thought and the figure of Jonathan Edwards.

## THE TRANSCENDENTAL DECLARATION OF INDEPENDENCE 161

This reception has reached its national apex in contemporary figures such as Harold Bloom, who insists that Emerson is entirely 'native' and that nothing could be more properly American – be it in philosophy, literature or theology. Moreover, Bloom in *Agon* does this in a way that rejects the previous accounts that stated that Emerson is fundamentally a puritanical thinker. For Bloom, Emerson should be identified neither with his puritanical heritage *nor* with his influences from abroad. He thus states that due to the 'native strain in Emerson' he distrusts 'the received scholarship that sees Emerson as the American disciple of Wordsworth, Coleridge and Carlyle, and thus indirectly a weak descendant of High German Transcendentalism of Fichte and Schelling' (Bloom 1982: 162). For Bloom, this disregards that 'the mind of Emerson is the mind of America' (ibid. 145).

Indeed, Bloom reconfigures Emerson by denying that he was in fact a philosopher like his predecessors in Germany (for instance, Kant) or the USA (for instance, Jonathan Edwards), someone inheriting the philosophical tradition that preceded him. Emerson, according to Bloom, may have read German Idealists and thinkers influenced by them, but Emerson's point of departure, his project, was in the end something that transcended these Germanic philosophical influences, including the very notion of transcendental philosophy. As Bloom puts it, 'Emerson is an experiential critic and essayist, and not a Transcendental philosopher. This obvious truth always needs restating, perhaps now more than ever, when literary criticism is so *overinfluenced* by contemporary heirs of the German tradition or Transcendental philosophy' (Bloom 1993: 148; my emphasis).

Bloom's use of Emerson in journals like *The New York Review of Books* in the 1980s to counter the rise of overseas influence in America – more specifically, the work of Derrida – might appear marginal and inconsequential if Bloom's academic work earlier in his career had not outlined his belief that Emerson was one of the most important figures to suffer what Bloom has famously called the 'anxiety of influence', the paradoxical resistance to all '*ideas*-of-influence' whilst being 'uniquely open to influence' (Bloom 1975: 138). Bloom thus belligerently declares 'the war of American poets *against influence* is part of our Emersonian heritage, manifested first in the great triad of "The Divinity School Address", "The American Scholar", and "Self-Reliance"' (ibid. 131; my emphasis). For Bloom, these three essays accordingly constitute the holy trinity of American independence, and form what he calls the 'American Religion' (Bloom 1982: 145). In fact, like Tocqueville, who stated that the inhabitants of the USA are Cartesians without needing to read Descartes, Bloom states that 'Americans pay something, whether or not they have read Emerson, since his peculiar relevance now is that we seem to read him merely by living here, in this place still somehow his, not our own' (ibid. 142). To live in America, for Bloom, is thus to be an Emersonian – he is as much part of the American landscape as Mount Rushmore, or rather, he *is* the American landscape for Bloom, presiding over it even in his absence.

But Bloom does not deny that Emerson has immense philosophical significance even if Emerson does not inherit philosophy for America, on behalf of America, for as he puts it, 'Emerson is the mind of our climate, the principal source of the American difference in poetry, criticism, and pragmatic post-philosophy' (Bloom 1993: 148). Emerson's significance for Bloom is thus that he is the thinker who comes to announce the end of European philosophy and traditional metaphysics. Rather than inheriting philosophy, from Europe and elsewhere, Emerson pursues a post-philosophical project, one that abandons traditional epistemology in favour of a neo-pragmatic point of view, the kind later favoured and outlined, for example, by Richard Rorty. Bloom thus declares that not only is Emerson the founder of what comes *after* philosophy, but that he 'fathered our national philosophy of Pragmatism' (Bloom 2007: xii).

The belief that Emerson was trying to exclude the 'foreign' and embrace the 'native' has usually found its basis in the aforementioned trilogy of essays invoked by Bloom. Some scholars have even feared that Emerson seems to suggest in these essays that one is nationalistically duty bound to stay at home and that all forms of travelling are to be denigrated and criticised. 'The American Scholar' has in particular been described as a text promoting an overtly nationalised culture hostile to the foreign; as Pamela Schirmeister notes, it is in fact 'considered America's primary document of literary nationalism' (Schirmeister 1999: 12). One of the passages in 'The American Scholar' that inspires such readings, for example, is when Emerson declares: 'I ask not for the great, the remote, the romantic; what is doing in Italy or Arabia; what is Greek art, or Provençal minstrelsy; I embrace the common, I explore and sit at the feet of the familiar, the low' (Emerson 1983: 68). This is usually coupled with another moment when Emerson seems to be disdainful of the foreign, namely, the passage in 'Self-Reliance' when Emerson declares that:

> It is for want of self-culture that the superstition of Travelling, whose idols are Italy, England, Egypt, retains its fascination for all educated Americans. They who made England, Italy, or Greece venerable in the imagination, did so by sticking fast where they were, like an axis of the earth. In manly hours, we feel that duty is our place. The soul is no traveller: the wise man stays at home, and when his necessities, his duties, on any occasion call him from his house, or into foreign lands, he is at home still, and shall make men sensible by the expression of his countenance, that he goes the missionary of wisdom and virtue and visits cities and men like a sovereign, and not like an interloper or a valet. (Emerson 1983: 277)

The problem, however, with those who read Emerson as a literary or cultural nationalist is that Emerson makes constant recourse to the trope of travelling and to the foreign, even in the same texts that seemingly denigrate travelling abroad. It is thus helpful to differentiate rather than level or amalgamate all forms of travelling and the foreign in such texts. For instance, if it is clear in the passage above that Emerson underscores that the USA should replicate the success of Italy, England and Egypt, rather than simply imitate these countries, it is perhaps less clear what kind of travelling is under discussion. How can someone travel while still staying at home? What does Emerson mean when he speaks of a method of travelling – and it is a question of method, the becoming-road of the method – which progresses by remaining immobile? The first thing to note is that Emerson in this itinerary-that-is-not-an-itinerary critiques the idea of travelling primarily understood as physical displacement, travelling as a form of sightseeing, in contrast to the traversal (real or imaginary) embedded in any experience. What is in question in his critique, in other words, is the mere act of being physically elsewhere – the idea of touring.

This indicates that for Emerson, one cannot simply inherit the thought of Europe – for example, its culture, its literature, its philosophy – simply by touring the continent. The problem with this conception of travelling is noted in what Emerson calls a 'proverb' in 'The American Scholar': 'He that would bring home the wealth of the Indies, must carry out the wealth of the Indies' (ibid. 59). What we discover in such passages (from the very same texts that are supposedly against travelling and the foreign) is that travelling as physical displacement lends itself to thinking that one can appropriate the culture of another – that travelling is about handling foreign goods (the wealth of the Indies) and shipping them back home. This proverb thus contrasts travelling in terms of the power to grasp something, seize it (travel as appropriation), with the power to receive something, the power to carry or bear something in one's hands (travel as hospitality). One first all of needs to work on one's own power to receive, before one can grasp something outside of oneself.

I shall further differentiate the means of transportation outlined by Emerson into four categories later in this chapter when I consider the issue of Manifest Destiny and the race question, but for now, we can note that Emerson's views of travelling are further distorted if one does not also read the essay which precedes 'Self-Reliance' in his *Essays: First Series*, namely, 'History'. For in that essay, Emerson declares that 'nomadism and agriculture are the two antagonist facts' and that the 'two tendencies' are no 'less active in individuals' than in 'nations' (ibid. 247). Every individual and nation thus faces, according to Emerson, the double bind of experiencing the foreign and paying attention to one's own time and place, or again, the call of cosmopolitanism and the call to engage with one's own republic.

This duality and tension is found throughout Emerson's writings and is perhaps most aptly captured in two texts that appeared after his *Essays*, namely, his 1863 Civil War address 'Fortune of the Republic' and his chapter on Shakespeare from his 1850 *Representative Men*. In the former, he states, using the language of fraternity, that:

> the truly cultivated class [. . .] exist in England, as in France, in Italy, in Germany, and in America. The inspirations of God, like birds, never stop at frontiers or languages, but come to every nation. This class, like Christians, or poets, or chemists, exists for each other, across all possibly nationalities, strangers to their own people, – brothers to you. (Emerson 2005: 324)

In the latter essay he writes, in contrast, that the poet – one of the categories invoked above alongside the Christian and the scientist who supposedly crosses frontiers and languages – must be 'in unison with his time and country' (Emerson 1983: 710). How then is one to resolve this dilemma of the cosmopolitical and the national?

If we return to the essay 'History', we find Emerson observing that nomadism has been traditionally feared in history, due to the fact that 'nomads were the terror of all those whom the soil or the advantages of a market had induced to build towns' (ibid. 246). Nomadism thus periled the 'state', and it, in turn, curbed the forces of nomadism so as to 'invigorate the national bond' (ibid. 247). However, if Emerson opposes nomadism with the national bond, the bond that ties someone to a place, he also clearly refuses to settle in either camp. A clear instance of this refusal is in his essay 'Plato', when he writes that 'Poetic creativeness' is not 'found in staying at home, nor yet in travelling, but in transitions from one to the other, which must therefore be adroitly managed to present as much transitional surface as possible' (ibid. 641). Creativity, on this outline, cannot be found in the space of one's own four walls, but neither can it be found in simply experiencing the foreign: one needs to implicate oneself in the foreign.

Thus Emerson even turns what is considered to be most foreign, most 'German' in his own thought, namely, his Transcendentalism, into something even more foreign when he relates its history and genesis not simply back to Kant, but to the Stoics, that is, pointedly, those philosophers who first spoke of the 'citizen of the world'. Transcendentalism, in other words, is deracinated itself; it is no longer held to be purely 'German' or 'native' to Germany, but something that traverses the entire history of philosophy from the Romans, that is, the culture that itself got philosophy from elsewhere. No autochthonal roots are thus found in this lineage of Transcendentalism: it has no native ground. This makes it, we might say, at once more and less American, at once more home-grown and foreign. Bloom's appropriation of Emerson, his

'Americanisation' of him ('Emerson is the mind of America'), can thus be critiqued within Emerson's own terms. As Emerson writes:

> This way of thinking [called Transcendentalism], falling on Roman times, made Stoic philosophers; falling on despotic times, made patriot Catos and Brutuses; falling on superstitious times, made prophets and apostles; on popish times, made protestants and ascetic monks, preachers of Faith against preachers of Works; on prelatical times, made Puritans and Quakers; and falling on Unitarian and commercial times, makes the peculiar shades of Idealism which we know now. (Emerson 1983: 198)

Hence, as Lawrence Buell points out, the strange logic of the essay 'History', an essay that warns about the danger of needlessly touring outside of one's country for inspiration, but where

> 'Boston Bay' is the only local reference in an otherwise heady catalogue of globe-circling names, place and world events, as Emerson skitters from Hastrubal to Caesar Borgia, Solomon, Alcibiades, Shakespeare, Burke, Thucydides, Xenophon, Pindar, Zoroaster, Menu; and transports us to London, Rome, Greece, Peru, Assyria, St. Helena. (Buell 1993: 51)

One can also read Emerson's lines about the necessity of nomadism – and Transcendentalism itself as a form of nomadism, going constantly from one culture to another nomadically – alongside the need to build towns and 'systems', to be obliquely responding to Kant's notion of cosmopolitanism. This response is oblique not only because it does not name Kant, as Emerson explicitly does in 'The Transcendentalist', but because it takes issue not with the Kant of *Perpetual Peace*, as we might expect Emerson to do, but with the Kant of the *Critique of Pure Reason*. For in the opening paragraphs of the preface to the first *Critique* Kant in fact uses the imagery of nomadism, and he does so to specifically narrate the *history* of metaphysics. Kant does this by comparing metaphysics to the principle of monarchy, that is, he compares the search for the ultimate *arche* to what is itself based on the rule of *arche*. If philosophy is 'the Queen of all the sciences', as Kant puts it, philosophy has also in the contemporary world lost its right to reign as sovereign (Kant 1933: A viii). Kant, accordingly, traces the history of her 'government', and states that at first it was 'despotic' since her administration was ruled by the 'dogmatists'; however,

> inasmuch as the legislation still bore traces of the ancient barbarism, her empire gradually through intestine wars gave way to complete anarchy; and the *sceptics*, a species of nomads, despising all settled modes of life,

broke up from time to time all civil society. (Kant 1933: A ix; original emphasis)

Kant thus associates nomadism with the end of metaphysics, with the coming of the sceptics and the breakdown of authority – the dissolution of the *arche*. It is thus no surprise that elsewhere Kant states that philosophy dispenses with the need to travel – it knows the world, it encompasses the globe, without having to travel. Philosophy is about settling, settling land and settling issues; it regulates travels to foreign lands (the right of hospitality), but it has no need for nomads (the right of inhabitation). As Derrida reminds us, this indifference to travelling in Kant crosses the boundaries of Kant's many texts, and it can even be found in the very text that considers the boundary, not only territorial boundaries, but the conceptual boundary between philosophy and anthropology – namely, Kant's *Anthropology from a Pragmatic Point of View*. Derrida writes:

> Travelling with Kant: his cosmopolitanism dispenses with travel or travel narratives. Observing one's fellow citizens and companions is enough – especially, Kant notes in the preface to his *Anthropology from a Pragmatic Point of View*, if one inhabits a large city as exemplary as Königsberg, at the centre of a state, with parliamentary assemblies, a university, sea traffic, inland commerce on its rivers, neighbours speaking foreign languages, and so forth. One can thus come to know the world and write one's anthropology [and then Derrida cites Kant's *Anthropology*] '*ohne zu reisen*' without travelling – not even in Europe, like a lowly Descartes. (Derrida 2005a: 323)

It is thus Kant, and not Emerson, as is often thought, who has no need for travelling. While Derrida mentions the traveller known as Descartes, I will now turn to discuss Tocqueville, to whom, I will suggest, Emerson was in fact responding in several of his works.

## THE EMERSONIAN ESSAY VERSUS THE METHOD

Although we cannot be certain that Emerson was familiar with Tocqueville before writing 'Self-Reliance', we do know that Emerson had read Tocqueville by 1841, because he cites *Democracy in America* in his journals and in his lectures from April 1841, one month after *Essays: First Series* was published. This section will thus argue that Emerson is using the language of the method (the step and the path) not to follow the Cartesian route opened by Tocqueville – even if Emerson is drawn to some of what Tocqueville says about 'the popular' and the democratic philosophical culture of America – but to challenge some of the very tenets of the American philosophical method as outlined by Tocqueville. An idea central to this section, and an idea fully contested by Emerson, is Tocqueville's idea of the 'general' as well as the role that 'likeness' plays in any method. In contrast to Tocqueville's emphasis on generalising by means of method, it will be argued that Emerson preserves the notion of (to use Adorno's term) the non-identical – that which cannot be treated methodically or generally – by using the essay form in his philosophical compositions.

Adorno, in 'The Essay as Form', contrasts the composition of the essay with that of the academic thesis or treatise. He argues that the essay form has always been sidelined in philosophy because 'the academic guild accepts as philosophy only what is clothed in the dignity of the universal and the enduring' (Adorno 1991: 3). Rather than claiming that the essay form does in fact fit the traditional model of philosophical discourse, Adorno argues that the essay challenges how we are to present and conceive of philosophy – that philosophy should be neither an art nor a science but a halfway house between both. Adorno thus privileges the essay form as it underscores for him that the medium of philosophy (unlike art) is essentially tied to concepts but (unlike science) cannot remain indifferent to its conceptual exposition because the arrangement (or constellation) of concepts – their sequence, order, and relation to one another – is a fundamental philosophical task. Adorno takes this as a lesson that the writing of philosophy should not be mapped out in advance, proceeding in a linear fashion, as the following of the Cartesian method would seemingly dictate, but should find instruction about how best to present itself from the subject matter it is engaged with. In other words, it should respond to what it is writing about. With regard to the essay form, Adorno thus states:

> Luck and play are essential to it. It starts not with Adam and Eve but what it wants to talk about; it says what occurs to it in that context and stops when it feels finished rather than when there is nothing to say. Hence it is classified as a trivial endeavour. (Adorno 1991: 4)

Adorno's comments on the essay form and its affinity with the transient and ephemeral (or, as we might reword it, with the ordinary and everyday) can be useful when considering Emerson's *Essays* as well as Tocqueville's remark that Americans distrust 'forms'.[2] The fact that an essay starts, according to Adorno, with a certain specific interest (rather than from Cartesian first principles) and that it comes to a stop when it feels it has said what it wanted to say (rather than attempting to exhaust what is to be said on the matter, following the fourth rule of the Cartesian method) has many affinities with Emerson's writings. Indeed, one might say that Emerson's essays, as Cavell has shown, develop in a distinctly paratactic way (akin to Hölderlin's poetry, as analysed by Adorno), ensuring that no sentence within them (including the first and last) has an undisputed mastery as a point of genesis or terminus. As Adorno writes, the essay 'has to be constructed as though it could always break off at any point. [. . .] Discontinuity is essential to the essay; its subject matter [*Sache*] is always a conflict brought to a standstill' (ibid. 16). Adorno's notion of an aporetic 'standstill' expresses Cavell's point that the gulf between sentences in an Emersonian essay is as wide as the gulf between his individual essays. Each sentence in a given essay can be read as the 'last', that is, the one that brings philosophy to a close, at least for today, or as a shoemaker's form, and so a mould by which to read the rest of the essay, as if the essay were 'fitted' around this mould.

Another interesting affinity between Adorno's 'The Essay as Form' and Cavell's reading of Emerson's *Essays* is that Adorno, like Cavell, contrasts epistemologies that believe 'all knowledge can potentially be converted into science' with those resisting such a claim, and associates these antipositivistic epistemologies with those that acknowledge that the presentation (*Darstellung*) of philosophical discourse matters – that one's writing may have some essential role in the philosophical work advanced (ibid. 8). One could thus suggest that one of the ways Emerson seeks to disrupt and derail the equation of knowledge with science that was gaining ground in the USA when he was writing (as described by Tocqueville and later, by Adorno), is in the very act of choosing to write essays as opposed to other forms of philosophical composition. One could suggest, further, that he intends his essays to reorient the possibilities that an American difference to philosophy might still harbour.

Best capturing this reorientation, perhaps, is 'experience', a word that for Adorno expresses the essence of what the essay makes possible. Adorno notes that 'the essay invests experience [*Erfahrung*] with as much substance as traditional theory does mere categories [. . . and this] experience is mediated through the essay's own conceptual organisation, the essay proceeds, so to speak, methodically unmethodically' (ibid. 10–13). What we garner from experience, according to Adorno, are not 'arbitrary hunches'. Neither is it the case, however, that the insights of an essay are to be grounded in 'the verification of assertions through repeated testing [that is, the application of a method], but rather individual human experience, maintained through hope and disillusionment' (ibid. 8). Adorno's comments are noteworthy not only because 'experience' is a key Emersonian word (along with 'hope'), but also because the word invokes, as noted before, the notion of travel. This motif of onward movement in experience, of a path cleared or blocked, is most apt because Adorno also presents the essay form as a specific critique of the Cartesian method. As Adorno writes:

> In the realm of thought it is virtually the essay alone that has successfully raised doubts about the absolute privilege of method. The essay allows for the consciousness of non-identity [. . .] in refraining from any reduction to a principle, in its accentuation of the partial against the total, [and] in its fragmentary character [. . .] [so much so, the essay] might be interpreted as a protest against the four rules established by Descartes' *Discourse on Method*. (Adorno 1991: 9–14)

The non-identity for Adorno that the method evaporates is the recognition that our knowledge of an object does not exhaust it, that there is some remainder, some excess that does not, and can never, fit the concepts we already have of it. Dennis Redmond, in his online list of the keywords of Adorno's *Negative Dialectics*, puts this well: non-identity

> doesn't just mean the opposite of identity, that is to say, the nonequivalent, or what doesn't fit into certain categories, which is usually just a metaphor for a *different* identity which isn't the same as the first identity, but refers to what escapes or eludes *every* sort of identity, but which nevertheless exists in the shadow or penumbra of identity, as the fleeting reminder or glimpse of unrealized possibilities, of what that identity locked out, excluded, or can't quite become.[3]

It is perhaps this aspect of Emerson, the essay writer who is attuned to the non-identity of things – despite remaining, crucially, committed to concepts – that has concerned most philosophers and led them to liken Emerson's prose to a 'mist' (Cavell 1990: 22). But it is also this aspect of Emerson that remains the most important, not only because it challenges the dominant philosophical idea that concepts fully 'capture' or exhaust the object to which they refer, but because it acknowledges the force of the utterly singular – that which is not amenable to the generalising technique of the Cartesian method – that Tocqueville eradicates through his emphasis on general ideas. To recall, general ideas for Tocqueville are based on similarity, on the logic of the *semblable*, as is the very idea of the Cartesian method, which is to treat non-singular things. This is exactly what the Emersonian essay can be said to strive to disrupt in its rendering of the non-identical, that which resists the identifiable and substitutable. In sum, Emerson's critique of Tocqueville is that the American philosophical method he describes, and indeed, the democratic culture he outlines, does not place sufficient importance on singularities, for that which escapes the logic of the *semblable*.

Hence, one conclusion we may reach (and something I would urge Emerson is suggesting in his writings) is that the essay has certain affinities with the experiment of democracy as such, insofar as democracy is not just about treating individuals as equals, and so as fundamentally similar, but as singularities, and so as fundamentally different. As Derrida astutely puts it, 'There is no *democracy* without respect for irreducible *singularity* or alterity but there is no democracy without [. . .] the calculation of majorities, without identifiable, stabilisable, representable subjects, all *equal*' (Derrida 2005c: 22). Taking the democratic aspect of the essay seriously, we might say that what Emerson shows in choosing to write essays is that it is the democratic respect for singularities that Tocqueville sacrifices in the idea that democracy is likeness politically manifested.

However, if Emerson is responding to a novel form of political Cartesianism, as outlined above, he is also responding to that dimension of Cartesianism that is concerned with how one lives one's life outside of the school. For Cavell, Descartes marks the turning of scepticism from a problem concerning the way one lives one's life to an academic thesis one may or may not hold. As Cavell writes:

> from the time of Descartes [. . .] scepticism is no longer, as it were in the ancient world, a way of life, something to be achieved through spiritual exercise – scepticism becomes a possible intellectual fate that must be warded off, to be managed by argument or by distraction, since the world is after all supposed to be abjectly subject to human knowledge, as modern science is supposed to show. (Cavell 2010: 528)

One may contrast this view – which is also, interestingly, held by Michel Foucault – with that of Pierre Hadot, who has argued that:

> when Descartes chose to give one of his works the title *Meditations*, he knew perfectly well that the word designated an exercise of the soul within the tradition of ancient spirituality [exemplified by Marcus Aurelius' *Meditations*]. Each *Meditation* is indeed a spiritual exercise – that is, work by oneself and upon oneself which must be finished before one can move to the next stage. (Hadot 2004: 264)

Indeed, in discussing exceptions to the waning influence of philosophy conceived as a spiritual exercise, Hadot has himself mentioned the names of Emerson and Tocqueville alongside names like Descartes. I thus want to suggest that, *contra* Cavell, one reader who does *not* take Descartes to be proffering only a thesis (in his *Meditations*, or elsewhere) is in fact Emerson. Hence Tocqueville and Emerson present competing inheritances of Descartes and the idea of philosophy not as an academic pursuit, but as a way of life; Emerson, in effect, reorienting and redirecting the paths both pursued and opened up by Descartes, in order to contest the uses Tocqueville makes of Descartes

THE TRANSCENDENTAL DECLARATION OF INDEPENDENCE 171

in describing the USA and the American philosophical method. Whatever one makes of these competing Cartesian inheritances, the Tocqueville–Emerson relationship, I want to suggest, can no longer be ignored. For what Tocqueville and Emerson are arguing about is nothing less than the very idea of the American way of life, and how the USA might (still yet) transform the idea of philosophy as much as philosophy might (still yet) transform the USA. This raises the question of what the USA is politically for Emerson, and the kind of bond that exists there.

RESOLVING TO SOLVE THE BOND OF THE USA

Emerson emphasises the political undertones to the idea of turning in his lecture 'The Anglo-American' when he states that 'Every election is a revolution' (Emerson 2005: 197). Elections thus always turn for Emerson on the figure of the turn, but this revolution which is initiated by reformers is never complete; it is not singular and non-repeatable – as he carefully notes, *every* election counts as a revolution. The force behind this turn of phrase is, however, already evident in 'Self-Reliance', when he states that 'the reformers summon conventions and vote and resolve in multitude' (Emerson 1983: 281). The democratic revolution is on this picture constant, always reforming itself, perfecting itself, returning to itself so as to perfect itself. Emerson reiterates the repetition built into the idea of 'election' by his repetitive use of words beginning with the prefix re-, as in 'revolution', 'reform' and 'resolve'. The last word is particularly decisive since it invokes the very idea of decision, the decision reached by a formal vote, the 'resolution' made by a deliberative body and the other meaning of the word 'resolution', used primarily in chemistry and mathematics, of separating components, and so loosening and dissolving the bond.

The bond, for example, of political unity, the bond appealed to in his essay 'Politics' when he states that 'This is the history of governments – one man does something which is to bind another' (ibid. 567). Emerson thus resolves to solve the bond by respecting a double bind: a multitude comes together when resolved, it gathers many into one, but at the same time, it separates and dissolves that which is gathered into one. The resolve is thus one and not one, or as he puts it in his essay on 'Plato' in *Representative Men*:

> Two cardinal facts lie forever at the base; the one, and the two. – 1 Unity, or Identity; and, 2. Variety. We unite all things by perceiving the law which pervades them; by perceiving the superficial differences, and the profound resemblances. But every mental act, – this very perception of identity or oneness, recognises the difference of things. Oneness and

otherness. It is impossible to speak, or to think, without embracing both. (Emerson 1983: 637)

As a result, Emerson's bond is the kind of bond that disbands unity – it is united in not being finally united. As Emerson would later write in 'Poetry and Imagination', 'All multiplicity rushes to be resolved into unity' (Emerson 2010: 3). Rather than rushing into unity, Emerson calls for us to be vigilant, to be resolved to resolution, to keep faith with it, and not to seek false unity. The issue of the bond reappears in 'Fate', when Emerson discusses the Nordic myth about Fenris or Fenrir, the monstrous and voracious wolf that was so dangerous that the gods decided to bind it. As Emerson relates:

> When the gods in the Norse heaven were unable to bind the Fenris Wolf with steel or with weight of mountains, – the one he snapped and the other he spurned with his heel, – they put *round his foot a limp band softer than silk or cobweb*, and this held him: the more he spurned it, the stiffer it drew. So soft and so stanch is the *ring* of Fate. Neither brandy, nor nectar, nor sulphuric ether, nor hell-fire, nor ichor, nor poetry, nor genius, can get rid of this *limp band*. (Emerson 1983: 952; my emphasis)

Emerson thus invokes a 'limp band' that is paradoxically stronger than steel or the weight of mountains, say, the might of the brute force (military strength) or the might of geography (physical landscape), and names it 'Fate'. The strongest bond that unites will neither be found in military might, and so in physical strength, nor in the idea of 'natural borders', and so a border created by 'natural' formations like mountains. Once again, Emerson takes recourse to circular images, and highlights that the Wolf is made immobile by the binding of his foot, that he cannot move, that he is paralysed due the 'ring of Fate', which is a circular band. We can receive instruction on how to read this image of the limp band in Emerson's *English Traits* (1856), since the image had already appeared in that work, and moreover, it was written at the same time as 'Fate'. Emerson is discussing the rising importance of technoscientific forces, such as roads, locomotives and telegraphs, and states that:

> By these new agents our social system is moulded. By dint of steam and of money, war and commerce are changed. Nations have lost their old omnipotence; the patriotic tie does not hold. Nations are getting obsolete, we go and live where we will. Steam has enabled men to choose what law they will live under. Money makes place for them. The telegraph is a limp band that will hold the Fenris-wolf of war. For now that a telegraph line runs through France and Europe from London, every message it

transmits makes stronger by one thread the band which war will have to cut. (Emerson 1983: 854)

The forces of modern science have thus dislocated the patriotic tie for Emerson, unbinding the very thing – the patriotic tie – that unites a nation as a nation. Notably, Emerson does not specify a nation, he does not single out a nation among others even though he is discussing English traits – he describes this transformation as a more global phenomenon, in fact the becoming-global of the dissolution of patriotic ties. Emerson thus observes in the middle of the nineteenth century what Derrida over a century and a half later called the forces of 'dislocation, expropriation, delocalisation, deracination, disidiomatisation and dispossession [. . .] that the tele-techno-scientific machine does not fail to produce' (Derrida 2002a: 81). In particular, the 'limp band', the loose but unbreakable band that ties the Fenris Wolf down is given a name: the telegraph, that which writes at a distance – the very thing that transforms distance and the space between things, and so what had been till then the proper boundaries of something, say, the division of territory by means of mountains. This silken band is thus a form of teletechnology that criss-crosses territories in such a way as to make war increasingly difficult in an age of transnational communication. The speed and expanse of transmission as well as migration ('we go and live where we will') have thus transformed, for Emerson, our notion of attachment, the place of attachment, and, indeed, our very attachment to the notion of attachment.

In a lecture entitled 'The Young American' from 1844 that is usually read as endorsing American expansionism, and so what would be called 'Manifest Destiny' only a year later, Emerson asks:

> Who has not been stimulated to reflection by the facilities now in progress of construction for travel and the transportation of goods in the United States? This rage for road building is beneficent for America, where vast distance is so main a consideration in our domestic politics and trade, inasmuch as the great political promise of the invention is to hold the Union staunch, whose days seemed already numbered by the mere inconvenience of transporting representatives, judges, and officers across such tedious distances of land and water. Not only is distance annihilated, but when, as now, the locomotive and the steamboat, like enormous shuttles, shoot every day across the thousand various threads of national descent and employment, and bind them in one web, an hourly assimilation goes forward, and there is no danger that local peculiarities and hostilities should be preserved. (Emerson 1983: 213)

Emerson thus resorts to the imagery of weaving ('shuttles', 'threads', 'bind', 'web') – whose origins go all the way back to Plato's text, *Statesman* – to convey the sense of political bonding and assimilation that the technoscientific machine affords – the mechanical to-and-fro that makes the national possible as such. But one can perhaps distinguish at least four different kinds of transportation in Emerson. Two can be described as positive and two as perverse. The two positive types are those occurring within national boundaries (domestic transport) so as to form the national unit; and those that cross national boundaries (cosmopolitical transport) so as to ensure that the national unit is not indivisible and self-enclosed. The two perverse types are, we might say, the mirror-reverse of the above, and both are connected to racism. The first violates the ability of anyone to go 'live where we will' within a national territory (fugitive slave transport), and the second violates national boundaries so as to appropriate and steal (slave transport). We have already seen an instance of the first above (domestic transport); the second (cosmopolitical transport) can also be found near the end of 'The Young American', when Emerson states that:

> A heterogeneous population crowding on all ships from all corners of the world to the great gates of North America, namely, Boston, New York, and New Orleans, and thence proceeding inward to the prairie and the mountains, and quickly contributing their private thought to the public opinion, their toll to the treasury, and their vote to election, it cannot be doubted that the legislation of this country should become more catholic and cosmopolitan than that of any other [. . .] she should speak for the human race. (Emerson 1983: 217)

The second kind of transportation (cosmopolitan transport) thus differentiates and diffuses the population of a given territory by encouraging the flow of international migration. We shall return to Emerson's pronouncements on cosmopolitical legislation later on in this chapter, but we can for now draw attention to the third type of transportation Emerson invokes, the transport of fugitive slaves within a national territory. This type of transport is, we might say, the kind envisaged in the Fugitive Slave Act of 1850 – the so-called Bloodhound Law – that made it a duty of any official, including those in the North, to arrest anyone suspected of being a runaway slave and to return them forcibly to their 'owners'. The fourth type, namely, slave transport, also derives, like 'The Young American', from a lecture Emerson gave in 1844, namely, the 'Emancipation of the Negroes in the British West Indies'. Emerson writes that 'Public attention [. . .] was drawn that way [to the West Indies], and the methods of the stealing and the transportation [of slaves] from Africa became noised abroad' (Emerson 1995: 33). Emerson in the same year thus opposes two ways of arriving in America: one way promises to make the USA the cosmopolitical nation *par excellence*, the other threatens to ruin the USA and to make it the nation of bondage and captivity. As he states in 'Address to the Citizens of Concord', 'America, the most prosperous country in the universe, has the greatest calamity, negro slavery' (Emerson 2008: 138).

Indeed, the so-called race issue in America has a number of ties to other passages in *English Traits*, above all when Emerson relays a conversation he had with Wordsworth. He states that Wordsworth

> had much to say of America, the more that it gave occasion for his favourite topic [. . .] He has even said, what seemed a paradox, that they needed a civil war in America, to teach the necessity of knitting the social ties stronger. (Emerson 1983: 775–6)

The import of this passage, significant in itself with its political language of knitting and ties, is transformed when one considers that Emerson may be writing back, sending his own telegraph, his own message back to the USA in the word of another, as if these words of Wordsworth were picking up something up in the air, so to speak, rather than disclosing a private opinion of Wordsworth. In fact, in the essay 'Fate', Emerson emphasises that Fenris is a war-chief, an animal of war, and so a sovereign animal (following the idea that he who wages war, who makes the decision to go to war, is sovereign). The bondage of Fenris, his paralysis, is thus also about the bond of the Union, the sovereignty of the Union in the face of war.

One finds evidence for this relation between 'Fate' and *English Traits* when one considers that the latter was published in August of 1856, and that Emerson's 'Kansas Relief Meeting' was delivered in September later that year. In that latter talk, Emerson discloses that a 'systematic war' is already taking place in America and that the 'testimony of the *telegraphs* from St. Louis and the border confirm the worst details' (Emerson 2002: 111–12; my emphasis). Rather than pursuing Wordsworth's claim that war would strengthen the tie of the social bond, Emerson suggests that it is news about the 'question of the times', namely, the question of race, which is simultaneously gathering people together and dividing them. The 'limp band' which brings news from St. Louis is thus not acting as an agency of national cohesion in this case, but in fact disseminating the news that there 'is no Union' (ibid. 114). The telegraphs in this scene, rather than binding, are thus instruments for dissolving the union, but, paradoxically, by eliminating distance, by making this disunion known, they are making territorial and local calamities national affairs. The reason for Emerson's claim that there 'is no Union' is, as we saw earlier, that language itself is no longer representative, that due to words like 'Manifest Destiny' people are deceived by 'every new link in the chain which is forged for their limbs by the plotters in the Capitol' (ibid. 114). Emerson, relying on the double meaning of forged, suggests that the bond is not only counterfeit, but something forged specifically 'for their limbs'. The bond of all society in the USA, is, in other words, pictured as a prison chain, a form of bondage, and society itself is viewed as one large chain gang.

The problem Emerson has with this notion of dissolving, rather than his notion of the resolve to resolution in society, lies above all with its method of division. For this division, be it in the form of racial division, or in the form of those who are pro- or anti-slavery, is for Emerson the wrong kind of division insofar as it divides collectives rather than individuals. This malevolent form of division, even if it divides the individual, is not the kind of division that enshrines the individual; it is instead the one that divides society into two separate and homogenous camps (White and non-White). The issue of counting – the difficulty of counting individuals and accounting for the influence of race – is indeed pivotal in Emerson's description of the problem in 'Fate'. For instance, the expression 'the question of the times' is repeated – we might say multiplied beyond all calculation – when Emerson declares in its opening that the 'question of the times resolved itself into a practical question of the conduct of life. How shall I live? We are incompetent to solve the times' (Emerson 1983: 943).

Emerson thus once again joins separation *with* reparation. However, this time, the separation is not the kind that divides society into two camps – as if there were only two camps worth fighting for; rather, it is one that makes union, the Union, possible in the first place. The separation in this case is thus not opposed to reparation. His method is consequently to join two 'opposing' poles by the double bond of resolve ('resolve in multitude') and conduct ('the conduct of life'). We have already noted the power of resolve and resolution, but the notion of conduct is also crucial, since Emerson no doubt relies on the fact that 'conduct' derives from the Latin *conducere*, 'to lead or bring together', and indeed, sure enough, the question 'How shall I live?' is followed immediately by the first person plural: 'We are incompetent to solve the times.' The question of the times is thus also another version of the question Emerson asked some years earlier in 'Experience': 'how many individuals can we count in society?' (ibid. 472). The question also raises the issue of who will count as an individual – whom will *we* value in these times in order to give the vote? That the subtext of civil war connects *English Traits* to the essay 'Fate' several years later in many surprising ways is also evident in both texts' preoccupation with the notion of 'air'. In *English Traits* Emerson had written 'Already it [the all-giving machine] is ruddering the balloon, and the next war will be fought in the air' (ibid. 954). This might be read literally as an insightful prediction concerning the future of war, and the importance that flying machines would play in future conflicts, but more importantly, it also speaks to a number of the other terms that relate to air, and the being-with that air suggests for Emerson, namely, conspiracy, spirit and breathing.

Let us take the first term, 'conspiracy'. Emerson in 'Self-Reliance' had famously stated that 'Society everywhere is in *conspiracy* against the manhood of every one of its members' (ibid. 261). The word 'conspiracy' comes from the Latin *conspirare*, 'to agree, unite, plot', and literally means 'to breathe together', from *com-* 'together' and *spirare* 'to breathe'. 'Self-Reliance' thus pictures the danger of society to every one of its individual members to be asphyxiation; society leaves little room for the individual to breathe. In his 1851 'Address to the Citizens of Concord', Emerson states:

> The last year has forced us all into politics [due to the Fugitive Slave Act], and made it a paramount duty to seek what is often a duty to shun [namely, politics as a collective and unified action]. We do not breathe well. There is infamy in the air. (Emerson 2008: 135)

He thus casts the Fugitive Slave Act as the worst form of conspiracy, a conspiracy that affects all and not simply those it targets and wounds ('We do not breathe well').

We can now consider the relation of the term 'conspiracy' to the second and third terms as they appear in 'Fate'. In this latter essay Emerson uses the expression 'The Spirit of the Times' (Emerson 1983: 943), and claims that 'if we rise to a spiritual culture, the antagonism takes a spiritual form' (ibid. 952). That the same issues raised in 'Address to the Citizens of Concord' – conspiracy, being-with, breathing, race, and so on – are at stake in 'Fate' is revealed by the fact that the word 'spirit' is also connected, like 'conspiracy', to breath, since it derives from the Latin *spiritus*, 'soul, courage, vigour, breath', which, in turn, is related to *spirare* 'to breathe'. Indeed, already in his 1836 *Nature*, Emerson had highlighted that '*Spirit* primarily means *wind*; *transgression*, the crossing of the *line*' (ibid. 20). 'The Spirit of the Times' can thus be understood to be transgressive; it is a struggle ('the antagonism takes spiritual form'), and it is a struggle about the spirit of man, the relation of men to the air they breathe together, as 'Fate' declares in (unattributed) quotation marks, '"The air is full of men"' (ibid. 951). The central importance of air to Emerson is underscored in one of his earlier essays from 1844, namely 'Manners'. In it he states that the 'Persian Lilla' was 'a solvent powerful [enough] to reconcile all heterogeneous persons into one society: like air or water, an element of such a great range of affinities, that it combines readily with a thousand substances' (ibid. 531). Air is thus paradoxically the 'solvent' that 'reconcile[s]' for Emerson, it is the element that achieves reconciliation not by binding men together, but by expressing the ruptured bond.

Stanley Cavell acknowledges the importance of air to Emerson – even if he does not explore it is as motif outside of Emerson's essay 'Fate' – in his 'Emerson's Constitutional Amending' (Cavell 2003). One of the things Cavell underlines in his reading of the essay is that Emerson is claiming to know what everyone knows, that Emerson's knowledge is not posited as furtive or hidden, as some form of expertise, but something in the air, available to all, as a kind of 'public spirit'. Indeed, Emerson, in the poem preceding the essay 'Fate', no doubt relies on the double meaning of *ornis*, meaning 'bird', on the one hand, and on the other, 'omen', when he writes in its opening line that 'delicate omens traced in the air / To the lone bard true witness bare' (ibid. 941). Cavell highlights another sentence by Emerson that invokes air and relates it to time, and so 'The Spirit of the Times', namely, 'The truth is in the air, and the most impressionable brain will announce it first, but all will announce it a few minutes later' (ibid. 965). This formulation in 'Fate' can once again be seen to recall his earlier 'Address to the Citizens of Concord', and its claim that:

> There are men who are sure of indexes of the equity of legislation and of the sane state of public feeling, as the barometer is of the weight of the air; and it is a bad sign when these are discontented. For, though they snuff oppression and dishonor at a distance, it is because they are more impressionable: the whole population will in a short time be as painfully affected. (Emerson 2008: 135)

Emerson thus imagines certain men to be measures (barometers) of what is in the air, but that these men, these indexes, are only exemplary in showing what will soon be felt by all ('the whole population'). They are thus witnesses, giving what we might call testimony. Their privileged position is thus not that they are superior to us, but only that they read themselves before others do, and that this reading is figured in terms of law (they are 'indexes of the equity of legalisation'). That what they read (in themselves) is above us, in the air, is also crucial, and hints at what Emerson calls later in the same address a 'Higher Law' (ibid. 140): law that is simply not man-made, or restricted to being posited in a given area, but which is universal in expressing justice.

One can thus appeal, Emerson suggests, to this 'Higher Law' that is more sovereign than any present national covenant – say, the US constitution – in order to challenge man-made laws that countenanced slavery; there is thus 'no virtue that is final: all are initial' (Emerson 1983: 411). Indeed, in his much later lecture 'Fortune of Republic' from 1863, he states that:

> The end of all political struggle, is, to establish morality as the basis of all legislation. 'Tis not free institutions, 'tis not a republic, 'tis not a democracy, that is the end, – no, but only the means: morality is the object of the government [. . .] a state of things which allows every man the largest liberty compatible with the liberty of every other man. (Emerson 2005: 325–6)

However, it should also be borne in mind that the USA was privileged in a cosmo-national manner for Emerson precisely because he thought it advanced the liberty of every man. This is not only indicated, as cited earlier, when he states in 'The Young American' that it 'cannot be doubted that the legislation of this country should become more catholic and cosmopolitan than that of any other', but also, in the same lecture, when he announces that 'here, in America, is the home of man' (Emerson 1983: 228). This is a problematic claim by Emerson – even if one is charitable, and thinks that Emerson is overturning the common idea of 'home' as the being-with of the common, as examined elsewhere in this chapter – given that he argues in *Representative Men* that no representative of man is complete, that 'Man' is, so to speak, a project that no man can hope to overcome or finish. Moreover, this privileging of the USA is not a singular instance, as is evident from his 1863 lecture 'Fortune of the Republic'.

However, it should also be noted that the idea of 'Higher Law' is crucial for Emerson when he wishes to express civil disobedience and criticise the USA. The position of 'Higher Law' is thus deeply ambiguous in Emerson's work; on the one hand, it privileges the USA above all other territories (it is the cosmopolitical nation), and on the other, it is used to show up the failings of the USA (it is a nation failing to live up to cosmopolitical standards). The idea of civil disobedience, famously outlined by Emerson's fellow Transcendentalist, Henry David Thoreau, is expressed by Emerson when he opposes the Fugitive Slave Act in the name of a 'Higher Law' – a form of so-called natural law. As he writes:

> An immoral law makes it a man's duty to break it, at every hazard. For virtue is the very self of every man. It is therefore a principle of law [the Law written in the air, so to speak] that an immoral contract is void, and that an immoral statute is void. (Emerson 1983: 138)

The language of this passage highlights in particular that the issue in question is the social bond, the false bond of an 'immoral law' which it is one's duty to 'break'. Emerson thus sketches a picture where we are constantly coming together, say, enchaining one another, and constantly separating, say, emancipating one another, banding together in a manner that separates us (the idea of 'resolve') rather than aggregates us (the idea of a 'collective').

We can thus contrast Emerson's use of the word 'resolve' to his use of the word 'statistics'. He states in 'Fate' that:

> One more fagot [that is, a bundle of sticks that is bound together] of these adamantine bandages, is, the new science of Statistics. It is a rule, that the most casual and extraordinary events – if the basis of population is broad enough – become matter of fixed calculation. (Emerson 1983: 950)

Emerson thus emphasises that certain bandages operate as bands, but that they can tie us together so strongly that they become illicit and contraband – like the mythical hard material 'adamant' that these statistical bandages are made of.

Emerson thus limits the laws of statistics in order to leave room for what he calls, in 'Circles', 'The last chamber, the last closet', the one that is 'never opened', the one where 'there is always a residuum unknown, unanalyzable' (ibid. 405–6). For Emerson, everyone thus contains within them something that cannot be broken down further, something 'unanalyzable', something beyond the reach of the totalising logic of the *semblable* and self-same, the kind, for example, extolled by Tocqueville. This is revealed above all in the prefatory essay to *Representative Men*, 'Uses of Great Men', when Emerson states that 'there are no common men', but instead, there is 'secret liking' (ibid. 630, 618): a form of liking, of likeness, that partakes of the secret, that goes with the secret, a being-with that goes with the very thing that sets things apart, the secret, the thing that separates (*se*, one's own). This secret is 'unanalyzable', Emerson suggests, not because this residence of self has a solid foundation, an indivisible bottom line – since this would be to disregard, as he puts it in 'Circles', that 'Every thing looks permanent until its secret is known' and that 'this surface on which we stand, is not fixed, but sliding' – but because this secret separates oneself not only from others, but from oneself (ibid. 404). This secret place ('the last closet'), rather than being the place of one's true self, is thus repositioned as a kind of portal, an opening, the opening to another self. The last chamber is as a result, somewhat paradoxically, always empty. As Emerson puts it in 'History', the inner sanctum of the self is nothing but the pursuit of the 'unattained but attainable self' (ibid. 239). There is no final home in this domestic picture, precisely because the 'last chamber' is not a home, because it is not situated as the home-of-oneself. The 'last chamber' consequently is never the proper identity of oneself since it is already different from itself – insofar as it is constituted *by* this difference to itself. The self, for Emerson, thus inscribes a secret in itself, in the self-same.

Emerson consequently ensures that the role of the singular, the individual, the 'unknown', is respected even in movements of social and political reform; there is, for Emerson, no reform without respect for singularity and no singularity without respect for reform. As he puts it in the 'Kansas Relief Meeting', a meeting about (social) reform: 'First, the private citizen, then primary assembly, and the government last' (Emerson 2002: 113). But the fact that Emerson strives to respond to both unity and diversity, the singularity of reform and the reform of singularity, and that he does so by linking a certain diversity with unity, a 'with' that divides unity in constituting it, makes the description he gives of Plato in *Representative Men* fitting as a self-description, one that turns on itself to describe itself (Emerson 1983: 641). As he writes, Plato was 'resolved that the two poles of thought shall appear in his statement.

His argument and sentence are self-poised and spherical' (ibid. 641). Instead of two poles, two extreme edges, two opposites that never meet, we thus find a sphere, something balanced between two points, that is, yet another circular form.

Rather than taking the metaphor of the 'election' literally, we might then say that Emerson is turning the metaphor of 'election' around. It is therefore not a matter of inverting the metaphorical meaning of election, going straight from the metaphor to the literal meaning, as Becovitch (1975) would have it, but of determining the turn that makes election possible in the first place. Emerson thus does not inverse the 'metaphor' of election – and so the idea of an 'elect people' – as displace it altogether, in a word, move it elsewhere. The elect have not already been elected. Emerson is as a result continuously converting the trope of election rather than relying on the pre-established idea of conversion. He thus disrupts those who wish to settle the USA in the name of a 'national election' that holds this-land-to-be-ours. There is thus no single place, no single circumlocution, where election is finally gathered together or settled in Emerson. The process of election that replaces one heading for another is itself endlessly replaced. This absence of an assembly point around 'election', its resolve to resolution, rather than paralysing democracy is instead for Emerson the very chance of democracy.

Emerson thus proposes an amendment to the constitution, the constitution of self and the Constitution of the USA. And he does this by emphasising the routes instead of the roots of language – circulation instead of belonging. The fact that the cords of unity are to be resolved rather than tied together, for Emerson, the fact that words like 'election' constantly circulate, dissolve and resolve, means for this sage of Concord that our concord together at a given place will never be the result of some accord about language or through language. As Emerson puts it in 'Experience', 'Our love of the real draws us to permanence, but health of body consists in circulation. We need change of objects' (Emerson 1983: 476). The body politic thus by necessity requires circulation to remain healthy – to think otherwise for Emerson is to allow into the heart of politics the threat of bad blood.

Indeed, in his essay 'Politics', Emerson declares that 'society is fluid; there are no such roots and centres; but any particle may suddenly become the centre of the movement, and compel the system to gyrate round it' (ibid. 559). One way to read this passage, one that shuns the language of centres in favour of circumnavigation and transition, is as a rewording of the democratic body politic and the rotation of office; the rotation promised and premised in all forms of democracy, the rotation, for example, that informs us that one's position in society, one's standing in it, may not be the same as the one society finds you in or assigns you to. Derrida emphasises that the space of the circle is essential for thinking about and through democracy when he states:

> It seems difficult to think the desire for or the naming of any democratic space without what is called in Latin a *rota*, that is, without rotation or rolling, without the roundness or rotating rondure of something round that turns round in circles, without the circularity, be it pretechnical, premechanical, or pregeometrical, of some automobilic and autonomic turn or, rather, return to self, toward the self and upon the self; indeed, it seems difficult to think such a desire for or naming of democratic space without the rotary motion of some quasi-circular return or rotation toward the self, toward the origin itself, toward and upon the self of the origin, whenever it is a question, for example, of sovereign self-determination. (Derrida 2005d: 10)

What is in question in Emerson is thus something larger than – though it includes – the constitutional concept of rotation; as Emerson puts it in 'Self-Reliance', 'greater self-reliance must work a revolution in all the offices and relations of men' (Emerson 1983: 275). Emerson thus democratises the very movement of self-reliance; it is not elite-centric, or State-centric, but makes its office with the *demos* at large, with any particle of the *demos*, not merely with those who *govern* democracy ('there are no common men'). In fact, Judith N. Shklar observes in her 'Emerson and the Inhibitions of Democracy' that 'rotation in office was *the* great watchword of Jacksonian democracy' (Shklar 1990: 608; original emphasis). It is thus perhaps all the more telling that Emerson does not restrict this office to the 'political office' as such – self-reliance is not merely a matter of political participation or reform for Emerson, it is not, for instance, exhausted in the idea of political virtue. Rather, like the democracy spoken by Tocqueville, it speaks to *all* areas of life – all 'relations of men' – including one's cultural and intellectual life, one's so-called inner life.

It also important to note that the image Emerson uses is once again a circle, and crucially, it is not simply a matter of ever expanding circles, circles going ever outwards like a ripple – since this might simply equate to imperialistic expansion, and so, the 'empire' of 'immense egotism' that Emerson opposes – but the fact that a further circle can be drawn anytime and anywhere, that the encircling of circles can never claim to be finished or at an end (Emerson 1983: 219). The circles described by Emerson thus do not settle anything, instead, they perfect something, improve it, without bringing that process to an end. They may thus be said to resist capitalising on the figure of the capital, the figure of the centre, the *caput* – the Capitol, the central figure for the seat of government ('any particle may suddenly become the centre'). We cannot even know, Emerson suggests, where a further circle can be drawn, or where it will be drawn to, or where it will lead, or what it will encompass, until it is drawn. In other words, there is no constant centre, no unmoved mover at the centre of an Emersonian circle. This kind of circle therefore resists rather than assists the political heading known as centralisation, not in the name of mere individual egoism but in the name of attaining one's unattained but attainable self.

## EMERSON AND THE POET

If Emerson has not been often viewed as a political philosopher, he has not been ignored in the field of language and literature; indeed, this is normally one of the reasons *why* he is not viewed as a (political) philosopher. The significance of Emerson's language is registered by Stanley Cavell when he writes that:

> For an American, the discovery of such a language [namely, one that can be said to be *without* authority, or that authorises itself only by *continuing* to question itself] [. . .] presents a double task, since America, as Emerson was beginning to write, had as yet to inherit effectively a patrimony in European philosophy; no one had proven that the encounter of America with philosophy (beyond its occurrence in certain political doctrines) was feasible, hence had shown what it might sound like. To express America's difference (one could say, to justify its existence, its independence) was for Emerson's generation most pressing in its call for a mode of literature that expresses the American experience. Emerson, in effect, established both modes of expression, suggesting that, for America, philosophy and literature would bear a relation to each other not envisioned in the given, outstanding traditions of philosophy in England and in Germany. Or, if it were said that this relation was in fact precisely envisioned in the movement called romanticism [. . .] it would have to be added that in both standing traditions the development of literary practise unfolded in the presence of, in a process of withstanding, established philosophy. (Cavell 2003: 3–4; my emphasis)

What Cavell highlights in his illuminating reading of Emerson, is that philosophy and literature could bear a relation to each other otherwise than in Europe, since the USA would name the place where literature was no longer subordinate to philosophy, determined by it in advance. One can usefully compare this with Derrida's views on literature, where what might be thought to be 'literature' up until at least the nineteenth century, even when resisting philosophy, was a further development of philosophy, yielding from the outset to the constraints philosophy imposed on it. In short, the concept of mimetological literature that Aristotle and Plato produced in the name of philosophy, so as to fix the essence of literature once and for all, to make it stand still, so as to stabilise conclusively the ontology of literature. If Derrida examines a contortion or folding back of this notion of *mimesis* in writers like Stéphane Mallarmé in the middle of the nineteenth century, one might say that for Cavell it is Emerson who plays this role in and for America, that it is Emerson who discloses that the USA can be the place where literature is not entirely determined or fixed in advance by the concept of literature produced by philosophy; where the authority of philosophy to name the being of literature and the idiom is put into question; where the idea of *mimesis* as literary-being of literature, its essence, is interrogated.

Cavell, moreover, emphasises in the passage above, through his use of the word or morpheme 'standing', the unsettling nature of this Emersonian event, not only to certain long-standing accounts of philosophy – philosophy as the establishment, as Descartes would have it, of an Archimedean point, somewhere to 'stand still', a firm and immobile point, a standpoint, in which to move the world – but also to accounts of language, and so, for example, the understanding of language at work in such diverse texts as Locke's *Essay Concerning Human Understanding* and Leibniz's *New Essays Concerning Understanding*. The USA is hence one of the places where the standing of literature and philosophy – and their mutual misunderstandings – was radically revised.

In addition, Cavell turns to Kant's notion of schematism several times when describing Emerson's form of writing. Claiming that Emerson has his own form of schematism, Cavell argues that Emerson is seeking to determine the conditions that make speaking together possible. As Cavell writes in 'Finding as Founding':

> Kant's demonstration requires what he calls a 'schematism' to show how objects are subsumed under or represented in a concept. Emerson's schematism, let me call it, requires a form or genre that synthesises or transcendentalises the genres of the conversion narrative, of the slave narrative, and of the narrative of voyage and discovery. For Emerson the forms that subsume – undertake – subjects under a concept [the world under a genre] become the conditions of experience, for his time. My association of Emerson with Kant on the necessity of schematism [or temporalisation] of forms [for Kant, the forms of judgement, which mark concepts; for Emerson the genres of texts, which mark narratives] is a proposal for work to be done. (Cavell 2003: 128; Cavell's interpolations)

Cavell returns to this topic in 'Aversive Thinking', once again linking Emerson's schematism to the conditions of experience outlined by Kant:

> Emerson is transfiguring Kant's key term 'condition' so that it speaks not alone of deducing twelve categories of the understanding but of deriving

– say schematising – every word in which we speak together (speaking together is what the word *condition* says), so that the conditions or terms in our language stand to be derived philosophically, deduced. (Cavell 2003: 147; original emphasis)

The parallel that Cavell makes between Kant's schematism and Emerson's schematism allows us to rethink the importance of language in Emerson's writings and the conditions associated with it. One of these conditions could be said to be Emerson's picturing of words as 'living things' rather than merely instrumental tools for communication. Emerson does this when he identifies words with horses in his essay 'The Poet', stating that 'in every word he says [that is, the poet] he rides on them as horses of thought' (Emerson 1983: 456). As Cavell puts it, words are thus 'declared to be horses on which we ride, suggesting both that they obey our intentions and that they work beyond our prowess' (Cavell 2003: 3). It thus leads Cavell to ask:

> what does speaking of words as horses rule out? Apart from other animals, it rules out, or differs from, for example, speaking of words as tools or saying that they are the bearers of meaning [. . .] Given that the idea of 'every word' is not a generalisation but bespeaks an attitude towards words as such, toward the fact of language, the horse suggests that we are in an attitude or posture of a certain grant of authority, such as humans may claim, over a realm of life not our own (ours to own), in view of some ground to cover or field to take. That words are under a *certain* control, one that requires that they obey as well as that they be obeyed. (Cavell 1990: 22; original emphasis)

Cavell consequently emphasises that Emerson's picturing of words as horses avoids the technoscientific account of language we find, for example, in Descartes, where words are primarily understood as tools, a simple, neutral and external instrument. While we cannot, as Emerson states, do anything we like with words, neither can we fully master them – their projections from one context to another, their context transcendence, will always outrace us.

But we may go further and suggest that Emerson's locution – horses of thought – is in fact a transfiguration, a rereading, of a passage found in Descartes' *Meditations*. Descartes is discussing the puzzle that one knows more distinctly about 'things' in the world, things foreign to oneself, than oneself – the ego that thinks, that allows 'things' in the world to be thought about in the first place. He diagnoses the source of the problem in the fact that:

> my mind enjoys wandering off [in French, *s'égarer*; in Latin, *aberrare*] and will not yet submit to being restrained within the bounds of truth. Very

well then; just this once let us give it a completely free rein [loosen its bridle one more time: *relâchons-lui donc encore une fois la bride*; *laxisimass habenas ei permittamus*], so that after a while, when it comes to tighten the reins [when it is led back], it may more readily submit to being curbed [it will let itself be ruled more easily]. (Descartes 1988b: 83–4)

Descartes thus confesses that his mind, the driver of his thought, is always falling into error, being sidetracked, diverted and driven astray. Descartes, in other words, compares – using an ancient Platonic image – his mind to a wayward horse. He states that he will provide it with *some* slack, so to speak, but only to facilitate its control more easily later on. The only time straying is permitted, in other words, is when it would allow us to keep *more* rigidly on the path, on the straight and narrow. As Georges Van den Abbeele notes, the Latin original of the *Meditations* cannot – and indeed does not – distinguish between the two senses of *erro*: to wander or to err (Van den Abbeele 1992: 45). Wandering, in short, is always an error – one must always keep to the path. One should therefore, according to Descartes, *exhaust* the potential for any deviation so as to ensure that the right path is all the easier to follow. The theme of the bridle is therefore about the mastery of truth and the vanquishing of error.

Emerson in his counter-reading of Descartes, one which is *contra* Descartes but which uses Descartes' own diction to undermine him, thus reclaims the right to wander, for words to wander, for philosophy to begin by wandering, not so as to deny that words must also be obeyed and followed, or to deny the intent of an author, but so as to acknowledge the possibility that words can at any time slip or stray from our reins. If words are horses in this outline, the individual lines of a page are the reins of any particular word, and these lines can be made more or less slack, more or less oblique. So the author, even the one who affords no leeway, no deviation, no wandering, cannot guarantee that 'his' words, the vehicles of thought, will not bolt away, find new meanings in unforeseen contexts; indeed, that others might master his words, find ways of whispering to them, about them, better than he does. Emerson insists, in other words, that words can escape from the straight and narrow, and yet not be errors, that the path laid out by words is not always so straightforward (*recte*). That we can learn as much from the roguish movement of words, from one field to another, as we can when we are rigorous, when we harness their equivocal and equine nature and ensure that they are clear and distinct, which is to say, immobile and fixed.

The image of the rein and the bridle is further characterised by Emerson later on in the essay when he states:

As the traveller who has lost his way, throws his reins on his horse's neck, and trusts to the instinct of the animal to find his road, so must we do with the divine animal who carries us through this world. (Emerson 1983: 460)

One can compare this to Descartes' image of the lost traveller who follows the straight road:

> [U]pon finding himself lost in a forest, [the lost traveller] should not wander about turning this way and that, and still less stay in one place, but should keep walking as straight as he can [*le plus droit*] in one direction, never changing it for slight reasons even if mere chance made him choose it in the first place; for in this way, even if he does not go exactly where he wishes, he will at least end up in a place where he is likely to be better off than in the middle of the forest. (Descartes 1988a: 32)

One should thus avoid – if one wants to progress – retracing one's steps, according to Descartes, for fear of doubling back on oneself. The straight road even *without* a planned itinerary is thus better than the meandering path. For Emerson, on the other hand, to rein in the meaning of a word is sometimes to entrust oneself to its unexpected route. Emerson thus counsels us – like Derrida does to 'the reader' in *The Postcard* – not to predestine our writings or our readings, not to foretell them. As Emerson puts in 'The American Scholar':

> One must be an inventor to read well [. . .] There is then creative reading as well as creative writing. When the mind is braced by labour and invention, the page of whatever book we read becomes luminous with manifold allusion. Every sentence is doubly significant, and the sense of our author is as broad as the world. (Emerson 1983: 59)

It is important to emphasise that Emerson in speaking of 'creative reading' does not deny that the author has some intent in the meaning of his words; after all, Emerson speaks of expanding our notion of authorship, and the lost traveller Emerson describes does not *abandon* his reins, he does not, in other words, decide to ride it out on his own. Rather, the process of reading is one of give and take, it must be handled well, and cannot be predestined – while not all progress is therefore methodical, this does not mean it is without method. In an instructive passage on the method of the reader, Derrida states:

> Because I still like him, I can foresee the impatience of the bad reader: this is the way I name or accuse the fearful reader, the reader in a hurry to be determined, decided upon deciding (in order to annul, in other words to bring back to oneself, one has to wish to know in advance what to expect (oneself)). Now, it is bad, and I know no other definition of the

bad, it is bad to predestine one's reading, it is always bad to foretell. It is bad, reader, no longer to like retracing one's steps. (Derrida 1987b: 4)

Following on from this, one might say that if Descartes is in too much of a 'hurry to be determined', 'decided upon deciding', Emerson, in contrast, leaves room to retrace 'one's steps', including the steps to come, the ones not yet taken. He therefore leaves room for what we might call the revisitation of the unexpected. But this attachment to language is not absolute, for while he states that we must attend to 'forms', he also informs us that 'they must be held lightly, and be very willingly translated into the equivalent terms which others use' (Emerson 1983: 464). The danger that poetic forms present is thus to think that they cannot be translated at all – given a new shape, reformulated or transformed in another language, be it in intra-lingual or inter-lingual terms. Emerson thus distinguishes that which is not translatable, that which is not convertible, and sides it with mysticism, and what is translatable and convertible, and sides it with philosophy. Emerson declares, 'let us have a little algebra, instead of this trite rhetoric, – universal signs, instead of these village symbols, – and we shall both be gainers' (ibid. 464). Emerson contrasts the territoriality of rhetorical symbols with universal and placeless signs, adding that the symbolism of algebra is still privileged in relation to philosophy insofar as it is universal, shared by all men and not simply the inhabitants of a single village. One should thus dwell on forms and symbols, but not use them to establish dwellings. As Emerson puts it earlier on in the essay, while 'talent may frolic and juggle; genius realizes and adds' (ibid. 451). Emerson thus uses the language of mathematics – for example, double, quadruple, centuple, equivalent, algebra, gainers, adding – to suggest that we will always gain a handsome return in returning to a text and multiplying its meanings, that we will never be overdrawn in our interpretations so long as we maintain our interest in them. He thus writes of Plato:

> This citizen of a town in Greece is no villager nor patriot. An Englishman reads and says, 'how English!' a German, – 'how Teutonic!' an Italian, – 'how Roman and Greek!' As they say that Helen of Argos had that universal beauty that every body felt related to her, so Plato seems, to a reader in New England, an American genius. His broad humanity transcends all sectional lines. (Emerson 1983: 634)

Emerson thus banks on the fact that genius broadens and expands our circle of reading; it reads creatively, so as to carry on – literally 'translate' – the project of universality for all men. Emerson's understanding of universality, his continual hope for it, is thus that it may speak to all men, not by generalising them, treating them as a collective or as an assembly that is self-identical – be it in terms of race, class, party, nation, and so on – but by allowing all men to speak in their own singular way. Emerson, in other words, addresses culture as an unending series of singularities. And yet, for Emerson each of these singularities, each of these idioms, is not an island, but part of the continent. The poet's job is not to be 'original', to cultivate or guard his originality, or to ensure it is not repeatable, but to find and experience one's own idiom in the idiom of the other. The poet thus ensures that the idiom – be it 'his' idiom, or a 'national' idiom – is neither his alone nor even simply the possession of a nation. Shakespeare's singular achievement, for Emerson, thus 'consists in not being original at all; in being altogether *receptive*; in letting the world do all, and suffering the spirit of the hour to pass unobstructed through the mind' (ibid. 711; my emphasis).

Hence the poet gets himself across by crossing himself out; the task of the poet, in other words, is to transverse experience, to be always at the crossroads, turning this way or that, to be crosswise at any given moment. As Derrida notes, the word 'experience' in fact implies 'passage, traversal, endurance, and rite of passage' (Derrida 1993a: 13). There is thus no idiom that is not already contained in or bound up with the idiom of the other, the experience of the other. The idiom is thus what responds to the other, it names a certain kind of hospitality, the 'the power to receive' as Emerson puts it in 'The Poet'. The power of the poet is thus to receive *more* than other men, for 'the poet is the Namer, or Language-maker, naming things sometimes after their appearance, sometimes after their essence, and giving to every one its own name and not another's, thereby rejoicing the intellect, which delights in detachment or boundary' (Emerson 1983: 456–7).

The poet thus makes hospitality possible in the first place by drawing boundaries, by differentiating things, by defining limits. But this 'delights' the intellect, that is, philosophy, since Emerson defines the philosopher as the definer *par excellence*:

> At last comes Plato, the distributor, who needs no barbaric paint, or tattoo, or whooping; for he can define. He leaves with Asia the vast and superlative; he is the arrival of accuracy and intelligence. 'He shall be as a god to me, who can rightly divide and define.' This defining is philosophy. (Emerson 1983: 637)

Yet the intellectual power to demarcate, to draw boundaries, to make things clearer, can also, paradoxically, limit our understanding, for Emerson. We thus find that this power to receive and define is tempered in the epigraph to 'Experience' by the experience of the other, which is not experienced as the definition of the other, but the other of definition, the other *without* name. For in the epigraph of that essay, one that follows on from the 'The Poet', Emerson names that experience which is '[o]mnipresent without name', namely, the experience of the other that exceeds the intellect, the other that exceeds the boundary of self but which cannot be detached since it is everywhere (ibid. 469).

In fact, in 'Self-Reliance', Emerson had already drawn on the nameless figure to describe the figure of the good. He writes:

> When good is near you, when you have life in yourself, it is not by any known or accustomed way; you shall not discern the foot-prints of any other; you shall not see the face of man; you shall not hear any name; – the way, the thought, the good shall be wholly strange and new. It shall exclude example and experience. You take the way from man, not to man. (Emerson 1983: 271)

Emerson thus differentiates what has gone before, custom, the footprints of another, the way, the method, the experience of the prior example, with the singular, the wholly strange and new, in sum, the unforeseen. This also means, as Emerson puts it, that 'all symbols are fluxional; all language is vehicular and transitive, and is good, as ferries and horses are, for conveyance, not as farms and houses are, for homestead' (ibid. 463). What Emerson declares in this passage is that there is no such thing as an idiom free of the vehicular; that it is the essence of language to be transitive, and that paradoxically, what is most idiomatic, what is most proper to language, cannot be claimed as or held to be property. We thus should not – cannot – appropriate words, appropriate them as national symbols, symbols of the homestead. Words, for Emerson, are thus never fully domesticated; symbols cannot be tied down to boundaries of the household and to its associated values – to put it somewhat economically, the familiar values of familial property and the homeland. Words and symbols cannot consequently be fenced off; they cannot be held steadfast – they will always derive and be further derived. Words as vehicles (or horses) are thus as viable in New England as in England.

This 'property' of symbols is in fact what allows them to convey things to others, to cross idioms, to carry things across the threshold of self. As Emerson states, 'In our way of talking, we say, "That is yours, this is mine", but the poet knows well that it is not his; that it is as strange and beautiful to him as to you' (ibid. 466). The poet's words can thus be as strange and foreign to the poet, the one who writes them, as to the reader, the stranger in strange lands. The poet consequently strangely resembles a stranger himself, a foreigner, one making 'his' own native tongue appear foreign to itself – out of place and out of joint. Emerson thus believes in the force of the uncanny and the unhomely (*das Unheimlich*).

The poet's success, accordingly, is not measured simply in terms of how well he represents us, but in the effect of estrangement he produces in his representation of our shared home, the home-of-one's-own. The secret of the poet is thus that he publicly shows us that language can never be walled up, sealed within the four walls of a dwelling or a homestead. As Emerson warns in 'Self-Reliance', we should never idolise a given thinker's 'classification' of things so that it 'passes for the end', otherwise we will be like, so to speak, one of those captives in Plato's cave where 'the walls of the system blend to their eye in the remote horizon with the walls of the universe' (ibid. 277). As a result, Emerson continually channels his energy into pointing out false limits – our unending ability to deceive ourselves, to limit ourselves by taking our current horizon as the limit of the possible, what all too readily passes, as he puts it, for the end (e.g. *telos, terminus, eskhatos*). He thus writes in 'Experience' that: 'we have not arrived at a wall, but at interminable oceans' (ibid. 486).

For Emerson, one must abandon claims of propriety, of belonging, of ownership, not in order to embrace a technolanguage of universal communication, one which is *atopos*, but in order to cultivate the *oikos* that is not identical to itself, that does not belong to someone, the abode that is constituted only as passage to the outside world. What Emerson calls for, therefore, is a new respect for the idiom in the republic – a republic that respects the singularity of the idiom, and a singular idiom that does not permanently estrange itself from the republic. In short, a situation where the poet abides in the commonwealth, with the commonwealth, and sometimes against the commonwealth. The poet's demonstrations, his protests as well as exhibitions, are therefore not simply private, they are not removed from public demonstrations, shut away from the demonstrations we find, for example, on the street, or elsewhere in the republic. The poet's civil disobedience is, accordingly, not reducible to 'mere' symbolism, but neither is the disobedience demonstrated in the language of poet, the symbols he uses, external to his standpoint. He stands with us by standing against us, by *with*standing us. For Emerson, loving your country thus means calling it out – and calling out to it – when it is wrong.

Emerson is hence not so much the mind of America, as a thinker of hospitality. That Emerson deracinates rather than guards his own tradition, namely Transcendentalism, claiming that each instantiation of this movement in culture is singular, but also repeatable. Rather than merely return to the originary, as Fichte does, or claim that his movement is uniquely methodical and repeatable, as Tocqueville does, Emerson pursues a path that shows how indebted and hospitable American thought is to 'foreign philosophy'. He thus does not equate the USA with the philosophical as such, nor claim that Transcendentalism is the 'American Way', something properly or purely American. Transcendentalism is thus not the philosophical equivalent of Manifest Destiny as Simpson (1986) claims. While there is a residual cosmonationalism strain in Emerson, it is one tempered by his continual critique of the USA, and its failures to adequately deal with the question of the times – that is to say, slavery.

Perhaps what is most instructive, however, is the manner in which Emerson writes – his use of language in philosophy. If Kant claimed that philosophy must be written in natural language, but failed to analyse the philosophical and political consequences of this, and if Fichte claimed that language to be German in spirit or *Geist*, and Tocqueville, in turn, French in method, Emerson does not claim that one language is the language of philosophy, as much as disrupt the very notion that philosophy has a home, a native language to return to or be projected towards. His strategy of embracing both unity and variety, oneness and otherness, is thus analogous to Derrida's notion of '*plus d'une langue*' – more than one language, no more than one language, no longer of one language, more of one language (Derrida 1986: 15).

## NOTES

1. Derrida (1984–8), Box 18, Folder 2, Seminar 3, p. 1.
2. The philosophical topic of 'forms' is, of course, a vast one, and will not be developed methodically here, but one should note, at the very least, that forms and footprints have, so to speak, crossed paths with one another since at least Plotinus, due to his claim that 'the trace is the form of the formless' (*to gar ikhnos tou amorphous morphe*), since the Greek word *ikhnos*, as well as meaning 'trace', can also mean 'track' or 'footprint'. For an analysis of this statement by Plotinus, see Derrida 1982: 172f.
3. Dennis Redmond, 'ND Keywords', available at <http://members.efn.org/~dredmond/ND_Keywords.html> (last accessed 20 July 2017).

# Bibliography

Abizadeh, Arash (2005), 'Was Fichte an Ethnic Nationalist? On Cultural Nationalism and Its Double', *History of Political Thought*, 26.2, summer, 334–59.
Adorno, Theodor W. (1983), *Negative Dialectics*, trans. E. B. Ashton, London: Continuum.
Adorno, Theodor W. (1991), 'The Essay as Form', in *Notes to Literature, Volume 1*, ed. Rolf Tiedemann, trans. Shierry Weber Nicholsen, New York: Columbia University Press.
Adorno, Theodor (2005), 'On the Question: "What Is German?"', in *Critical Models: Interventions and Catchwords*, trans. Henry W. Pickford, New York: Columbia University Press.
Allen, Barbara (2005), *Tocqueville, Covenant and the Democratic Revolution*, Lanham, MD: Lexington Books.
Anderson, Benedict [1983] (2006), *Imagined Communities*, rev. edn, London: Verso.
Anderson, Douglas R. (2006), *Philosophy Americana: Making Philosophy at Home in American Culture*, New York: Fordham University Press.
Arendt, Hannah (1990), *On Revolution*, London: Penguin.
Aristotle (1996), *Politics*, trans. Jonathan Barnes, Cambridge: Cambridge University Press.
Arsić, Branka (2010), *On Leaving: A Reading in Emerson*, Cambridge, MA: Harvard University Press.
Arsić, Branka and Cary Wolfe (2010), *The Other Emerson*, Minneapolis: University of Minnesota Press.
Azouvi, François (1992), 'Descartes', in Pierre Nora (ed.), *Les lieux de mémoire*, vol. 3, Paris: Gallimard.
Azouvi, François (1998), 'Descartes', in Pierre Nora and Lawrence D. Kritzman (eds), *Realms of Memory*, vol. 3, trans. Arthur Goldhammer, New York: Columbia University Press.
Azouvi, François (2002), *Descartes et la France*, Paris: Librairie Arthème Fayard.
Azouvi, François and Dominique Bourel (1991), *De Königsberg à Paris: la réception de Kant en France*, Paris: Librairie philosophique J. Vrin.
Balibar, Étienne (1994), 'Fichte and the Internal Border', in *Masses, Classes, Ideas: Studies on Politics and Philosophy before and after Marx*, trans. James Swenson, London: Routledge.
Balibar, Étienne (2000), 'What Makes a People a People? Rousseau and Kant', in *Masses,*

*Classes, Ideas: Studies on Politics and Philosophy before and after Marx*, ed. Mike Hill and Warren Montag, London: Verso.
Balibar, Étienne and Immanuel Wallerstein (1991), *Race, Nation and Class: Ambiguous Identities*, trans. Chris Turner, London: Verso.
Bambach, Charles (2005), *Heidegger's Roots: Nietzsche, National Socialism, and the Greeks*, Ithaca, NY: Cornell University Press.
Barnard, Frederick M. (2003), *Herder on Nationality, Humanity, and History*, Montreal: McGill-Queen's University Press.
Beardsworth, Richard (1996), *Derrida and the Political*, London: Routledge.
Beck, Lewis White (1969), *Early German Philosophy*, Cambridge, MA: Harvard University Press.
Becovitch, Sacvan (1975), 'Emerson the Prophet: Romanticism, Puritanism, and Auto-American-Biography', in David Levin (ed.), *Emerson: Prophecy, Metamorphosis, and Influence*, New York and London: Columbia University Press.
Bennington, Geoffrey (2000), *Interrupting Derrida*, London: Routledge.
Berlin, Isaiah (1979), *Against the Current: Essays in the History of Ideas*, ed. Henry Hardy, London: Hogarth Press.
Berlin, Isaiah (1990), *The Crooked Timber of Humanity: Chapters in the History of Ideas*, ed. Henry Hardy, London: John Murray.
Berlin, Isaiah (1996), *The Sense of Reality: Studies in Ideas and their History*, ed. Henry Hardy, London: Chatto and Windus.
Berlin, Isaiah (2002), *Freedom and Its Betrayal*, Princeton: Princeton University Press.
Berman, Antoine (1992), *The Experience of the Foreign*, trans. S. Heyvaert, New York: State University of New York Press.
Bernasconi, Robert (2001), 'Who Invented the Concept of Race? Kant's Role in the Enlightenment Construction of Race', in Robert Bernasconi (ed.), *Race*, Oxford: Blackwell.
Billig, Michael (1995), *Banal Nationalism*, London: Sage Publications.
Bloom, Harold (1975), 'The Freshness of Transformation: Emerson's Dialectics of Influence', in David Levin (ed.), *Emerson: Prophecy, Metamorphosis, and Influence*, New York and London: Columbia University Press.
Bloom, Harold (1982), *Agon: Towards a Theory of Revisionism*, Oxford: Oxford University Press.
Bloom, Harold (1984), 'Mr. America', *New York Review of Books*, 22 November, 19–24.
Bloom, Harold (1993), 'Emerson: Power at the Crossing', in Lawrence Buell (ed.), *Ralph Waldo Emerson: A Collection of Critical Essays*, Englewood Cliffs, NJ: Prentice Hall.
Bloom, Harold (2007), 'Introduction', in Harold Bloom (ed.), *Ralph Waldo Emerson*, New York: Infobase Publishing.
Bloom, Harold, Paul de Man, Jacques Derrida, Geoffrey Hartman and J. Hillis Miller (1979), *Deconstruction and Criticism*, New York: Continuum-Seabury Press.
Breazeale, Daniel and Tom Rockmore (eds) (2008), *After Jena: New Essays on Fichte's Later Philosophy*, Evanston: Northwestern University Press.
Breuilly, John (2000), 'Nationalism and the History of Ideas', in *Proceedings of the British Academy*, Oxford: Oxford University Press.
Breuilly, John (2006), 'Introduction', in Ernest Gellner, *Nations and Nationalism*, Oxford: Blackwell.
Buell, Lawrence (ed.) (1993), *Ralph Waldo Emerson: A Collection of Critical Essays*, Englewood Cliffs, NJ: Prentice Hall.
Buell, Lawrence (2003), *Emerson*, Cambridge, MA: Harvard University Press.

Buell, Lawrence (ed.) (2006), *The American Transcendentalists: Essential Writings*, New York: The Modern Library.
Buell, Lawrence (2010), 'Manifest Destiny and the Question of the Moral Absolute', in Joel Myerson, Sandra Harbert Petrulionis and Laura Dassow Walls (eds), *The Oxford Handbook of American Transcendentalism*, Oxford: Oxford University Press.
Cadava, Eduardo (1997), *Emerson and the Climates of History*, Stanford: Stanford University Press.
Cadava, Eduardo (2010), 'The Guano of History', in Branka Arsić and Cary Wolfe (eds), *The Other Emerson*, Minneapolis: University of Minnesota Press.
Carroll, David (ed.) (1994), *States of Theory*, Stanford: Stanford University Press.
Cassin, Barbara (ed.) (2004), *Vocabulaire européen des philosophies*, Paris: Editions du Seuil; Le Robert.
Cassin, Barbara, Emily Apter, Jacques Lezra and Michael Wood (eds) (2014), *Dictionary of Untranslatables: A Philosophical Lexicon*, Princeton: Princeton University Press.
Cassirer, Ernst (1945), *Rousseau, Kant, Goethe: Two Essays*, Princeton: Princeton University Press.
Cavallar, Georg (1999), *Kant and the Theory and Practice of International Right*, Cardiff: Cardiff University Press.
Cavell, Stanley (1981), *The Senses of Walden*, San Francisco: North Point Press.
Cavell, Stanley (1988), *In Quest of the Ordinary: Lines of Skepticism and Romanticism*, Chicago: University of Chicago Press.
Cavell, Stanley (1990), *Conditions Handsome and Unhandsome: The Constitution of Emersonian Perfectionism*, Chicago: University of Chicago Press.
Cavell, Stanley (1996), *A Pitch of Philosophy: Autobiographical Exercises*, Cambridge, MA: Harvard University Press.
Cavell, Stanley (2003), *Emerson's Transcendental Etudes*, Stanford: Stanford University Press.
Cavell, Stanley (2004), *Cities of Words: Pedagogical Letters on a Register of the Moral Life*, Cambridge, MA and London: The Belknap Press of Harvard University Press.
Cavell, Stanley (2010), *Little Did I Know: Excerpts from Memory*, Stanford: Stanford University Press.
Caygill, Howard (2008), 'Introduction: Kant and the Language of Philosophy', in Howard Caygill (ed.), *Kant Dictionary*, Oxford: Blackwell.
Cheah, Pheng (2003), *Spectral Nationality*, New York: Columbia University Press.
Cheah, Pheng (2006), *Inhuman Conditions*, Cambridge, MA: Harvard University Press.
Cheah, Pheng and Suzanne Guerlac (eds) (2009), *Derrida and The Time of The Political*, Durham, NC and London: Duke University Press.
Cicero (1991), *On Duties*, trans. M. T. Griffins and E. M. Atkins, Cambridge: Cambridge University Press.
Cicero (1999), *On the Commonwealth*, trans. James E. G. Zetzel, Cambridge: Cambridge University Press.
Cohen, Edward E. (2002), *The Athenian Nation*, Princeton: Princeton University Press.
Cohen, Hermann (1915), *Deutschtum und Judentum mit grundlegenden Betrachtungen über Staat und Internationalismus*, Giessen: Töpelmann.
Cohen, Hermann (1993), *Reason and Hope: Selections from the Jewish Writings of Hermann Cohen*, trans. and ed. Eva Jospe, Cincinnati: Hebrew Union College Press.
Conant, James (2005), 'Cavell and the Concept of America', in Russell B. Goodman (ed.), *Contending with Stanley Cavell*, Oxford: Oxford University Press.
Conant, James (2006), 'The Recovery of Greece and the Discovery of America', in Alice Crary and Sanford Shieh (eds), *Reading Cavell*, London: Routledge.

Crary, Alice and Sanford Shieh (2006), *Reading Cavell*, London: Routledge.
Crépon, Marc (1996), *Les géographies de l'esprit: enquête sur la caractérisation des peuples de Leibniz à Hegel*, Paris: Bibliothèque philosophique Payot.
Crépon, Marc (1998), 'L'Idée de "philosophie nationale"', in André Jacob (ed.), *Encyclopédie philosophique universelle, IV, Le Discours Philosophique*, Paris: Presses universitaires de France.
Crépon, Marc, Barbara Cassin and Claudia Moatti (2014), 'People/Race/Nation', in Barbara Cassin (ed.), *Dictionary of Untranslatables: A Philosophical Lexicon*, trans. Steven Rendall et al., Princeton: Princeton University Press.
Critchley, Simon (2006), 'Frankfurt Impromptu – Remarks on Derrida and Habermas', in Lasse Thomassen (ed.), *The Derrida-Habermas Reader*, Edinburgh: Edinburgh University Press.
Cumming, Robert Denoon (1979), *Starting Point*, Chicago: University of Chicago Press.
Deledalle, Gerard (1996), 'Can Philosophy Have a Nationality?', in Robert W. Burch and Herman J. Saatkamp (eds), *Frontiers in American Philosophy*, vol. 2, College Station: A & M University Press.
de Man, Paul (1996), *Aesthetic Ideology*, ed. and with an introduction by Andrzej Warminski, Minneapolis and London: University of Minnesota Press.
Derrida, Jacques (1967), *L'Écriture et la différence*, Paris: Seuil.
Derrida, Jacques (1972a), *La Dissémination*, Paris: Seuil.
Derrida, Jacques (1972b), *Marges de la philosophie*, Paris: Editions de Minuit.
Derrida, Jacques (1974), *Of Grammatology*, trans. Gayatri Chakravorty Spivak, Baltimore: Johns Hopkins University Press.
Derrida, Jacques (1978), *Writing and Difference*, trans. Alan Bass, Chicago: University of Chicago Press.
Derrida, Jacques (1980), *La Carte postale: de Socrate à Freud et au-delà*, Paris: Flammarion.
Derrida, Jacques (1981a), *Dissemination*, trans. Barbara Johnson, Chicago: University of Chicago Press.
Derrida, Jacques (1981b), *Positions*, trans. Alan Bass, Chicago: University of Chicago Press.
Derrida, Jacques (1982), *Margins of Philosophy*, trans. Alan Bass, Chicago: University of Chicago Press.
Derrida, Jacques (1983), 'La langue et le discours de la méthode', in *Recherches sur la philosophie et le langage*, no. 3, Grenoble: Groupe de recherche sur la philosophie et le langage.
Derrida, Jacques (1984), *Signéponge/Signsponge*, bilingual edn, trans. Richard Rand, New York: Columbia University Press.
Derrida, Jacques (1984–8), *Nationalité et nationalisme philosophiques*, unpublished seminars held in UC Irvine Special Collections and Archive. (Jacques Derrida Papers, MS-C01, Special Collections and Archives, The UC Irvine Libraries, Irvine, CA, USA.)
Derrida, Jacques (1986), *Glas*, trans. John P. Leavey, Jr. and Richard Rand, Lincoln: University of Nebraska Press.
Derrida, Jacques (1987a), *De l'esprit*, Paris: Galilée.
Derrida, Jacques (1987b), *The Post Card*, trans. Alan Bass, Chicago: University of Chicago Press.
Derrida, Jacques (1988), *The Ear of the Other: Otobiography, Transference, Translation*, trans. Peggy Kamuf, Lincoln: University of Nebraska Press.
Derrida, Jacques (1989), *Of Spirit*, trans. Rachel Bowlby, Chicago: University of Chicago Press.
Derrida, Jacques (1990), *Du droit à la philosophie*, Paris: Galilée.

Derrida, Jacques (1992a), 'Onto-Theology of National-Humanism (Prolegomena to a Hypothesis)', trans. Geoffrey Bennington, *Oxford Literary Review*, 14, 3–23; also in Jacques Derrida (2007), *Jacques Derrida: Basic Writings*, ed. Barry Stocker, London: Routledge.
Derrida, Jacques (1992b), *The Other Heading*, trans. Pascale-Anne Brault and Michael B. Naas, Bloomington and Indianapolis: Indiana University Press.
Derrida, Jacques (1992c), 'This Strange Institution Called Literature', in Derek Attridge (ed.), *Acts of Literature*, trans. Geoffrey Bennington and Rachel Bowlby, London: Routledge.
Derrida, Jacques (1993a), *Aporias*, trans. Thomas Dutoit, Stanford: Stanford University Press.
Derrida, Jacques (1993b), 'Back from Moscow, in the USSR', in Mark Poster (ed.), *Politics, Theory and Contemporary Culture*, New York: Columbia University Press.
Derrida, Jacques (1993c), 'On a Newly Apocalyptic Tone in Philosophy', in Peter Fenves (ed.), *Raising the Tone of Philosophy*, Baltimore: Johns Hopkins University Press.
Derrida, Jacques (1993d), *Spectres de Marx*, Paris: Galilée.
Derrida, Jacques (1994a), *Politiques de l'amitié*, Paris: Galilée.
Derrida, Jacques (1994b), 'Some Statements and Truisms about Neologisms, Newisms, Positisms, Parasitisms, and other Small Seismisms' in David Carroll (ed.), *The States of 'Theory'*, Stanford: Stanford University Press.
Derrida, Jacques (1994c), *Specters of Marx*, trans. Peggy Kamuf, New York: Routledge.
Derrida, Jacques (1995a), 'Khôra', in Thomas Dutoit (ed.), *On the Name*, Stanford: Stanford University Press.
Derrida, Jacques (1995b), 'Passages – from Traumatism to Promise', in Elisabeth Weber (ed.), *Points: Interviews 1974–1994*, trans. Peggy Kamuf et al., Stanford: Stanford University Press.
Derrida, Jacques (1996), *Le Monolinguisme de l'autre*, Paris: Galilée.
Derrida, Jacques (1998a), 'Fidelité à plus d'un', *Idiomes, nationalités, déconstruction: Rencontre de Rabat avec Jacques Derrida*, special issue, *Cahiers INTERSIGNES*, 13.
Derrida, Jacques (1998b), *Monolingualism of the Other*, trans. Patrick Mensah, Stanford: Stanford University Press.
Derrida, Jacques (1999), *Adieu to Emmanuel Levinas*, trans. Michael Naas and Pascalle-Anne Brault, Stanford: Stanford University Press.
Derrida, Jacques (2000), *Of Hospitality: Anne Dufourmantelle Invites Jacques Derrida to Respond*, trans. Rachel Bowlby, Stanford: Stanford University Press.
Derrida, Jacques (2002a), *Acts of Religion*, ed. Gil Anidjar, trans. Samuel Weber, London: Routledge.
Derrida, Jacques (2002b), *Ethics, Institutions, and the Right to Philosophy*, trans. and ed. Peter Pericles Trifonas, Lanham: Rowman & Littlefield.
Derrida, Jacques (2002c), *Who's Afraid of Philosophy?: Right to Philosophy 1*, trans. Jan Plug, Stanford: Stanford University Press.
Derrida, Jacques (2002d), *Without Alibi*, ed., trans. and with an introduction by Peggy Kamuf, Stanford: Stanford University Press.
Derrida, Jacques (2003a), *Philosophy in the Time of Terror: Dialogues with Jürgen Habermas and Jacques Derrida*, ed. Giovanna Borradori, Chicago: University of Chicago Press.
Derrida, Jacques (2003b), *Psyché: inventions de l'autre, II*, Paris: Galilée.
Derrida, Jacques (2003c), *Voyous: Deux essais sur la raison*, Paris: Galilée.
Derrida, Jacques (2004a), *Eyes of the University: Right to Philosophy 2*, trans. Sylvia Söderlind, Stanford: Stanford University Press.
Derrida, Jacques (2004b), *For What Tomorrow . . . A Dialogue*, trans. Jeff Fort, Stanford: Stanford University Press.

Derrida, Jacques (2005a), *On Touching – Jean-Luc Nancy*, trans. Christine Irizarry, Stanford: Stanford University Press.
Derrida, Jacques (2005b), *Paper Machine*, trans. Rachel Bowlby, Stanford: Stanford University Press.
Derrida, Jacques (2005c), *Politics of Friendship*, trans. George Collins, London: Verso.
Derrida, Jacques (2005d), *Rogues*, trans. Pascale-Anne Brault and Michael Naas, Stanford: Stanford University Press.
Derrida, Jacques (2005e), *Sovereignties in Question: The Poetics of Paul Celan*, ed. Thomas Dutoit and Outi Pasanen, New York: Fordham University Press.
Derrida, Jacques (2007a), *Jacques Derrida: Basic Writings*, ed. Barry Stocker, London: Routledge.
Derrida, Jacques (2007b), *Psyche: Inventions of the Other, Volume 1*, ed. Peggy Kamuf and Elizabeth Rottenberg, Stanford: Stanford University Press.
Derrida, Jacques (2008), *Psyche: Inventions of the Other, Volume 2*, ed. Peggy Kamuf and Elizabeth Rottenberg, Stanford: Stanford University Press.
Derrida, Jacques (2009), *The Beast and the Sovereign*, trans. Geoffrey Bennington, Chicago: University of Chicago Press.
Derrida, Jacques (2010), 'We Other Greeks', in Miriam Leonard (ed.), *Derrida and Antiquity*, Oxford: Oxford University Press.
Derrida, Jacques (2011), *Parages*, trans. Tom Conley, James Hulbert, John P. Leavey and Avitall Ronell, Stanford: Stanford University Press.
Derrida, Jacques and John D. Caputo (1997), *Deconstruction in a Nutshell: A Conversation with Jacques Derrida*, New York: Fordham University Press.
De Sanctis, Francesco M. (1992), 'The Question of Fraternity in *Democracy in America*', in Eduardo Nolla (ed.), *Liberty, Equality, Democracy*, New York: New York University Press.
Descartes, René (1988a), 'Discourse on Method', in *Descartes: Selected Philosophical Writings*, trans. John Cottingham, Robert Stoothoff and Dugald Murdoch, Cambridge: Cambridge University Press.
Descartes, René (1988b), 'Meditations on First Philosophy', in *Descartes: Selected Philosophical Writings*, trans. John Cottingham, Robert Stoothoff and Dugald Murdoch, Cambridge: Cambridge University Press.
Descartes, René (1988c), 'Principles of Philosophy', in *Descartes: Selected Philosophical Writings*, trans. John Cottingham, Robert Stoothoff and Dugald Murdoch, Cambridge: Cambridge University Press.
Descartes, René (1988d), 'Rules for the Direction of our Native Intelligence', in *Descartes: Selected Philosophical Writings*, trans. John Cottingham, Robert Stoothoff and Dugald Murdoch, Cambridge: Cambridge University Press.
Dewey, John (1903), 'Emerson – The Philosopher of Democracy', *International Journal of Ethics*, 13.4, 405–13.
Dewey, John (1915), *German Philosophy and Politics*, New York: Henry Holt.
Dumont, Louis (1986), *Essays on Individualism: Modern Ideology in Anthropological Perspective*, Chicago and London: University of Chicago Press.
Eigen, Sarah and Mark Larrimore (eds) (2006), *The German Invention of Race*, Albany: State University of New York Press.
Eldridge, Richard (ed.) (2003), *Stanley Cavell*, Cambridge: Cambridge University Press.
Elias, Norbert (1994), *The Civilising Process: The History of Manners*, trans. Edmund Jephcott, Oxford: Basil Blackwell.
Emerson, Ralph Waldo (1983), *Essays and Lectures*, ed. Joel Porte, New York: Library of America.

Emerson, Ralph Waldo (1995), *Emerson's Antislavery Writings*, ed. Len Gougeon and Joel Myerson, New Haven, CT and London: Yale University Press.
Emerson, Ralph Waldo (2002), 'Kansas Relief Meeting', in *Emerson's Antislavery Writings*, ed. Len Gougeon and Joel Myerson, New Haven, CT: Yale University Press.
Emerson, Ralph Waldo (2005), *The Selected Lectures of Ralph Waldo Emerson, 1843–1871, Volume 1*, ed. Ronald A. Bosco and Joel Myerson, Athens: University of Georgia Press.
Emerson, Ralph Waldo (2008), *Emerson: Political Writings*, ed. Kenneth Sacks, Cambridge: Cambridge University Press.
Emerson, Ralph Waldo (2010), *The Collected Works of Ralph Waldo Emerson: Letters and Social Aims, Volume VIII*, Cambridge, MA: Harvard University Press.
Espagne, Michel (1990), 'Die Rezeption der politischen Philosophie Fichtes in Frankreich', *Fichte-Studien*, 2, 193–222.
Espagne, Michel (1999), *Les Transferts culturels franco-allemands*, Paris: Presses universitaires de France.
Faull, Katherine (ed.) (1995), *Anthropology and the German Enlightenment*, Lewisburg: Bucknell University Press.
Fenves, Peter (1991), *Peculiar Fate: Metaphysics and World-History in Kant*, Ithaca and London: Cornell University Press.
Fenves, Peter (ed.) (1993), *Raising the Tone of Philosophy*, Baltimore: Johns Hopkins University Press.
Fenves, Peter (1998), 'The Scale of Enthusiasm', in Lawrence E. Klein and Anthony J. La Vopa (eds), *Enthusiasm and Enlightenment in Europe, 1650–1850*, San Marino: Huntington Library.
Fenves, Peter (2003), *Late Kant: Towards another Law of the Earth*, London: Routledge.
Fiala, Andrew (2008), 'Fichte and the *Ursprache*', in Daniel Breazeale and Tom Rockmore (eds), *After Jena: New Essays on Fichte's Later Philosophy*, Evanston: Northwestern University Press.
Fichte, Johann Gottlieb (1895), *Discours à la nation allemand*, trans. Léon Philippe, Paris.
Fichte, Johann Gottlieb (1922), *Addresses to the German Nation*, trans. R. F. Jones and G. H. Turnbull, London: Open Court.
Fichte, Johann Gottlieb (1923), *Discours à la nation allemande*, trans. J. Molitor, Paris: Costes.
Fichte, Johann Gottlieb (1952), *Discours à la nation allemand*, trans. S. Jankélévitch, Paris: Aubier, Éditions Montaigne.
Fichte, Johann Gottlieb (1971), 'Der Patriotismus und sein Gegenteil [Dialogues on Patriotism and Its Opposite]', in *Fichtes Werke*, vol. 11, Berlin: Walter de Gruyter.
Fichte, Johann Gottlieb (1978), *Reden an die deutsche Nation*, Hamburg: Meiner.
Fichte, Johann Gottlieb (1982), *Science of Knowledge*, trans. Peter Lauchlan Heath and John Lachs, Cambridge: Cambridge University Press.
Fichte, Johann Gottlieb (1992), *Discours à la nation allemand*, trans. Alain Renaut, Paris: Aubier, La Salamandre.
Fichte, Johann Gottlieb (2000), *Foundations of Natural Right*, trans. Michael Baur, Cambridge: Cambridge University Press.
Fichte, Johann Gottlieb (2005), *Gesamtausgabe der Bayerischen Akademie der Wissenschaften*, ed. R. Lauth and H. Gliwitzky, Stuttgart-Bad Cannstatt: Frommann.
Fichte, Johann Gottlieb (2008), *Addresses to the German Nation*, trans. Gregory Moore, Cambridge: Cambridge University Press.
Fichte, Johann Gottlieb (2013), *Addresses to the German Nation*, trans. Isaac Nakhimovsky, Béla Kapossy and Keith Tribe, Indianapolis and Cambridge: Hackett.
Forster, Michael N. (2014), 'Kant's Philosophy of Language?', in Frank Schalow and Richard

Velkley (eds), *The Linguistic Dimension of Kant's Thought*, Evanston: Northwestern University Press.
Foucault Michel (2003), *Society Must Be Defended*, trans. David Macey, London: Penguin.
Foucault Michel (2008), *Introduction to Kant's Anthropology*, trans. Roberto Nigro and Kate Briggs, Los Angeles: Semiotext(e) and MIT Press.
Fredickson, George M. (1997), *The Comparative Imagination and the History of Racism, Nationalism and Social Movement*, Berkeley: University of California Press.
Friedman, Michael (2000), *A Parting of the Ways: Carnap, Cassirer, and Heidegger*, Chicago: Open Court.
Gasché, Rodolphe (1986), *The Tain of the Mirror*, Cambridge, MA: Harvard University Press.
Gellner, Ernest (1994), *Encounters with Nationalism*, Oxford: Blackwell.
Gellner, Ernest [1983] (2006), *Nations and Nationalism*, 2nd edn, Oxford: Blackwell.
Geuss, Raymond (1999), *Morality, Culture and History*, Cambridge: Cambridge University Press.
Glendinning, Simon (ed.) (1999), *The Edinburgh Encyclopaedia of Continental Philosophy*, Edinburgh: Edinburgh University Press.
Glendinning, Simon (2006), *The Idea of Continental Philosophy*, Edinburgh: Edinburgh University Press.
Glendinning, Simon and Robert Eaglestone (eds) (2008), *Derrida's Legacies*, London: Routledge.
Goetschel, Willi (2011), 'Derrida and Spinoza: Rethinking the Theologico-Political Problem', *Bamidbar: Journal for Jewish Thought and Philosophy*, 1.2, 9–25.
Goodman, Russell (ed.) (2005), *Contending with Stanley Cavell*, Oxford: Oxford University Press.
Green, Nancy L. (2008), 'Tocqueville, Comparative History, and Immigration in Two Democracies', *French Politics, Culture & Society*, 26.2, summer, 1–12.
Greenfeld, Liah (1992), *Nationalism*, Cambridge, MA: Harvard University Press.
Griffiths, A. Phillips (ed.) (1987), *Contemporary French Philosophy*, Cambridge: Cambridge University Press
Groot, Jean De (ed.) (2004), *Nature in American Philosophy*, Washington, DC: The Catholic University of America Press.
Guéroult, Martial (1974), *Études sur Fichte*, Paris: Aubier.
Hacking, Ian (1990), *The Taming of Chance*, Cambridge: Cambridge University Press.
Hadot, Pierre (2004), *What Is Ancient Philosophy?*, trans. Michael Chase, Cambridge, MA: Harvard University Press.
Hamann J. G. (2007), *Writings on Philosophy and Language*, ed. and trans. Kenneth Haynes, Cambridge: Cambridge University Press.
Harth, Erica (1992), *Cartesian Women: Versions and Subversions of Rational Discourse in the Old Regime*, Ithaca: Cornell University Press.
Hedge, Frederic Henry (2006), 'The Significance of Kantian Philosophy', in Lawrence Buell (ed.), *The American Transcendentalists: Essential Writings*, New York: The Modern Library.
Heidegger, Martin (1968), *What Is Called Thinking*, trans. Fred D. Wieck and J. Glenn Gray, New York: Harper & Row.
Heidegger, Martin (1988), *The Basic Problems of Phenomenology*, trans. Albert Hofstadter, Bloomington and Indianapolis: Indiana University Press.
Heidegger, Martin (1992), *Kant and the Problem of Metaphysics*, trans. Richard Taft, Bloomington: Indiana University Press.
Heidegger, Martin (2000), *Introduction to Metaphysics*, New Haven, CT: Yale University Press.

Heine, Heinrich (1959), *Religion and Philosophy in Germany*, trans. John Snodgrass, Boston: Beacon Press.
Helvétius, Claude Adrian (1970), *De l'esprit*, New York: Burt Franklin.
Henrich, Dieter (2003), *Between Kant and Hegel*, Cambridge, MA: Harvard University Press.
Henry, Freeman G. (2008), *Language, Culture and Hegemony in Modern France*, Birmingham, AL: Summa Publications.
Herbert, Joseph L., Jr. (2007), 'Individualism and Intellectual Liberty in Tocqueville and Descartes', *The Journal of Politics*, 69.2, May, 525–37.
Herder, Johann Gottfried (2002), *Philosophical Writings*, ed. Michael N. Forster, Cambridge: Cambridge University Press.
Hollander, Dana (2008), *Exemplarity and Chosenness*, Stanford: Stanford University Press.
Hume, David (1998), 'Of National Characteristics', in *Selected Essays*, ed. Stephen Copley and Andrew Edgar, Oxford: Oxford University Press.
Husserl, Edmund (1995), 'Fichte's Ideal of Humanity', *Husserl Studies*, 12, 111–33.
Janara, Laura (2002), *Democracy Growing Up: Authority, Autonomy, and Passion in Tocqueville's Democracy in America*, Albany: State University of New York Press.
Jardin, André (1989), *Tocqueville: A Biography*, trans. Lydia Davis with Robert Hemenway, New York: Farrar, Straus and Giroux.
Kant, Immanuel (1933), *Critique of Pure Reason*, trans. Norman Kemp Smith, London: Macmillan.
Kant, Immanuel (1934) [AK 19], *Moral Philosophy, Philosophy of Law, and Philosophy of Religion Nachlaß*, ed. Friedrich Berger, Immanuel Kant: Gesammelte Schritten, Berlin: Königlich Preußischen Akademie der Wissenschaften.
Kant, Immanuel (1952), *Critique of Judgement*, trans. with analytical indexes by James Creed Meredith, Oxford: Clarendon Press.
Kant, Immanuel (1979), 'The Conflict of the Faculties', in *Religion and Rational Theology*, Cambridge: Cambridge University Press.
Kant, Immanuel (1991), *Kant: Political Writings*, ed. Hans Reiss and Hugh B. Nisbet, Cambridge: Cambridge University Press.
Kant, Immanuel (1993), 'Announcement of the Near Conclusion of a Treaty for Eternal Peace in Philosophy', in Peter Fenves (ed.), *Raising the Tone of Philosophy*, Baltimore: Johns Hopkins University Press.
Kant, Immanuel (1996a), *Metaphysics of Morals*, trans. Mary J. Gregor, Cambridge: Cambridge University Press.
Kant, Immanuel (1996b), 'On a Supposed Right to Lie from Philanthropy', in *Practical Philosophy*, ed. and trans. Mary J. Gregor, Cambridge: Cambridge University Press.
Kant, Immanuel (1997), *Critique of Practical Reason*, trans. Mary J. Gregor, Cambridge: Cambridge University Press.
Kant, Immanuel (1998), 'Vigilantius', in *Lectures on Ethics*, trans. Peter Heath and J. B. Schneewind, Cambridge: Cambridge University Press.
Kant, Immanuel (1999), *Correspondence*, trans. Arnulf Zweig, Cambridge: Cambridge University Press.
Kant, Immanuel (2001), 'Religion within the Boundaries of Mere Reason', in *Religion and Rational Theology*, Cambridge: Cambridge University Press.
Kant, Immanuel (2004), *Lectures on Logic*, ed. J. Michael Young, Cambridge: Cambridge University Press.
Kant, Immanuel (2006), *Toward Peace and Other Writings on Politics, Peace, and History*, ed. Pauline Kleingeld, trans. David L. Colclasure, New Haven, CT and London: Yale University Press.

Kant, Immanuel (2007), 'Observations on the Feeling of the Beautiful and the Sublime', 'Anthropology from a Pragmatic Point of View' and 'Idea for a Universal History with a Cosmopolitan Aim', in *Anthropology, History and Education*, Cambridge: Cambridge University Press.
Kant, Immanuel (2012), *Lectures on Anthropology*, ed. Allen W. Wood, trans. Robert R. Clewis, Robert B. Louden, G. Felicitas Munzel and Allen Wood, Stanford: Stanford University Press.
Kaufmann, Eric (2004), *The Rise of Anglo-America: The Decline of Dominant Ethnicity in the United States*, Cambridge, MA: Harvard University Press.
Kedourie, Elie [1960] (1993), *Nationalism*, rev. edn, Oxford: Wiley-Blackwell.
Kelly, George Armstrong (1969), *Idealism, Politics and History*, Cambridge: Cambridge University Press.
Klein, Lawrence E. and Anthony J. La Vopa (1998), *Enthusiasm and Enlightenment in Europe, 1650–1850*, San Marino, CA: Huntington Library.
Kleingeld, Pauline (1999), 'Six Varieties of Cosmopolitanism in Late Eighteenth-Century Germany', *The Journal of the History of Ideas*, 60.3, 505–24.
Kleingeld, Pauline (2003), 'Kant's Cosmopolitan Patriotism', *Kant-Studien*, 94.3, 299–316.
Kohn, Hans (1967), *Prelude to Nation-States: The French and German Experience, 1789–1815*, Princeton: Princeton University Press.
Kohn, Hans (2005), *The Idea of Nationalism: A Study in Its Origins and Background*, New Brunswick, NJ: Transaction Publishers.
Kramnick, Isaac (ed.) (1995), *The Portable Enlightenment Reader*, New York: Viking Penguin.
Krell, David Farrell (2015), *Phantoms of the Other: Four Generations of Derrida's Geschlecht*, Albany: State University of New York Press.
Kuklick, Bruce (1985), 'Does American Philosophy Rest on a Mistake?', in Marcus G. Singer (ed.), *American Philosophy*, Royal Institute of Philosophy Supplement, 19, Cambridge: Cambridge University Press.
Kuklick, Bruce (2003), *A History of American Philosophy: 1720–2000*, Oxford: Oxford University Press.
Lamberti, Jean-Claude (1989), *Tocqueville and Two Democracies*, Cambridge, MA: Harvard University Press.
Lawler, Peter Augustine (2004), *Democracy and Its Friendly Critics*, Oxford: Lexington Books.
Leonard, Miriam (ed.) (2010), *Derrida and Antiquity*, Oxford: Oxford University Press.
Levin, David (ed.) (1975), *Emerson: Prophecy, Metamorphosis, and Influence*, New York: Columbia University Press.
Loraux, Nicole (1986), *The Invention of Athens: The Funeral Orations in the Classical City*, trans. Caroline Levine, Cambridge, MA: Harvard University Press.
Loraux, Nicole (1993), *The Children of Athena: Athenian Ideas about Citizenship and the Division between the Sexes*, trans. Caroline Levine, Princeton: Princeton University Press.
Loraux, Nicole (2000), *Born of the Earth: Myth and Politics in Athens*, trans. Selina Stewart, Ithaca, NY: Cornell University Press
Loraux, Nicole (2002), *Divided City: On Memory and Forgetting in Ancient Athens*, trans. Corinne Pache with Jeff Fort, New York: Zone Books.
Lyotard, Jean-François (2009), *Enthusiasm: The Kantian Critique of History*, trans. Georges Van den Abbeele, Stanford: Stanford University Press.
McKim, Robert and Jeff McMahan (eds) (1997), *The Morality of Nationalism*, Oxford: Oxford University Press.
McQuillan, Martin (ed.) (2007), *The Politics of Deconstruction*, London: Pluto Press.
McQuillan, Martin (2009), *Deconstruction after 9/11*, London: Taylor & Francis.

McWilliams, Wilson Carey (2004), 'National Character and National Soul', in Peter Augustine Lawler (ed.), *Democracy and Its Friendly Critics*, Oxford: Lexington Books.
Manent, Pierre (1996), *Tocqueville and the Nature of Democracy*, trans. John Waggoner, Lanham: Rowman & Littlefield
Manent, Pierre (2006), 'Tocqueville, Political Philosopher', in Cheryl B. Welch (ed.), *The Cambridge Companion to Tocqueville*, Cambridge: Cambridge University Press.
Mansfield, Harvey (2004), 'Nature and Fact in Tocqueville's Democracy in America', in Jean De Groot (ed.), *Nature in American Philosophy*, Washington, DC: The Catholic University of America Press.
Martyn, David (1997), 'Borrowed Fatherland: Nationalism and Language Purism in Fichte's *Addresses to the German Nation*', *Germanic Review*, 74.2, 303–15.
Marx, Karl and Friedrich Engels (1938), *German Ideology*, ed. and introduced by R. Pascal, London: Lawrence and Wishart.
Meinecke, Friedrich (1970), *Cosmopolitanism and the National State*, trans. Robert B. Kimber, Princeton: Princeton University Press.
Mélonio, Françoise (1997), 'Nations et nationalismes', *La Revue Tocqueville/The Tocqueville Review*, 18.1, 61–75.
Mill, John Stuart (1989), 'The Subjection of Women' (1869), in *'On Liberty' and Other Writings*, Cambridge: Cambridge University Press.
Miller, Perry (1993), 'From Edwards to Emerson', in Lawrence Buell (ed.), *Ralph Waldo Emerson: A Collection of Critical Essays*, Englewood Cliffs, NJ: Prentice Hall.
Milton, John (2016), 'The Doctrine and Discipline of Divorce' (1643), in *Areopagitica and Other Prose Works*, Mineola, NY: Dover Publications.
Montesquieu, Charles de Secondat (1989), *Spirit of the Laws*, **trans.** Anne M. Cohler, Basia Carolyn Miller and Harold Samuel Stone, Cambridge: Cambridge University Press.
Munzel, Felicitas (1999), *Kant's Conception of the Moral Character*, Chicago: University of Chicago Press.
Nancy, Jean-Luc (1993), *The Birth to Presence*, trans. Brian Holmes et al., Stanford: Stanford University Press.
Nancy, Jean-Luc (2008), *The Discourse of the Syncope*, trans. Saul Anton, Stanford: Stanford University Press.
Nietzsche, Friedrich (2001), *Gay Science*, trans. Josefine Nauckhoff and Adrian Del Caro, Cambridge: Cambridge University Press.
Nietzsche, Friedrich (2002), *Beyond Good and Evil: Prelude to a Philosophy of the Future*, trans. Judith Norman, Cambridge: Cambridge University Press.
Nolla, Eduardo (1992), *Liberty, Equality, Democracy*, New York: New York University Press.
Nora, Pierre (ed.) (1992), *Les Lieux de mémoire, tome 3*, Paris: Gallimard.
Nora, Pierre (1998), *Realms of Memory*, vol. 3, English language edn, ed. Lawrence D. Kritzman, New York: Columbia University Press.
Norton, Andrews (2006), 'From "The New School in Literature and Religion"' (1838), in Lawrence Buell (ed.), *The American Transcendentalists: Essential Writings*, New York: The Modern Library.
Nussbaum, Martha (1997), 'Kant and Stoic Cosmopolitanism', *The Journal of Political Philosophy*, 5.1, 1–25.
Nussbaum, Martha and Joshua Cohen (eds) (1996), *For Love of Country: Debating the Limits of Patriotism*, Boston: Beacon Press.
O'Neill, Onora (1989), *Constructions of Reason: Explorations of Kant's Practical, Philosophy*, Cambridge: Cambridge University Press.
Özkirimli, Umut (2017), *Theories of Nationalism*, 3rd edn, London: Palgrave Macmillan.

Pagden, Anthony (ed.) (2002), *The Idea of Europe: From Antiquity to the European Union*, Cambridge: Cambridge University Press.
Perkins, Mary Anne and Martin Liebscher (eds) (2006), *Nationalism Versus Cosmopolitanism in German Thought and Culture, 1789–1914: Essays on the Emergence of Europe*, New York: Edwin Mellen Press.
Pierson, George Wilson (1996), *Tocqueville in America*, Baltimore: John Hopkins University Press.
Pinkard, Terry (2002), *German Philosophy, 1760–1860: The Legacy of Idealism*, Cambridge: Cambridge University Press.
Plato, (1997), 'The Republic', 'Menexenus' and 'Timaeus', in *Plato: Complete Works*, trans. G. M. A. Grube, Paul Ryan and Donald H. Zeyl, Indianapolis and Cambridge: Hackett.
Porte, Joel and Saundra Morris (eds) (1999), *The Cambridge Companion to Emerson*, New York: Cambridge University Press.
Poster, Mark (ed.) (1993), *Politics, Theory and Contemporary Culture*, New York: Columbia University Press.
Powell, J. G. F. (1999), 'Cicero's Translations from Greek', in *Cicero the Philosopher*, Oxford: Oxford University Press.
Rajchman, John and Cornel West (1985), *Post-Analytic Philosophy*, New York: Columbia University Press.
Rand, Richard (ed.) (1992), *Logomachia*, Lincoln, NE: University of Nebraska Press.
Redfield, Marc (2003), *Politics of Aesthetics*, Stanford: Stanford University Press.
Rickard, Peter (1989), *A History of the French Language*, 2nd edn, London: Routledge.
Ripley, George [1838] (2006), 'Victor Cousin and the Future of American Philosophy', in Lawrence Buell (ed.), *The American Transcendentalists: Essential Writings*, New York: The Modern Library.
Rivarol, Antoine [1784] (1968), 'Discours sur l'universalité de la langue française', in *Œuvres complètes*, vol. 2, Paris: Slatkin.
Rousseau, Jean-Jacques (1997a), 'Discourse on the Origin and Foundation of Inequality among Men *or* Second Discourse', in *The Discourses and Other Early Political Writings*, trans. and ed. Victor Gourevitch, Cambridge: Cambridge University Press.
Rousseau, Jean-Jacques (1997b), 'The Social Contract', in *The Social Contract and Other Later Political Writings*, trans. and ed. Victor Gourevitch, Cambridge: Cambridge University Press.
Sacks, Kenneth (2003), *Understanding Emerson: 'The American Scholar' and His Struggle for Self-Reliance*, Princeton: Princeton University Press.
Saxton, Alexander (1990), *Rise and Fall of the American Republic*, New York: Verso.
Schall, James V. (1962), 'Cartesianism and Political Theory', *The Review of Politics*, 24.2, April, 260–82.
Schirmeister, Pamela (1999), *Less Legible Meanings*, Stanford: Stanford University Press.
Shell, Susan Meld (2004), 'Organizing the State: Modern Transformations of the Body Politic in Rousseau, Kant and Fichte', *Internationales Jahrbuch des Deutschen Idealismus/ International Yearbook of German Idealism*, 2, 49–75.
Shell, Susan Meld (2009), *Kant and the Limits of Autonomy*, Cambridge, MA: Harvard University Press.
Shell, Susan Meld (2011), 'Kant's Conception of the Nation-State and the Idea of Europe', in Charlton Payne and Lucas Thorpe (eds), *Kant and the Concept of Community*, Rochester, NY: University of Rochester Press.
Shell, Susan Meld (2014), '*Nachschrift eines Freundes*: Kant on Language, Friendship, and the

Concept of a People', in Frank Schalow and Richard Velkley (eds), *The Linguistic Dimension of Kant's Thought*, Evanston: Northwestern University Press.
Shklar, Judith (1990), 'Emerson and the Inhibitions of Democracy', *Political Theory*, 18, 601–14.
Siedentop, Larry (1994), *Tocqueville*, Oxford: Oxford University Press.
Simpson, David (1986), *The Politics of American English, 1776–1850*, Oxford: Oxford University Press.
Singer, Marcus G. (ed.) (1985), *American Philosophy*, Royal Institute of Philosophy Supplement, 19, Cambridge: Cambridge University Press.
Smith, Anthony [1971] (1983), *Theories of Nationalism*, London: Duckworth.
Smith, C. J. (2006), *Roman Clan: The Gens from Ancient Ideology to Modern Anthropology*, Cambridge: Cambridge University Press.
Steiner, George (1977), *After Babel*, Oxford: Oxford University Press.
Suckiel, Ellen Kappy (1985), 'Emerson and the Virtues', in Marcus G. Singer (ed.), *American Philosophy*, Royal Institute of Philosophy Supplement, 19, Cambridge: Cambridge University Press.
Surber, Jere Paul (1996), *Language and German Idealism*, Atlantic Highlands, NJ: Humanities Press.
Swiggers, Pierre (1990), 'Ideology and the "Clarity" of French', in John E. Joseph and Talbot J. Taylor (eds), *Ideologies of Language*, London: Routledge.
Taylor, Charles (1997), 'Nationalism and Modernity', in Robert McKim and Jeff McMahan (eds), *The Morality of Nationalism*, Oxford: Oxford University Press.
Thomassen, Lasse (ed.) (2006), *The Derrida-Habermas Reader*, Edinburgh: Edinburgh University Press.
Thomson, Alex (2005), *Deconstruction and Democracy*, London and New York: Continuum Press.
Tocqueville, Alexis de (1986), *De la démocratie en Amérique*, Paris: Flammarion.
Tocqueville, Alexis de (2000), *Democracy in America*, trans. Harvey Mansfield and Delba Winthrop, Chicago: University of Chicago Press.
Tocqueville, Alexis de (2004), *Democracy in America*, trans. Arthur Goldhammer, New York: Library of America.
Tocqueville, Alexis de (2010), *Democracy in America*, bilingual edn, trans. James T. Schleifer, Indianapolis: Liberty Fund.
Tully, James (2002), 'The Kantian Idea of Europe: Critical and Cosmopolitan Perspectives', in Anthony Pagden (ed.), *The Idea of Europe: From Antiquity to the European Union*, Cambridge: Cambridge University Press.
Van den Abbeele, Georges (1992), *Travel as Metaphor: From Montaigne to Rousseau*, Minneapolis: University of Minnesota Press.
Vann, Richard T. (ed.) (1967), *Century of Genius: European Thought 1600–1700*, Englewood Cliffs, NJ: Prentice Hall.
Voltaire [François-Marie Arouet] (1972), *Philosophical Dictionary*, ed. and trans. Theodore Besterman, London: Routledge.
Voltaire [François-Marie Arouet] (2003), *Philosophical Letters: Letters Concerning the English Nation*, trans. Ernest Dilworth, Mineola, NY: Dover Publications.
Welch, Cheryl B. (2001), *De Tocqueville*, Oxford: Oxford University Press.
Welch, Cheryl B. (2006), 'Tocqueville on Fraternity and Fratricide', in Cheryl B. Welch (ed.), *The Cambridge Companion to Tocqueville*, Cambridge: Cambridge University Press.
West, Cornel (1989), *The American Evasion of Philosophy*, Madison: University of Wisconsin Press.

Wolin, Sheldon (2001), *Tocqueville between Two Worlds*, Princeton: Princeton University Press.
Zammito, John H. (2002), *Kant, Herder and the Birth of Anthropology*, Chicago: University of Chicago Press.

# Index

Abizadeh, Arash, 95–6, 99–103, 106–7, 109
Adorno, Theodor W., 15, 24–5, 29, 72, 95, 110, 157, 167–9
  *Essay as Form*, 167–8
American Transcendentalism, 12, 155–6, 159
Anderson, Benedict, 6, 11, 35, 38
Arendt, Hannah, 157
Aristotle, 1, 8, 10, 17, 117, 183
Athens, 1, 35–7, 38, 97, 148
Azouvi, François, 81, 127

Babel, 31–3, 57, 72, 74, 86
Balibar, Étienne, 44, 94, 100
Bennington, Geoffrey, 16–17
Berlin, Isaiah, 11, 30
Bloom, Harold, 15, 155, 156, 157, 158, 161–2, 164
Buell, Lawrence, 160, 165

Cartesianism, 12, 20, 81, 116–21, 124–5, 127, 128, 133
Cavell, Stanley, 14, 155, 156, 158, 167–9, 170, 177–8, 183–5
Cheah, Pheng, 90n, 114n
Christianity, 51, 63, 97, 145, 164
Cicero, 38, 50–2
Cohen, Hermann, 94–5
Constant, Benjamin, 59–61
cosmo-nationalism, 5, 8, 9, 16, 17, 105, 191
cosmopolitanism, 5, 9, 13, 24, 29, 42, 50–1, 67, 104–6, 108, 113, 144, 163, 165, 166
cosmopolitical, 3, 5, 9, 29, 37, 42, 50, 51–2, 65, 70, 81–4, 93, 95, 104–5, 106, 108, 129, 164, 174, 179

*Darstellung*, 55, 57, 66, 70, 168
De Man, Paul, 55–6, 57–8
democracy, 22, 46, 124, 125, 132–4, 136–9, 143, 144–5, 147, 149–52, 153, 159, 169–70, 178, 181–2

Derrida, Jacques, 2, 3–4, 6–8, 11, 12, 14–16, 17, 18–20, 21–2, 24–6, 27–8, 33, 38, 39, 40, 48–9, 56–7, 58, 62, 69, 70, 72, 75–6, 79–81, 83, 85, 94, 96, 99–103, 107, 108, 114, 117, 118–20, 122–3, 126, 129, 130, 137–9, 142, 145, 146, 149, 150, 157–9, 161, 166, 170, 173, 181–2, 183, 187–8, 189, 192
  'Onto-Theology of National-Humanism (Prolegomena to a Hypothesis)', 2, 4, 7, 8, 12, 22, 75
  Philosophical Nationality and Nationalism seminars, 6–7, 15–18, 21–2, 24–6, 39, 48–9, 56–7, 72, 75, 83, 85, 120, 122–3, 126, 129, 130, 138, 139, 142, 145, 146, 157–8
Descartes, René, 79–80, 119, 121, 127, 129, 150, 161, 166, 170, 185–7
  *Discourse on Method*, 79, 121, 125, 128–30, 169
  *Meditations*, 170, 185–6
Dewey, John, 83, 156, 159
dogma, 117, 125, 136, 139, 141–3

Emerson, Ralph Waldo, 3, 9, 11, 13, 14, 15, 20, 22, 155–92
  'Address to the Citizens of Concord', 175, 177, 178, 179
  'The American Scholar', 162, 163, 187
  'The Anglo-American', 171
  'Circles', 180
  'Emancipation of the Negroes in the British West Indies', 174
  *English Traits*, 172–3, 175, 176
  'Experience', 176, 181, 191
  'Fate', 172, 176, 177, 178, 179
  'Fortune of the Republic', 164, 178
  'History', 163, 164
  'Kansas Relief Meeting', 175, 180
  'Manners', 177
  *Nature*, 177
  'Poet', 185–7, 188, 189–90

Emerson, Ralph Waldo (*cont.*)
  'Poetry and Imagination', 172
  'Politics', 181
  *Representative Men*, 164, 171, 179, 180–1, 188, 189
  'Self-Reliance', 162, 171, 177, 182, 190, 191
  'The Transcendentalist', 165
  'The Young American', 173, 174, 179
English language, 18–19, 101, 132, 146–53, 160
Enlightenment, 30, 61, 65, 81, 143–6
enthusiasm, 58, 65–9, 70, 72, 75, 82, 84
*esprit*, 11, 38, 46, 68, 69, 71–2, 76–80, 82, 121, 124, 126–7

family, 2, 31, 33, 34–5, 38, 42, 51, 53, 101, 128–9, 132–4, 135
Fenves, Peter, 67, 70, 78
Fichte, Johann Gottlieb, 3, 4, 6, 9, 11, 13, 14, 15, 17, 20, 22, 76, 84–5, 89, 92–115, 122–3, 161, 191, 192
Foucault, Michel, 21, 43, 56, 86–7, 170
France, 2–3, 12, 18, 20, 22, 25, 30, 43, 45, 58, 59, 62, 63, 64, 65, 67, 69, 71, 78–81, 139, 143–6
French language, 2–3, 18–20, 28–9, 38, 43, 62–3, 65, 69–73, 75, 76, 77, 78–81, 101, 110–12, 138, 147, 150–2, 159–60
French Revolution, 6, 13, 58, 65, 66–8, 75, 77, 105

Gellner, Ernest, 6, 7, 10, 11, 30
German Idealism, 12, 93–4, 103
German language, 4, 11, 13, 20, 21, 24, 26, 31, 33–4, 42, 70, 71, 73, 75–8, 80, 84–9, 95, 98–9, 100–4, 105, 108–14, 126
Germany, 7, 9, 12, 18, 20–2, 25, 30, 45, 83–4, 96, 98, 104, 119, 124, 159–61, 164, 183
Greece, 2, 40, 162, 165, 188
Greek language, 1, 8, 19–20, 32, 38–9, 118, 123, 147–8
Guéroult, Martial, 93, 100, 106, 108

Hadot, Pierre, 170
Hedge, Frederic Henry, 159
Heidegger, Martin, 7, 15, 17–20, 25, 118, 158
Heine, Heinrich, 127
Herder, Johann Gottfried, 10, 26, 27, 39, 51, 73
Hume, David, 42, 45–9, 50, 52, 53
Husserl, Edmund, 20, 93–5

idiom, 2, 15–16, 17–20, 29, 33, 49, 63, 72, 75–6, 89, 95, 99–103, 108, 109, 110, 112, 114, 151, 156–8, 184, 189, 190, 191
*idion*, 2, 99, 102, 156

Kant, Immanuel, 3, 4, 6, 8, 9, 10, 11, 12, 13, 14, 15, 20, 21, 22, 24–54, 55–91, 92, 94, 98, 104, 107, 109–10, 119, 126, 144, 158, 159, 161, 164, 165–6, 184–5, 192
  *Anthropology from a Pragmatic Point of View*, 36, 42, 46–8, 64, 70, 71, 76, 77, 78–80, 81–3
  *The Conflict of the Faculties*, 62, 66–7
  *Critique of Judgement*, 49, 56, 57–8, 66–9, 82

*Critique of Practical Reason*, 87
*Critique of Pure Reason*, 31–2, 49, 74–5, 77, 87, 165–6
'Idea for a Universal History with a Cosmopolitan Aim', 38–9, 40, 52, 64, 70, 85
*Lectures on Anthropology*, 59, 71, 77, 78, 79, 80, 84
*Metaphysics of Morals*, 32, 34, 36, 37, 41, 42, 50, 88–9
*Observations on the Beautiful and the Sublime*, 55–9, 68, 69, 77, 78, 83, 85
'On a Supposed Right to Lie from Philanthropy', 59–61
'Perpetual Peace', 48, 56, 69, 165
Kedourie, Elie, 4, 6, 11, 20–1, 30–1, 53, 70–1, 92–3, 95, 99–100
Kleingeld, Pauline, 34
Kohn, Hans, 92–3, 95

Latin, 3, 4, 28, 31, 34, 37, 40, 53, 60, 62–3, 71, 73, 75, 79–80, 85–7, 102, 109, 112, 147–8, 150, 176, 177, 182, 185–6
Loraux, Nicole, 35–8

Meinecke, Friedrich, 9

Nancy, Jean-Luc, 57, 74, 77–8
nationalism, 4–11, 13–17, 20–2, 24–5, 29, 30–1, 34, 49–50, 53, 58, 68, 84, 92–5, 99–101, 107–8, 114, 139, 157–8, 162
Nietzsche, Friedrich, 25, 55
Nussbaum, Martha, 42, 51

O'Neill, Onora, 29
Özkirimli, Umut, 5

Pinkard, Terry, 26
Plato, 1, 8, 10, 18, 34–6, 62, 125, 136, 140

Ripley, George, 159–60
Rivarol, Antoine, 151
Rousseau, Jean-Jacques, 41, 53, 55, 116, 117, 134

schema, 8, 11, 12, 17, 44, 49, 56, 82, 84, 157
schematic affiliation, 4–5, 17
schematism, 9, 13, 49, 68, 110, 144, 184–5
sovereignty, 13, 15, 17, 43, 68–9, 117, 135, 141–3, 152, 175
Smith, Anthony D., 6, 11

Taylor, Charles, 10
Tocqueville, Alexis de, 3, 6, 9, 11, 13, 14, 15, 17, 20, 22, 116–54, 157, 159, 161, 166–71, 180, 182, 191, 192

USA, 9, 12, 14, 21–2, 116, 117, 118–19, 120, 123–4, 126, 129, 131, 132, 135, 139, 157, 158, 160, 161, 163, 168, 171, 174–6, 179, 181, 183–4, 191–2

West, Cornel, 156, 158

EU representative:
Easy Access System Europe
Mustamäe tee 50, 10621 Tallinn, Estonia
Gpsr.requests@easproject.com